Islam, Education
and Reform in
Southern Thailand

The **Institute of Southeast Asian Studies (ISEAS)** was established as an autonomous organization in 1968. It is a regional centre dedicated to the study of socio-political, security and economic trends and developments in Southeast Asia and its wider geostrategic and economic environment. The Institute's research programmes are the Regional Economic Studies (RES, including ASEAN and APEC), Regional Strategic and Political Studies (RSPS), and Regional Social and Cultural Studies (RSCS).

ISEAS Publishing, an established academic press, has issued almost 2,000 books and journals. It is the largest scholarly publisher of research about Southeast Asia from within the region. ISEAS Publishing works with many other academic and trade publishers and distributors to disseminate important research and analyses from and about Southeast Asia to the rest of the world.

Islam, Education and Reform in Southern Thailand

TRADITION & TRANSFORMATION

Joseph Chinyong Liow

ISEAS

INSTITUTE OF SOUTHEAST ASIAN STUDIES

Singapore

First published in Singapore in 2009 by
Institute of Southeast Asian Studies
30 Heng Mui Keng Terrace
Pasir Panjang
Singapore 119614

E-mail: publish@iseas.edu.sg
Website: <http://bookshop.iseas.edu.sg>

The responsibility for facts and opinions in this publication rests exclusively with the author and his interpretations do not necessarily reflect the views or the policy of the publisher or its supporters.

ISEAS Library Cataloguing-in-Publication Data

Liow, Joseph Chinyong, 1972–
    Islam, education & reform in Southern Thailand : tradition & transformation.
    1. Islamic education—Thailand, Southern.
    2. Muslims—Education—Thailand, Southern.
    I. Title.
LC910 T4L76   2009

ISBN 978-981-230-953-2 (soft cover)
ISBN 978-981-230-954-9 (hard cover)
ISBN 978-981-230-965-5 (PDF)

Cover photo: Male students' quarters, Pondok Dalor, Pattani, Thailand (*Photo courtesy of the author*)

Typeset by Superskill Graphics Pte Ltd
Printed in Singapore by

Dedicated to the memory of

CHEAH FOOK MENG
(1964–2005)

CONTENTS

LIST OF TABLES

FOREWORD

In the 1960s and 1970s, Islamic education in Southeast Asia was not a topic of great scholarly or policy urgency. Although a few anthropologists recognized that Islamic boarding schools in Java, Malaysia, and southern Thailand played an important role in religious learning and the sustenance of local religious identities, the general assumption was that Islamic schooling was so incapable of keeping up with the demands of the modern age that it was just a matter of time before it was pushed from the national scene. In an otherwise thoughtful essay, one of today's most perceptive observers of Islamic affairs in Southeast Asia reached just such a pessimistic conclusion about the future of the Javanese variant of the Islamic boarding school known as the *pesantren*, writing, "The *pesantren* has enjoyed an unusually long life for a traditional school, but it may finally be threatened with disappearance."[1]

As it turns out, like its southern Thai counterpart, the Javanese *pesantren* did not disappear. Rather, like Islamic education across most of Muslim Southeast Asia, it has flourished and diversified since the great resurgence in Islamic piety of the 1970s and 1980s. At the same time, however, Muslim educational institutions are no longer seen as quaintly irrelevant institutions. Since the 9/11 attacks in the U.S. and the October 2002 Bali bombings in Indonesia in particular, the sense of wistful obsolescence that used to characterize discussions of Southeast Asia's Islamic schools has been replaced by an anxious and often unhelpful media frenzy.

The reasons for the change of perception are understandable enough. The teachers of the young men responsible for the October 2002 attack in Bali had educational ties to the al-Mukmin boarding school in Central Java, an institution alleged to have links to the terrorist Jemaah Islamiyah. The link led to widespread fears that some of Indonesia's 47,000 Islamic schools were being used to open a "second front" in the al-Qaʿida conflict with the West. In the Philippines, the Intelligence Chief of the Philippine Armed Forces blamed an upsurge in terror bombings in that country in the early 2000s on the southern Philippines' network of *madrasas*. "[T]hey are teaching the children, while still young, to wage a *jihad*. They will become the future suicide bombers."[2] In Cambodia, government officials discovered that between 2002 and 2004 the JI military chief, Riduan Isamuddin, alias Hambali, had visited several Islamic schools, allegedly attempting to recruit militants for armed attacks on Westerners.

Nowhere have the allegations surrounding Islamic schooling been more heated, however, than with regard to the Malay-Muslim schools in southern Thailand. As Joseph Chinyong Liow shows in this timely and important study, since January 2004 Thailand has been rocked by a renewed cycle of violence between state authorities and the Malay-Muslim population concentrated in the country's south. Government officials have accused particular Islamic schools of laying the groundwork for attacks on Thai government officials. Liow did not shy from the policy implications of these allegations in the course of his research on southern Thailand's *pondoks*. He wisely reminds us, however, that Islamic education in this region can only be understood by situating it in relation to three broader facts.

The first is that, contrary to many media commentaries, the *pondoks* are not at all backward-looking or unchanging "medieval" institutions. The question of reform now being debated with regard to the *pondoks* is not new either. Rather, the question of how to accommodate Islamic education to modern markets, polities, and forms of knowledge has raged for more than a century here in Thailand and for the better part of two centuries in some parts of Southeast Asia and the Middle East to which Muslims in southern Thailand have long travelled.

A second point among the many fine insights offered in this study is equally relevant for scholarship and policy discussion. It is that, rather than being uniform, Islamic schooling in southern Thailand shows a competitive diversity of institutions and cultures. In the early decades of the twentieth century, the classical Malay *pondok* was challenged by new Islamic institutions proposing to integrate some subjects of general ("secular") learning into their curriculum. The challenges to the more or less classical *pondok* have continued to this day. Indeed, Liow shows, they have intensified in recent years, with the appearance of Saudi-funded Salafi schools that challenge not only the traditional *pondok* curriculum but the traditionalist Shafiʿi Sunnism long dominant in southern Thailand and most of Muslim Southeast Asia. The outcome of this competition among rival variants of Islamic schooling and rival visions of Islam, Liow shows, will be a major influence on the future of Islam in southern Thailand.

The third and final point I would highlight from Liow's rich account concerns the relationship of Muslim society and education to the Thai state. As Liow demonstrates, the Malay Muslims in Thailand's southern provinces have an identity distinct from that of dispersed Muslim minorities found in some societies. The Malays are overwhelmingly concentrated in a border region where they comprise the demographic majority and where they identify themselves as the original inhabitants of the land. In the face of the Thai government's assertive programs of cultural assimilation (conducted at varying fever pitches over the course of the twentieth and early twenty-first centuries), these facts have guaranteed that Islamic schooling has come to be seen by the Malays as key symbols of their identity. This perception, and the often tense relationship between Malay Muslims and the Thai authorities, has in turn meant that government efforts to impose reforms on the Malay population's Islamic schools have often met with opposition. However, it is telling that the resistance has been selective in its focus. Elements of general education have, in fact, been welcomed into some schools. Indeed, for a while in the 1970s, it looked as if the south's Islamic schools might become a bridge between Muslims and the state rather than the front line in a culture war. Education in some Islamic schools was being brought into alignment with the national curricula; Malay enrolments in national colleges soared. The establishment of two state-assisted Islamic colleges in the south, with plans for a third, was also well received in the Muslim community. The colleges were designed to provide higher education in Islam as well as courses on Islam for non-Muslims, including government officials posted to the south.

Other educational trends, however, showed that education and politics in the Muslim south were being buffeted by less favourable winds. Beginning in the 1980s, growing numbers of students opted to complete their religious education in the Middle East, particularly in Saudi Arabia. According to reports Islamic leaders provided Liow, today, several dozen schools promulgate conservative Salafi teachings. However, Liow shows, the life history of the Saudi-trained reformist, Ismail Lutfi, demonstrates that not all of the Saudi-style *Salafis* are anti-integrationist. Lutfi is a gifted and warm speaker, and advocates a gradualist and contextualist approach to the understanding of Islamic law. But recent developments in the southern provinces also indicate that, hardened by the heavy-handed tactics of the Thai authorities, a small minority within the Islamic school system has concluded that compromise with the state is no longer an option.

No one can say for certain where political events in southern Thailand are likely to lead in years to come. What is certain, however, is that the cultures and organizations Liow has highlighted in this far-ranging study will be key determinants of whatever finally takes place. Having begun by introducing us to a small, educational tradition that policy makers a few years ago thought obsolescent, Liow ends by providing us with critical insights for understanding the issues at stake in southern Thailand. The readability, high scholarship, and policy relevance that characterize this book are a rare achievement in the academy, and its insights are of relevance well beyond the beautiful but troubled landscapes of southern Thailand.

Notes

[1]   See Sidney R. Jones, "The Javanese *Pesantren*: Between Elite and Peasantry," in Charles F. Keyes, ed., *Reshaping Local Worlds: Formal Education and Cultural Change in Rural Southeast Asia* (New Haven, CT: Yale Southeast Asian Studies, 1991), p. 36.

[2]   See "Defense, Deped to look into *madrasah*'s alleged role in breeding terrorists," *MindaNews* II, no. 40, June 16, 2003.

Professor Robert W. Hefner
Associate Director
Institute on Culture, Religion, and World Affairs, Boston University

PREFACE

Islamic education in southern Thailand has not been the subject of much scholarly attention and analysis as few have gone to print on it — whether in the English, Malay, or Thai languages. Currently, Hasan Madmarn's work on Islamic schools in Pattani, *The Pondok and Madrasah in Pattani*, stands out as the only book-length investigation of this phenomenon published in the English language. For that reason alone it remains a path-breaking study and a valuable contribution to our understanding of a very dynamic, yet reclusive, social-religious institution. The value of Madmarn's contribution is undoubtedly augmented by the fact that he himself was a product of the traditional *pondok* (Islamic school), an institution that remains the heartbeat of Thai Malay-Muslim culture and identity, even in this age of globalization. Madmarn's book provides important historical information about the development of the *pondok* in southern Thailand, as well as its gradual ascent to a position of eminence as a bastion of Islamic scholarship in Muslim Southeast Asia.

While it provides insight into the traditional curriculum in Islamic schools, Madmarn's laudable effort is by and large descriptive in nature. Little attempt is made to analyse and interrogate the much-vaunted legacy of traditional Islamic education in southern Thailand against the political context in which it is located, or to uncover the tensions and antinomies inherent in southern Thailand's dynamic Muslim society, which I suggest have both framed and been framed by Islamic education. By skirting these more complex issues, Muslim society is inadvertently portrayed as a somewhat monolithic entity when in fact it is deeply divided between forces of tradition, reform, and modernity. To be fair, Madmarn does hint at these cleavages when he introduces the *madrasah* as an alternative to the traditional *pondok*, but ultimately, the implications of its emergence on the overall landscape of Islamic education in the South is skirted.

Aside from Madmarn's work, broader studies on Muslim society, particularly of the Malay-Muslim southern provinces have touched on various aspects of Islamic education. The work of Michel Gilquin, Wan Kadir Che Man, Surin Pitsuwan, Uthai Dulyakasem, and Raymond Scupin come immediately to mind, as does a Ph.D. dissertation written in English by Ibrahim Narongraksakhet, available in the libraries of Universiti Malaya and Prince of Songkhla University, Pattani Campus. With the exception of Scupin and Narongraksakhet, who provide a great deal of detail about Islamic education institutions themselves, the attention given to education issues in these studies are usually addressed along any of the following three themes: (1) the revered status of Islamic education institutions, in particular the *pondok*, in Malay-Muslim society, (2) the role of Islamic education institutions in the broader ethno-nationalist and separatist struggle, and (3) state policies towards Islamic education. Thus far, no article or book-length study has attempted to explore the structure of Islamic education in terms of the types of schools, enrolment or funding trends, or issues of translocality. Nor has any effort been made to pry open the "black box" of Islamic education by dissecting the curriculum in Islamic schools, either through interviewing teachers and students or by interrogating key texts and ideas that circulate in these schools. This book hopes to fill this lacuna.

On top of a careful scrutiny of existing literature, the methods of inquiry adopted in this study revolve around in-depth interviews, ethnographic observation, and textual analysis. Fieldwork for this book was conducted on numerous occasions beginning in April 2004. This included visits to Islamic schools and religious institutions in Pattani, Yala, Narathiwat, Bangkok, and Chiang Mai. Over the course of these visits, extensive interviews were conducted by the author and his research assistants with religious teachers, *alim*, academics, students, and community leaders. Where possible, interviews were also conducted with Thai government and security officials in order to ascertain how the state views Islamic education and its overall place in Thai society against the backdrop of conflict in southern Thailand. Field researchers also provided further assistance in the form of critical follow-up interviews. During these field visits, I also had the opportunity to spend some time at various Islamic schools observing religious and vocational classes. This allowed me the opportunity not only to witness firsthand the conduct of lessons, but also to observe the relationship between religious teachers and their students.

Beyond interviews and ethnographic observation, this project also undertakes analysis of some popular texts used in Islamic education institutions. Specifically, I have examined and interrogated the ideas behind some religious texts in order to tease out the trends and tensions that have come to define Islamic education in Thailand, particularly the differences between so-called reformist and traditionalist Islam in southern Thailand. In order to facilitate a comparative analysis of these two streams in the context of religious education in southern Thailand, I have chosen to focus on texts associated with reformist-Salafi scholars and their ideas, given that these have received almost no scholarly treatment in the extant literature, rather than on the core texts of traditionalist Islam, several of which have already received fairly detailed treatment in major studies of traditional religion in Southeast Asia.

Unsurprisingly, research for this book proved immensely challenging. Not least of the obstacles was the security situation in southern Thailand, where violence continues to rage as a consequence of a potent concoction of competing interests, thereby making access exceptionally difficult. Conditions were further aggravated by a mood of suspicion and apprehension, and oftentimes locals were reluctant to talk, especially when approached by unfamiliar faces. Because my research began at about the same time that several local Malay-Muslims were apprehended on allegations of being Thai members of the terrorist organization Jemaah Islamiyah, this made it even more difficult to win the trust of local religious leaders and teachers. It is because of these constraints that I am especially grateful to a number of locals who trusted me enough to make introductions, open doors, and on many occasions, accompany me for meetings and interviews. Needless to say, without their help I would not have been able to uncover as much as I eventually did.

ACKNOWLEDGEMENTS

In writing this book I have accumulated a great many debts of gratitude.

It is with deep appreciation that I acknowledge the support of Barry Desker, Dean of the S. Rajaratnam School of International Studies, who granted me time away from heavy administrative responsibilities so that I could conduct field research and later write up my research findings.

Research for this book first began as part of a larger project on Islamic education in Southeast Asia. Concomitantly, a word of thanks is due to my fellow project members Bob Hefner, Rick Kraince, Tom McKenna, and Bjorn Blengsli, who laboured with me to better understand the complicated dynamics and nuances of Islamic education in the region. It was during our many meetings discussing this project that my interest in the Islamic schools of southern Thailand was nursed, and it was they who first forced me to think through this topic carefully in order to define and refine research questions and methodologies. Thanks also to the National Bureau of Asian Research for funding this Islamic education project, and to Michael Wills, Aishah Pang, and Mercy Kuo for supporting it.

The person who learns most from any book is its author. In the course of writing this particular one, I have learnt and profited a great deal from my interactions with friends and colleagues from the Thai studies, Islamic studies, Southeast Asian studies, and security studies communities who helped me think through the issues it raises. I am particularly indebted to Saroja Dorairajoo, Raymond Scupin, Duncan McCargo, Michael Montesano, Chaiwat Satha-Anand, Ibrahim Narongraksakhet, Nilor Wae-u-Seng, Hasan Madmarn, Sukri Langputeh, Imtiyaz Yusuf, May Mullins, Muhammad Arafat, Suleemarn Wongsuphap, Worawit Baru, Ahmad Somboon Bualuang, Michael

Vatikiotis, Pakorn Priyakorn, Surin Pitsuwan, Greg Fealy, Bob Hefner, Greg Barton, Farish Noor, Patricia Martinez, John Funston, Francesca Lawe-Davies, Christoph Marcinkowski, and Anthony Davis, for whatever may be of value in the book.

In Bangkok, Jim Klein patiently took me through the Asia Foundation's projects in Thailand's religious schools, while Alayas Haji Salah kindly accompanied me on visits to *pondoks* and Islamic schools in the city and its vicinity. Similarly, research for the brief discussion on Chiang Mai benefited from the kind assistance of Suchart Sethamalinee and Kannaporn "Pam" Akarapisan. Francesca Lawe-Davies shared her data on religious education, reproduced in Chapter Two, based on her own research on the National Reconciliation Committee. In Pattani, Kariya (Zakaria) Langputeh kindly hosted me at the Yala Islamic College, while prominent local Islamic scholars such as Ismail Lutfi Japakiya, Nidae Waba, and Abdurrahman Khahama patiently and candidly answered my many questions.

I wish also to acknowledge the valuable contribution to this work made by a number of people who assisted in research and translation. Ustaz Muhammad Haniff Hassan was kind enough to share with me parts of his own analysis of Ismail Lutfi Japakiya's doctoral dissertation, while Abdul Rahim Zakaria allowed me to use segments of his Master's dissertation on Haji Sulong. Shahirah Mahmood, Mohamed Nawab, and Afif Pasuni helped in the translation of some Arabic and Jawi material; Shahirah patiently assisted me by ploughing through the entire manuscript as I prepared it for publication. Don Pathan was characteristically generous with his own time, contacts, and insights. As administrative responsibilities made it difficult for me to visit the southern provinces as often as I would have liked, I had to rely on local help to sustain the research on the ground. Owing to the precarious security situation in southern Thailand, however, I am unable to acknowledge by name those who were instrumental in arranging interviews for me, and at times conducting them as well. They know who they are, and they know how important their contribution has been to this book. There are many others — religious teachers and local Malay-Muslim community leaders as well as government officials — whose names cannot be revealed here for personal and security reasons. To them I owe a heartfelt gratitude and appreciation for their candour and honesty in sharing with me their views on the topic. Preliminary findings of this research were presented at a research seminar at the S. Rajaratnam School of International Studies (2006), a panel at the Association of Asian Studies Annual Conference (2006), and the Thailand Update at the Australian National University (2007). I would like to express my gratitude to those who attended these sessions and for contributing suggestions and criticisms. A special word of gratitude is also due John Funston for his kind invitation to speak at the ANU Thailand Update.

Back at my RSIS home base, the pressures of balancing academic writing with other professional responsibilities were made much more bearable thanks to my colleagues. I thank in particular Tan See Seng, Kumar Ramakrishna, Ralf Emmers, Bernard Loo, Norman Vasu, Joey Long, Adrian Kuah, Ang Cheng Guan, and Khong Yuen Foong. A special word of thanks, too, to Adeline Lim, who assisted me with many of my administrative burdens when I took time off to write up the manuscript. I am grateful to the staff at ISEAS Publications Unit, especially Triena Ong, who provided much needed support and editorial assistance as the publishers of this volume.

To my dear wife, Ai Vee, thank you for all your patience, love, and understanding, which have helped me keep things in perspective. This work is as much the fruit of your labour as it is mine. To my two children, Euan and Megan, thank you for allowing Daddy to spend more time than he should have in the study. Finally, none of this would have been possible without the grace of my Lord and Saviour, Jesus Christ. My debt to him is truly beyond measure: to him be the glory.

INTRODUCTION

In his best-selling narrative history on the rise of Wahhabism, Charles Allen made the following observation of the pertinence of the *madrasah* to social and religious life in South Asia:

> the Taliban were youngsters orphaned by war, who had been brought up and educated in the hundreds of religious schools set up in Pakistan with funds from Saudi Arabia. For many thousands of young Pathan boys the *madrasah* had been their home and its male teachers ... their surrogate parents. Here the bonds and shared purpose had been forged which had given these 'searchers after truth' their extraordinary aura of invincibility, for the *madrasah* was not so much a school as a seminary, with curriculum made up entirely of religious instruction and the study of the Qur'an. Here they had spent their adolescence rocking to and fro as they learned to recite by heart an Arabic text whose meaning they did not understand but which they knew conferred on them absolute authority in all matters governing social behaviour.[1]

This excerpt echoes both the centrality of religious education in Muslim life as well as a common tendency among Western scholars towards orientalist narrations that perpetuate a stereotypical view of Islamic education as a stoic and static pursuit. Such a view on Islamic education has been advanced further with former U.S. Secretary of Defence Donald Rumsfeld's now infamous October 2003 memo that queried if the U.S. was "capturing, killing, or deterring and dissuading more terrorists every day than the *madrasahs* and the radical clerics are recruiting, training, and deploying against us?"[2] It is clear from the frenzy that Rumsfeld's controversial question stirred up in

1

the international media, policy circles, and the terrorism analysis communities, not to mention the caustic reactions across the Muslim world, that Islamic education is a highly controversial and contested issue, and that the institution of the Islamic school is subject to intense scrutiny.

Education has always been a key feature of Muslim life and society. In Islamic culture, however, knowledge has never been an end unto itself. Nor has the role of educational institutions been envisaged as a production line churning out individuals equipped to contribute to the bureaucracies and economies of the modern nation-state and global capitalist enterprise. Instead, Islamic education has had two overarching objectives at its core: the transmission of Islamic heritage and values on the one hand, and the spiritual, moral, and ethical transformation and advancement of Muslim societies on the other. This long-cherished traditional role of Islamic education has, however, come under immense pressure and scrutiny in this modern age of development, globalization, and the nation-state. Notwithstanding the fact that the lines between secular and religious education are often far more complex and fluid than have been popularly portrayed, secular governments, for whom education is an efficacious tool of modernity, increasingly demand that these religious institutions produce students who can contribute to the instrumental ends of economic prosperity and national development in the name of the "greater good". Since September 11, 2001, another factor has come to the fore, and Islamic schools throughout the Muslim world find themselves under the microscope of state surveillance for the declared purpose of "uprooting" the Islamic radicalism that fans the embers of terrorism. The subtext is of course clear — terrorism is rooted in the extremist religious ideology that some Islamic schools perpetuate.

These pressures on Muslim societies are, at least in part, symptomatic of the "crisis of modernity" that many pundits suggest confronts Islam today, and that continues to be the subject of great scholarly interest. This "crisis" itself has been dealt with substantively elsewhere and is not a matter of concern for us here. How the tensions that define this crisis have been mirrored in Islamic education, however, is. That the perceptions of Islamic education described above have been gaining currency should not detract from the fact that Islam remains fraught with tensions. Despite romanticized notions of it being a unified religion, the realm of Islamic education has long been an arena for the interplay of various, and often contending, social forces.[3] This book is an attempt to document and unpack this interplay in the context of Islamic education in Muslim-dominated southern Thailand. It will focus primarily on the Malay-Muslim provinces of Pattani, Yala, and Narathiwat, but will also allude to trends beyond these provinces.

Islamic schools in southern Thailand have a long, chequered history. Members of the Malay-Muslim intelligentsia, as well as of the political and religious elite in Thailand, have often impressed upon us how the *pondok* or traditional Islamic school has been, and continues to be, amongst the most revered religious institutions in Muslim Southeast Asia.[4] On the other hand, Islamic schools are viewed in many quarters of the Thai state as parochial institutions that not only contribute little to modern Thai society, but, more disturbing, nurse an exclusivist vision of the world and of the place of Malay-Muslims in the imagined Thai nation. At least to some extent, it can be said that Islamic schools lend themselves to the perpetuation of this view by virtue of the fact that they have intermittently been accused of, and at times found to be, complicit in the long-drawn Malay-Muslim separatist insurgency in the southern provinces.[5] That said, the unfortunate reality is that, in truth, very little is known about the nature of religious knowledge and education in the region. Unpacking this evident disjuncture in what Islamic schools represent through the prisms of the state and of the Malay-Muslim community, one is likely to find that the reality straddles the two extremes. In other words, this disjuncture captures the challenges confronting the community — questions of tradition, identity, religiosity, historical legacy, relations with the state, and responses to encroaching secularism and modernity. It is my contention that these dynamics and tensions at once both frame and are framed by what is happening to, and in, the Islamic school system in southern Thailand in particular and, to a lesser degree, in Islamic schools across the country in general. The purpose of this book is to describe and reflect on trends and tensions in Islamic education in Thailand which will allow us to further illustrate and critically evaluate the dynamics and tensions that have emerged in the Muslim community there.

OBJECTIVES OF THE BOOK

By way of the above as a point of entry, this book has four primary objectives. First, this book aims to be a first-of-its-kind resource book for Thai specialists and those working more broadly in the field of Islamic education. In particular, it accumulates and provides hitherto unpublished information on various aspects of Islamic education in southern Thailand, but also with an eye to comparison with other Muslim communities strewn throughout the country. The data amassed in this book, collected over a period of three years by the author and a team of local researchers, will be of significant use not only to scholars working on Muslim politics and community in Thailand, but for comparativists as well.

There are further localized reasons why mapping out the profile of Islamic schools in southern Thailand is an urgent and necessary exercise. The extant literature centres our understanding of Islamic education in southern Thailand on the *pondok* and its role and stature in the Malay-Muslim community. There are no doubt important reasons why this is so. The southern Thai kingdom of Patani Darussalam was historically significant as a centre of Islamic learning across the Malay-Muslim world from the sixteenth century onward, and the *pondok* has come to exemplify this tradition. Hence, any attempt to study Islamic education must necessarily begin with the institution of the *pondok* as a point of entry. Additionally, such is the centrality of the *pondok* in popular imagination that it has become the prevailing practice to label just about every institution of Islamic learning in southern Thailand a "*pondok*". This discursive practice obfuscates what has over the years developed into a highly complex and pluralistic system of religious education. Indeed, there has been a proliferation of Islamic schools in southern Thailand, both in number and kind, such that, at least in theory, students would be able to go from pre-school through to tertiary education along an exclusively "Islamic" track (even if they were pursuing an academic discipline, as opposed to Islamic studies). These schools can be differentiated not just in terms of standards, but also the nature and source of funding, qualifications of teaching staff, the focus of their respective curricula, and, most provocatively, ideological proclivities as well. There is an urgent need to sufficiently appreciate this plurality in order to better understand Islamic education in southern Thailand.

The second aim of this book is to provide an update on the nature of relations between the central Thai state and its Malay-Muslim periphery through the optic of Islamic education. While this is a topic that has garnered widespread interest over the years, the book looks to go beyond general impressions of this relationship to explore its dynamics in the specific case of education. Here, it is important also to register that the employment of education policies as the yardstick takes on greater salience since many of the problems associated with the conflict in southern Thailand today are a result of contested, polarized interpretations of history and identity, and it is the education system that often perpetuates both national dogma and local perspectives on these issues, rendering them progressively intractable.

Because an exclusive focus on relations between Bangkok and southern Thailand through the optic of state-society relations tends invariably to treat the Malay-Muslims as a monolithic group comprising empty, unreflective subjects somehow devoid of the ability to reflect on and analyse the existential conditions of their social, political, and economic predicaments, there is an equally urgent need to investigate dynamics within the Malay-Muslim community itself, as they pertain to the nature and authenticity of knowledge, and the legitimacy and authority of those empowered to transmit it. Bearing this in mind, the third objective of the book will be to investigate a dimension of Islamic education unexplored in recent times in studies on southern Thailand — the nature of relationships within the Malay-Muslim community.

Here, interest is given particularly to the effect that Muslim reformists have had on the traditional landscape. This arises out of observations that traditionalism and orthodoxy in the Malay-Muslim community of southern Thailand have in recent years come under pressure for change and transformation from a brand of Islamic reformism that is, paradoxically enough, rooted in puritanical and fundamentalist Salafi ideology. The tension and contestations arising from this "clash" is, this book argues, clearly evident in the education system, where the reformist attempt to transform the nature and transmission of Islamic knowledge has been interpreted by traditionalists as a challenge to age-old beliefs and practices, as well as to their authority and legitimacy as custodians of the faith. In order to trace the contours of this tension, the book will rely on extensive interviews with educators from both camps as well as the analysis of popular Islamic texts employed in the religious studies curriculum. Particular attention will be given here to texts identified with reformist thinking among the *ulama* community in southern Thailand. There are two issues at stake here. First, unlike the works of traditionalist scholars, which have been treated at some length by Hasan Madmarn, Azyumardi Azra, and Peter Riddell amongst others, the work of a current generation of reformist scholars such as Ismail Lutfi Japakiya has yet to come under similar scholarly scrutiny.[6] Second, while a bastion of traditional Shafi'i and Sufi Islam, the discursive landscape in southern Thailand has of late experienced considerable growth in Salafi-reformist scholarship that is gradually reconfiguring (not without resistance) the existing constellation of Islamic thought and praxis and threatening to eclipse the stature of traditionalist scholars.

Fourth, the book also charts out the transnational links and networks, both formal and informal, between Islamic education institutions and scholars in southern Thailand and the wider community of believers. Given the universal nature of Islam as faith, creed, and knowledge (in theory, at least), it follows that Islamic education would logically possess a transnational dimension in the way that local knowledge is to some extent or other plugged into the wider *ummah*. Furthermore, it is common knowledge that, insofar as mainstream thinking on questions of authenticity are concerned, the "universal" character of Islamic knowledge is also paradoxically predicated on the existence of a temporal "core" — the Middle East and Arab Peninsula, from which Islamic knowledge flows to all quarters of the Muslim world. The charting of these transnational links and networks entail, to the extent such information is obtainable, careful examination into the flow of Malay-Muslim students from Thailand to various centres of Islamic learning both regionally and globally, the nature of relationships between institutions in these centres with counterparts in southern Thailand, and the existence of alumni networks.

Finally, the book aims to bridge the gulf that exists between the fields of security and conflict studies on the one hand and area studies on the other. This objective arises from the observation that this gulf has grown wider today, in the age of the post-September 11 fascination with global *jihadi* terrorism, despite the fact that both fields have much to contribute to our understanding of violence and conflict — sanctioned with religious referents by its perpetrators — and of the nature and configuration of the societal structures that spawn them. While the study of Islamic education has in general gained greater currency these days, owing to concerns about a possible nexus between Islamic schools and Muslim militancy, the resultant cottage industry has produced few works that have attempted to open this "black box" (of Islamic education) by systematically and critically examining its content, nor has much been done to study the policies and procedural norms that inform it. This is certainly so in the case of southern Thailand, where persistent accusations made by the Thai government and by numerous security analysts and pundits — that Islamic schools are somehow spawning militants and perpetuating endemic violence — have not been followed by careful study of the ideas and ideologies these schools are supposedly propounding and instilling. While the immediate purpose here is not so much to test the validity of such claims, through careful interrogation of the religious texts employed in the curriculum as well as through interviews with the educators in these schools, this book hopes to provide a nuanced perspective of how Islamic schools may or may not be involved in the conflict in southern Thailand.

DEFINITIONS AND ARGUMENTS

Given that a key objective of this book is to investigate the tensions that have arisen between "traditionalist" and "reformist" Islam, some comments on the definition of these terms are perhaps appropriate here. For our purposes, traditionalist Islam in southern Thailand refers to the syncretic belief system that marries the Islamic creed with indigenous cultural beliefs and practices that were carried over from the pre-Islamic era of Southeast Asian history.

This syncretism underscores the brand of Sufi Islam commonly found across Islamic Southeast Asia including southern Thailand, even today. Additionally, it should further be noted that this brand of traditional Islam sits comfortably with the Shafi'i school of jurisprudence popularly practised across the region. As alluded to earlier, in the realm of education traditional Islam is expressed in the institution of the *pondok*, where the instruction provided is, save for some very elementary lessons in mathematics, exclusively focused on religion. Reformist Islam, on the other hand, can be conceptualized on (at least) two levels. In terms of pedagogy, it refers simply to moves to "reform" and change prevailing means of knowledge transmission. Hence, as we shall see in the following chapters, one of the imperatives behind the creation of the Islamic private school, for example, stems from the observed need to reform the traditional *pondok* by introducing academic and general subjects, improving pedagogical tools, and streamlining methods of assessment. At a deeper level, however, the concept of reformist Islam, as least as it is applied here, relates also to the very nature of knowledge itself. Following the tradition of the Islamic reform movement that gained prominence a century earlier and whose influence continues to linger, reformist Islam speaks among other things of the need to refocus knowledge away from the fixation on *fiqh* or jurisprudence back to the Qur'an and *sunnah*, the actions and teachings of the Prophet that are often recorded in the *hadith* (a series of authenticated sayings and declarations recorded by Muslim scholars from sources who heard the Prophet speak and watched him live). Furthermore, rather than a rejection of modernity, reformist Islam seeks to understand and embrace modernity by arguing the premise that modern knowledge is not unexplainable in Islamic terms. It should be noted here that to some, this model of reform is explicitly Salafi in nature in that the return to the Qur'an and *sunnah* accords in some respects with the Salafi practice of avoiding scientific rationalism and adopting faith and religion as the point of entry to the pursuit of understanding. In this regard, the interest in the intellectual and theological dimensions of the reform movement here is specifically with relation to the ideas and writings of Salafi-reformists, as identified in this book.

Bearing these objectives in mind, this study argues that, far from being a merely passive recipient of Western secular education paradigms or of foreign Islamic ideational and ideological influences, the Malay-Muslim community of the southern provinces has increasingly exercised agency in its attempt to navigate between pressures generated by the need to preserve culture, knowledge, and identity at one end, and the demands of modernization, nationalism, and reform at the other. Consequently, Islamic education in southern Thailand has been defined as much by the adaptation, synthesis, and appropriation of external models of education (by which I mean both "Western" and secular as well as reformist and Salafi) as it has by tradition, orthodoxy, and resistance to change. Beyond the simplistic caricature of Islamic schools as a breeding ground of Islamic militancy and terrorism — a view that has unfortunately gained much currency in the post-September 11 "age of terror" — this book contends that Islamic education in southern Thailand is a highly dynamic terrain which captures a variety of contestations emanating from within the structural, historical, and cultural parameters of the southern Thai Malay-Muslim community.

STRUCTURE OF THE BOOK

This book is divided into five chapters. Chapter One briefly describes the advent and configuration of Islam in southern Thailand, as well as the role that Islamic schools have played in the narratives of ethno-nationalism and separatism in the Malay-Muslim provinces. The chapter further discusses the major policies that the modern Thai state has formulated and instituted with regards to Islamic schools in the south, and the ramifications of these policies on state-society relations as well as on the Muslim community's own sense of identity and belonging. Chapter Two maps out the plural landscape of Islamic education in southern Thailand. It does so by identifying the structures and institutions of Islamic learning, in the process distinguishing their key traits. Chapter Three investigates the emergence and trends of Islamic reform in Thailand in general, and in the south in particular. Here, three major stages are identified: the advent of reformist ideas in Thailand, the emergence of a reformist movement in the southern provinces, and the resurgence of this reformist movement in recent times. It is suggested that the latter two stages are personified, first in the nationalist-reformist scholar Haji Sulong Abdul Kadir in the years immediately preceding World War Two, and later in the person of Dr. Ismail Lutfi Japakiya, the Saudi-trained cleric and current rector of Yala Islamic University. The chapter further focuses discussion on Lutfi's practice of Islam and considers it against the backdrop of allegations of his allegedly unstinting allegiance to Wahhabism, a distinct and highly puritanical stream of Salafism. Chapter Four charts the parameters of Islamic thought and practice in southern Thailand's Islamic schools on a range of issues, focusing on the contestations between Salafi-reformist and traditionalist approaches to the teaching and content of Islamic education in the southern provinces. The chapter explores these tensions through the optic of pedagogical and curricular emphasis. Particular focus is given to the key texts used by reformists which, as suggested earlier, have been insufficiently studied in the literature. These texts are introduced, analysed, and interrogated in terms of their transmission of ideas that in some instances challenge conventional and traditionalist thinking on a range of issues. Chapter Five maps out the transnational networks, both formal and informal, of Islamic education locally and internationally. It focuses on identifying the nature of these networks, as well as its features in terms of student associations and alumni groupings. The chapter also explores the cross-currents generated by alternative Islamic ideas and movements, primarily the *Jemaat Tabligh* and Shi'a groups, which have taken shape on the educational landscape in Muslim Thailand. In addition, the chapter undertakes a number of comparative investigations in order to consider trends in the southern provinces against those in other major concentrations of Muslims in Thailand, chiefly, Chiang Mai in the north and Bangkok in the central plains. The book concludes by drawing out key observations on the trends and tensions within Islamic education in southern Thailand. The Conclusion will attempt to illustrate that popular assumptions about how Islamic schools in southern Thailand are generating radicals and terrorists have been grossly exaggerated and misplaced. Such generalizations, the book argues, are fundamentally counter-productive, as they might engender policies that would do little other than deepen misunderstanding and resentment between the state and the Muslim communities of the southern provinces. Rather, the book concludes that there is a need to foster greater understanding of the challenges and constraints faced by southern Thailand's Islamic schools, not only in relation to the state and to history, but also in the context of developments and tensions within Muslim society itself.

Prior to the study proper, a few caveats on spelling, terminology, and research methods are in order. In this book, both the terms "Patani" and "Pattani" are used. "Patani" is used when there is a need to refer to the historical Muslim kingdom of Patani Darussalam that continues to resonate in the minds of Thailand's Malay-Muslims. "Pattani", on the other hand, is employed to describe the administrative unit of Pattani, which constitutes one of four or five (depending on how one chooses to define the area) provinces in the south. Because the subject of inquiry is Islamic education in the Malay-Muslim community, when exploring local concepts and ideas this study alludes to mostly Malay and, where appropriate Arabic, terminology as opposed to Thai. By the same token, while cognizant of the fact that as a religio-ethnic marker the notion of "Malay-Muslim" is by no means exclusive to southern Thailand, the phrase Malay-Muslim is used here specifically to refer to the Muslims in the three southern Thai provinces who are also almost entirely ethnic Malay. Likewise, the provinces covered under the rubric of "southern Thailand" here are primarily Pattani, Yala, Narathiwat, where Malay-Muslims form the majority of the population.

Finally, given the dearth of extant published literature on the topic in either English, Malay, or Thai, this study draws upon extensive field research conducted by the author as well as by a team of field researchers who conducted interviews and collected information over three years. Because of the sensitivity both of the information collected and of the situation in southern Thailand more broadly, it is difficult to divulge specific details of interviews and meetings without potentially compromising the security of interviewees. In particular, I have been careful not to divulge the names of those interviewed (except where I was explicitly permitted to do so), or of the schools in which they teach, and for that matter, of my field researchers. For purposes of methodological rigour and source verification, I have identified most of the schools in which interviews were conducted. For obvious reasons I have not been able to name the schools that either my field researchers or I identified that teach local Patani history in a way that is antagonistic towards the Thai state, at times to the extent of endorsing separatism.

Notes

[1]   Charles Allen, *God's Terrorists: The Wahhabi Cult and the Hidden Roots of Modern Jihad* (London: Abacus, 2007), p. 5.

[2]   Fred Kaplan, "Rumsfeld's Pentagon Papers", in *Slate*, October 2003 <http://slate.msn.com/id/2090250> (accessed 23 October 2003).

[3]   See, for example, Yadullah Kazmi, "Islamic Education: Traditional Education or Education in Tradition?", *Islamic Studies* 42, (2003): 259–88; Sherin Saadallah, "Islam, Religious Orientations, and Education", in *Educational Strategies Among Muslims in the Context of Globalisation*, edited by Holger Daun and Geoffrey Walford (Leiden: Brill, 2004), pp. 37–61.

[4]   Raymond Scupin, ed., *Aspects of Development: Islamic Education in Thailand and Malaysia* (Bangi: Institut Bahasa Kesusasteraan dan Kebudayaan Melayu, Universiti Kebangsaan Malaysia, 1989); Hasan Madmarn, *The Pondok and Madrasah of Pattani* (Bangi: Universiti Kebangsaan Malaysia, 1990).

[5]   Surin Pitsuwan, *Islam and Malay Nationalism: A Case Study of the Malay-Muslims of Southern Thailand* (Bangkok: Thai Khadi Research Institute, Thammasat University, 1985); Wan Kadir Che Man, *Muslim Separatism: The Moros of Southern Philippines and the Malays of Southern Thailand* (Singapore: Oxford University Press, 1990).

[6]   See Hasan Madmarn, *The Pondok and Madrasah in Pattani* (Bangi, Selangor:

Penerbit Universiti Kebangsaan Malaysia, 1999); Peter Riddell, *Islam and the Malay-Indonesian World: Transmission and Responses* (Singapore: Horizon Books, 2001), pp. 184–204; Azyumardi Azra, *The Origins of Islamic Reformism in Southeast Asia* (New South Wales: Allen & Unwin, 2004), pp. 122–26.

1

ISLAM AND MALAY-MUSLIM
IDENTITY IN THAILAND

Depending on the source, the percentage of Muslims in Thailand has been placed at around 4–8 per cent of a total population of approximately 65 million people. Islam is currently the largest minority religion in Thailand where (despite intermittent pressures by the Buddhist Sangha), Buddhism, a religion of great import in Thai society and the creed of the vast majority of Thais, has not been declared the official religion of the country. Muslims are concentrated in the southernmost provinces of Narathiwat, Pattani, Yala, and Satun, where they make up anywhere between 65–85 per cent of the local population and are mostly ethnic Malay. The region itself has become known in popular parlance, somewhat problematically, as the "deep south", "deepestmost south" or "far south" — terminology that further accentuates the perception of marginality to Thailand.[1] Other areas of major Muslim concentrations are in the North (Chiang Mai), the central plains (Bangkok and Ayutthaya), and the "upper" south (Songkhla, Nakhon Si Thammarat, Phuket). This narrative of the marginalization of Malay-Muslims is further underscored in the way that until recently they were also known pejoratively as *khaek* or "dark-skinned visitors" in colloquial discourse.[2] There is also a Buddhist minority in the Muslim-dominated southern provinces amounting to approximately 30 per cent of the population, depending on which of the southern provinces one is referring to. Despite their minority status in the south, Buddhists are concentrated chiefly in urban areas and town centres (though there are Buddhist-majority rural villages scattered across the southern provinces), while the Malay-Muslims have a weightier presence in rural areas where economic activity continues to revolve around farming, agriculture, and fishing, and where traditional Malay practices and lifestyles still hold sway despite the onslaught of development and modernization.[3]

UNDERSTANDING ISLAM'S PLACE IN THAI HISTORY

The question of the arrival of Islam to Patani continues to be debated by Thai historians.[4] According to some historical records, Muslim communities were present in Thailand as early as the thirteenth century — prior even to the conversion of Melaka — during the reign of King Ramkhamhaeng (1279–1298) who ruled the Sukhothai kingdom. Islam, as several scholars have noted, arrived in Thailand via a number of routes, namely, the Indo-Malay Archipelago, Yemen, Persia, South Asia, China, Burma, and Cambodia. In local Malay-Muslim folklore, however, the transformation of Patani into an Islamic kingdom is traced to the conversion of the Patani king Phraya Tu Nakpa by Syaikh Sa'eed, an *ulama* from Pasai.[5] The Patani king is said to have sought Syaikh Sa'eed's help in curing a skin disease that was plaguing him. In brief, the folklore tells of how the Patani king made a promise to convert to Syaikh Sa'eed's religion, Islam, if the latter were able to successfully rid him of the ailment. According to this narrative, after being cured Phraya Tu Nakpa failed to keep his promise and the disease returned. This cycle of healing and relapse happened three times, and it was only after the third occasion that the king honoured his commitment, and upon being permanently cured, converted to Islam and took the name Sultan Ismail Shah Zillulah Fi al-Alam.

In line with the rest of archipelagic Southeast Asia, the vast majority of Muslims in Thailand subscribe to the Shafi'i school of Islamic jurisprudence. The only major exception to this are Muslims in the north of the country, such as those populating Chiang Mai, who are mostly Hanafi in jurisprudential orientation. Beyond that, there remains a significant Sufi influence carried over from older traditions, and since Sufi Muslims also subscribe to one of the four accepted schools of Sunni jurisprudence, it is not uncommon to find that in Thailand Sufism overlaps at various points with the orthodox practices of the mainstream Shafi'i traditionalists.

In the sixteenth and seventeenth centuries Persian merchants brought Shi'a Islam to Thailand. The Ayutthaya era of Persian-influenced Islam may arguably be considered the "golden age" of Islam in Thai history, for Islam flourished at this time. During this period, the Muslim community in Ayutthaya was not only cosmopolitan but, as a result of its role in commerce, trade, and the bureaucracy, powerful and influential as well. With this influence came the introduction of the office of the Chularajmontri or *Sheikh ul-Islam*, whose task was to advise the court of Ayutthaya on matters pertaining to Islam. The Chularajmontri is today seen as the official, if titular, head of Thailand's Muslim community. He is appointed by royal decree and holds the office for a life term. In terms of institutional capacity, the Chularajmontri supervises Thailand's twenty-nine provincial Islamic committees and the Islamic Centre of Thailand, established in 1945 as an outgrowth of the Patronage of Islam Act. The Chularajmontri is elected by the presidents of the twenty-nine provincial Islamic committees (which together make up the Provincial Council of Islamic Affairs) and thirty-six members of the National Council of Islamic Affairs housed at the Islamic Centre. He is endorsed by the king via royal decree.[6] Persian influence over the court in Ayutthaya was not confined to the introduction of the office of the Chularajmontri. Shi'a Muslims from Persia also served as ministers at the court of Ayutthaya, managing the Ayutthayan navy and its maritime trade.[7] A small but increasingly active Shi'a community grew out of this legacy of Persian influence and can be found across several cities in Thailand today, with the largest concentrations found in Bangkok, Ayutthaya, and Nakhon Si Thammarat. At the same time as Persian influence flourished in the plains, Islam had also begun to command strong adherence across the Malay world, establishing another foothold in the process. The southern kingdom of Patani, while nominally a tributary of Ayutthaya, in fact enjoyed considerable autonomy and as a consequence gradually gravitated into the orbit of the Malay world. Along with sultanates in Kedah, Kelantan, and Terengganu, Patani underwent an Islamization process that took somewhat different form from that in the north.

Though Buddhism is not the official religion of Thailand, it is the majority religion, and while the king is officially the patron of all religions in Thailand, his stature and position is very much emblematic in the eyes of Thai society of the stature and recognition that Buddhism commands in the country. The primacy accorded to Buddhism is further expressed in the crafting of modern Thai national identity along the lines of "*Chat, Sassana, Pramahakasat*" or "Nation, Religion, and Monarchy", which clearly speaks to the central role that Buddhism was expected to play in the eyes of Thailand's modernizers in the early twentieth century.

The question of religious identity is also freighted with ethno-linguistic connotations. This is particularly pertinent in the context of southern Thailand, where such considerations have had ramifications for the place of Malay-Muslim culture and identity in the modern Thai nation. Since the modernization of Thailand was set in motion during the reign of King Rama V (King Chulalongkorn), the nomenclature employed to categorize Thailand's

Muslim population has been a subject of much debate. The official term for Muslims in Thailand, "Thai Islam", was a product of the Patronage of Islam Act enunciated in 1945 by the post-war democratic government. This term, however, caused some consternation in the ethnic Malay communities of the southern provinces. For them, it was seen as a perpetuation of the narrative of hegemony and subjugation that informed local understandings of history, and "Thai Islam" was interpreted as yet another means through which Bangkok contrived to dilute, if not altogether eradicate, Malay culture and identity in the south. As far as the southern provinces are concerned, locals have traditionally preferred to emphasize not only their religious but also their ethnic identity. So sensitive and controversial is the issue of nomenclature and the discourse on identity for southern Thailand that debates over how to identify the Muslims of the south continue to this day.

The latest permutation surfaced as recently as 2005, when this question became one of the key challenges faced by the National Reconciliation Commission. Members of the commission were compelled in the course of their deliberations to ponder the difficult questions of "who" exactly were the victims of conflict and whether the problems of the south were really rooted in historical consciousness.[8] At another level, this stress on "Malayness" speaks to the exclusiveness of Malay-Muslims' conceptions of self, for such terminology obviously aims to distinguish its referents from Thailand's non-Malay Muslims. It should be noted here that it is not the objective of this book to unpack the problems associated with terminology and nomenclature. Such an endeavour would demand a volume of its own and as such lies well beyond the scope of the current project. While recognizing the complex nature of the problem, this book will nevertheless employ the terminology of "Malay-Muslim" when referring to the Muslims of southern Thailand, simply because this is the label that is used most often by both scholars and locals, and it remains the least problematic term as far as the object of inquiry — the Muslim community of the southern provinces — is concerned.

While Malay-Muslims are our primary concern, we need to keep in mind that a significant component of the Muslim population in Thailand is for all intents and purposes Thai in terms of culture and social practice, including in the use of the Thai language. In other words, they share little by way of cultural and linguistic affinity with the ethnic Malays, aside from religion. In the south, they populate the upper provinces of Trang, Phang-nga, Songhkla and Satun, and, as suggested earlier, are commonly referred to among Thais as "Thai Islam". Compared to the Malay-Muslims of the three southern provinces, these Thai Muslims are considerably better integrated into contemporary Thai society. Their children speak Thai, as they do themselves, and attend Thai national schools. They participate in economic and social activities alongside Buddhists. While Muslim by creed, oftentimes their adherence to Islam is far less rigid than what is found among the Malay-Muslims in the three southern provinces, notwithstanding the prevalence of pre-Islamic cultural practices among the latter. For instance, Thai Muslims sometimes eat foods generally deemed to be prohibited in Islam, and they do not necessarily observe obligations of prayer and fasting very strictly. Moreover, the women are hardly ever found in the full *hijab*, whereas such dress has in recent times become increasingly popular in the Malay-Muslim communities of the three southern provinces, no doubt as a sign of the proliferation of Salafi influence in the region. Overall, some scholars have observed that Muslim communities in the upper southern provinces have generally developed a more relaxed mutuality with Buddhists, and the coexistence of people of both religions in many villages is notable.[9]

The heterogeneous character of Muslim society in Thailand becomes even more evident when one profiles Islam in the rest of the country. Bangkok, for instance, is home to approximately 500,000 Muslims from a variety of ethnic backgrounds, while Chiang Mai to the north has a population of around 30,000 to 35,000 Muslims, half of whom are ethnically Yunnanese while the rest consists of Persian, Bengali, Pathan, Indian, Cham, Malay, and Indonesian ethnicities. Because of this heterogeneity, decades of attempts at integration on the part of various Thai governments have given rise to a discourse that recognizes at once the ethnic plurality of Thailand's Muslims as well as the unity of their allegiances to the state and its conceptualization of national identity. As alluded to earlier, the essence of this is captured in the terminology of "Thai Islam" or "Thai Muslim" that has come to dominate the state's discourse on its Muslim religious minority. Again however, while this nomenclature is generally accepted by Muslims outside of the three southern provinces, it is widely rejected in Malay-Muslim circles because of the salience of their Malay ethnic identity, into which their allegiances to Islam are subsumed, in their conceptions of self.

From this sketch of the ethno-religious terrain, it is clear that one of the major fault lines in Southeast Asia's cultural landscape lies at the border between Thailand's upper southern provinces and its "deep south". It is at this junction that "Thai" ends and "Malay" begins, and where the question of ethnicity gains greater currency in the discourse on communal identities. As noted above, Muslims of the "deep south" are predominantly Malay, and it is to this ethnic identity that loyalty and primacy are pledged. Malay-Muslims maintain a strong identity distinct from that of other Thai Muslims, to say nothing of their Buddhist countrymen. Their claim to distinctiveness is based in large part on the construction and maintenance of an historical narrative of uniqueness. It begins with the argument that they are ethnically different ("*Melayu*") and, as *Anak Patani* (children of Patani), are Muslims of a particular stock and purity. This narrative is not only widely held to and celebrated among the Malay-Muslims of the south, it is also transferred from generation to generation via oral history as well as the local school curriculum (of which more will be discussed later) and thereby etched into the communal consciousness. Nowhere is this uniqueness and exclusivity more patently expressed than in the realm of language. Malay-Muslims speak a local dialect of Malay commonly but problematically referred to in Thai as "Jawi" or "Yawi". Local Malay-Muslims refer to it as "*Bahasa Tempatan*" or "the local language", and it is linguistically similar to the Malay dialect spoken in the neighbouring northern Malaysian state of Kelantan.[10] These significant linguistic disjunctures also carry religious overtones. Here, Omar Farouk observes:

> it is only in recent times that the Thai language has been elevated as the language of Islam in Thailand. Consequently, there is a growing corpus of Islamic religious literature in Thai. There have already been a few versions of translations of the Qur'an. Collections of *hadiths* too have been translated into Thai. The expanding role of the Thai language within Thailand's Muslim public sphere, however, has not dislodged the entrenched position of Malay as the traditional language of Islam, especially among the Malay Muslims of Thailand.[11]

To be sure, the centrality of language is not merely confined to the polemics of academic debate. From his research into the declassified documents of the Central Intelligence Office, Thanet Aphornsuvan has unearthed the Thai government's early fixation with language in their framing of the "problem" of the south. In Thanet's words:

> The classified report stated that apparently the 'Thai Islam' in the four southern provinces (including Satun) did not understand the system of government because many of them had learned little Thai from ancient times to the present. There was no interest in studying Thai language. The government bureaucracy did not seriously promote and encourage them to study Thai language, thus 'Thai Islam' only studied Islamic religion and Malay language with devotion. We could see that 'Thai Islam' in the four southern provinces hardly used the local dialect but preferred to use Malay. Therefore they had no opportunity to know and understand the development in the government system of administration.[12]

The salience of language in conceptualizations of self and other on the part of the Malay-Muslim community was also stressed in the observation of religious leaders that "if the government accepts our language, we can accept the Thai nation".[13] More recently, the controversial nature of questions of language recognition and legitimacy have been further captured in the debates surrounding the National Reconciliation Commission's proposal for Malay to be adopted as a "working language" in the south.

Notwithstanding the cultural divide epitomized by language, there have of course been some points of convergence between Malay and Thai Muslims. For instance, as is the case throughout the Muslim world, in Thailand the institution of the mosque lies at the heart of both Malay-Muslim and Thai-Muslim society. Clearly though, it has been the divergences that by and large seized both the Thai governments and the local communities.

If language is a clear expression of the exclusivity of the Malay-Muslim identity, then one could conceivably argue that separatism has become its chief consequence. To be sure, nowhere is this exclusivity of Malay-Muslim identity more profoundly demonstrated than in the long-drawn separatist struggle for liberation from a Bangkok which is portrayed in Malay-Muslim ethno-nationalist discourse as an alien colonizer. Predictably, the geographical parameters of this century-old separatist struggle have largely been defined by the ethno-religious boundaries of the "deep south" Malay-Muslim provinces of Narathiwat, Yala, and Pattani. While this is not to imply that a separatist spirit holds sway among the vast majority of Malay-Muslims in the south, the nexus between separatism and cultural identity nevertheless has proven sufficiently salient to warrant consideration here, particularly given the role that Islamic schools are believed to have played (and continue to play) in sustaining it.

ISLAM, IDENTITY, AND ETHNO-NATIONALISM

Historically, the kingdom of Patani consisted of the area that today roughly coheres geographically to the provinces of Pattani, Yala, and Narathiwat in southern Thailand. Between roughly the fifteenth and eighteenth centuries, the Kingdom of Patani was also known as Patani Darussalam, and was acknowledged across the Malay world not only as a Malay kingdom, but as an Islamic polity (Dar Al-Islam). At the same time, Patani was also a flourishing centre of commerce and trade, where traders from Southeast Asia met and transacted with counterparts from elsewhere on the Asian continent and Europe. More specifically, Patani Darussalam was during this time emerging as a major centre for Islamic learning in Southeast Asia

— to the extent that scholars would later describe it as the cradle of Islam in Southeast Asia. The *pondok* schools of southern Thailand played a particularly important role in establishing and sustaining this reputation. By the early twentieth century, just as a re-awakening of religious consciousness was underway across the Muslim world, the Patani region had the largest number of *pondok* schools in the Malay Peninsula, drawing students from all over the Southeast Asian region.[14]

Although Patani Darussalam was basically a tributary state of the Siamese kingdom after the Siamese invasion during the reign of Rama I (1737–1802), actual links were for the most part relatively weak. Consequently, Patani enjoyed a significant degree of independence which on several occasions was manifested in a refusal to pay tribute to Siam, and at times even in rebellion against Siamese rule. Gradually, however, as the modernization and bureaucratization of the central state took shape, the kingdom of Siam gained leverage over its outer peripheries, including Patani, and through the combined use of military force and administrative centralization, not to mention the occasional diplomatic machination, eventually managed to consolidate its grip over the southern region. As part of King Chulalongkorn's policies to transform his principality into a modern territorial nation-state with a Westernized bureaucracy, a modern educational system was created towards the end of the nineteenth century. The transformation of the education system was to serve two purposes. First, it was envisaged to provide a steady stream of educated officials and administrators for a Siamese bureaucratic service upon which the modern state was to be built. Second, the content of the existing education system was to be restructured so as to facilitate the integration of ethnic minorities into a coherent Siamese national identity. These efforts to transform education, however, did not always appeal to Siam's outer provinces. In fact, in the southern provinces of the former Patani Darussalam, these policies were for the most part not welcome at all. The initiatives were actively resisted on the account that they threatened local cultural and religious identity, expressed in the autonomous education system centred on the *pondok*, and ignited a spirit of resistance that in many respects carries on to this day. The dislocation threatened by these changes in education for the Malay-Muslim population was succinctly described by Raymond Scupin in the following manner:

> they (the changes) created fundamental dilemmas for the Malay Muslims of this southern region. The Thai compulsory education system was based upon the Thai language, a language foreign to most of the Malay Muslims of the South, and upon Buddhist values, which were intimately

associated with a traditional monastic curriculum developed by the
Buddhist Sangha. Therefore, in the eyes of many Muslims in these
southern provinces to become involved as a citizen participating in the
Thai polity necessitated a rejection of one's language and religion.[15]

Following the completion of administrative consolidation of Siamese
rule over the territories of the traditional Patani kingdom in 1909 (after the
signing of the Anglo-Siamese Treaty), a resistance movement emerged led by
displaced feudal Malay elites. Despite the recognizable role of this traditional
feudal leadership in the early stages of the Malay-Muslim rebellion against
Siam, religious leaders have always made a major contribution to the
articulation of challenge against the hegemony of the central state.[16] The
Siamese government's attempts to exert control over traditional institutions
such as the *pondok* and *shari'a* courts — the educational and judicial backbone
of Malay society — ensured that disenchanted religious teachers and jurists
provided a fertile source of intellectual and religio-cultural leadership for
movements opposing the incorporation of the southern provinces into the
Siamese central state.[17] Religious leaders were further emboldened by the
Islamic reformist movement of the early twentieth century that swept through
the Malay world. As we will see later, this reformist tide witnessed the influx
of ideas that transformed Muslim mindsets, pitting them against central
authorities who in any case never fully comprehended the implications of
Islamic reformism on Thai-Muslim consciousness.[18]

In order to grasp this fundamental antithesis in the historical consciousness
of the Malay-Muslim community, one has to appreciate not only the resilience
of Malay identity, but also the forceful nature of Bangkok's drive to craft a
distinct Thai nationality and impose it on ethnic minorities. The turn of the
twentieth century saw the Thai state seek to promulgate modernizing policies
that required the dilution of ethnic identities and loyalties, even as they
promoted the primacy of Buddhism. This phenomenon was most tellingly
demonstrated during the reign of King Vajiravudh (Rama VI, 1881–1925).
Upon succeeding Chulalongkorn, he initiated new policies aimed at
constructing a Thai national identity resting on three institutions, namely,
Nation (*Chaat*), Religion (*Saatsanaa*), and Monarchy (*Phra Mahaa Kasat*), as
its cornerstones.[19] Explaining the impetus behind this construction of identity,
Raymond Scupin surmised: "this Thai political and cultural code constituted
an iconic representation of the structure of Thai society that was formulated
to mediate actual ethnic ambiguities and contradictions within the country".[20]
The articulation of a new ideology of nationalism was followed by the
promulgation of compulsory Thai education for the purposes of indoctrinating

the values it encapsulated. In the Malay-Muslim provinces of the south, this attempt to form and consolidate a national identity clashed head on with prevailing educational practices which emphasized Islam and cultural identity. Instead, the articulation of this nationalist project marked "the beginning of a long and torturous struggle to widen the sphere and deepen the level of autonomy for the Malay-Muslims of Patani based on specific ethnic differences".[21] These tensions would later be aggravated by aggressive assimilationist policies during the administrations of Phibun Songgkram (1938–44; 1948–57) and Sarit Thanarat (1958–63). In these periods, civil law was imposed and Islamic law abolished. The office of the Dato Yutthitam (*qadi* or Islamic judge), that had governed family and inheritance issues in the Muslim community while still being subject to the final arbitration of a sitting Thai judge, was dismantled. Friday was abolished as a public holiday, and there were orchestrated attempts to convert Muslims to Buddhism.[22] In the case of Sarit, assimilationist policies were imposed for the purpose of cementing a new "development" ideology (*patanakarn*) that attempted to bring about integration and assimilation through social-economic development programmes.[23] The net effect of this historical legacy of marginalization was to bring about what Peter Gowing termed the "psychological death" of the community.[24] Needless to say, this new ideology, and the policies it spawned, did little more than to provoke strong Malay nationalist reactions.

Sandwiched between these authoritarian regimes, however, was a brief democratic reprieve which, though short-lived, did witness an attempted recalibration of policy towards the Malay-Muslim provinces of the south. In a move to temper the strains in the relationship, the government of Khuang Aphaiwong crafted the Patronage of Islam Act in 1945. Among the policies enunciated was the reinstatement of the office of the Chularajmontri discussed earlier, the right to observe Friday as a holiday, and the restoration of Islamic family and inheritance laws.[25] Under the Act, Dato Yutthitam was also reinstated as a government appointee, though many in the Muslim community criticized this on the grounds that a non-Muslim government should not have the authority to appoint a Muslim judge. The Patronage of Islam Act further legislated for the creation of a National Council for Islamic Affairs (NCIA) that was to be headed by the Chularajmontri. The NCIA functioned as an advisory body to the interior and education ministries on matters pertaining to the Muslim community and oversaw the activities of the various Provincial Councils for Islamic Affairs (PCIA).

The salience of Malay-Muslim ethno-cultural consciousness ensured that separatism in southern Thailand was naturally an exclusive affair, thereby reinforcing the uniqueness of the three southern provinces. Indeed, Malay-

Muslim resistance was premised exclusively on Malay identity and interpretations of history. Yet this exclusivist subtext to southern Thai separatism is sometimes missed in narratives of the struggle, particularly those purveyed in the conflict and terrorism studies fields, which tend to portray it as a phenomenon that covers the entire region of southern Thailand.[26] Despite forming 67 per cent or so of the population, a substantial portion of Satun's ethnic Malays, for reasons too complex to be elaborated here, no longer use the Malay language. In other words, Malay-Muslims in Satun are by and large assimilated Thai speakers, and this has had a tremendous effect on the place of Satun in Malay-Muslim conceptualizations of self and other. The relatively successful assimilation of Malay-Muslims in Satun provides a fairly persuasive explanation of why the province is largely peripheral in the socio-cultural imagination of the "deep" south. Against this backdrop, it is also no coincidence that Satun has always stood apart from the separatist activity that has plagued southern Thailand.[27] For instance, statistics compiled at Chulalongkorn University on the violence since January 2004 indicate that Satun has mostly been spared in the most violent year to date in the history of southern resistance. This reinforces the argument that the dynamics behind the conflict in southern Thailand remain primarily driven by ethnic identity and are confined to the Malay-speaking provinces of Narathiwat, Pattani, and Yala.[28] The question of Satun throws into greater relief the dichotomous identities at work in defining the essence of resistance and rebellion in the south.[29] At the heart of this, as Ruth McVey tells us, lies the tension "between Patani and those Muslims who do not share Patani's past".[30]

Popular attitudes towards the Chularajmontri further indicate the exclusionary nature of southern Thailand's Malay-Muslim community. Since the reintroduction of this office in 1945, no Malay-Muslim has ever occupied this office. This fact is not lost on locals in the Malay-Muslim provinces. Indeed, because of this, the Chularajmontri is not seen by local communities as an acceptable representative of their aspirations. Likewise, comments and statements made by non-Malay (and non Malay-speaking) Muslim political, community, and religious leaders are not deemed by Malay-Muslims to be legitimate articulations of their grievances.[31]

THE STATE AND ISLAMIC EDUCATION

Historically, education in Thailand primarily revolved around both religious and royal institutions. Buddhist monks provided basic education to boys in classes set within the compounds of monasteries, while children of the royal household and from the nobility were educated in formal institutions to serve at court and govern in the provinces. The mass of society was made up of farmers who had little access to formal education. Village history, lore, and local philosophy were transmitted orally. During the reign of King Chulalongkorn, the Thai education system was modernized and made more accessible to the general public for the purpose of staffing the growing bureaucracy with administrators and civil servants. This began with the 1898 Education Proclamation, which was strongly influenced by the British system and in which academic and vocational paths of education were made accessible to the general population.[32]

Islamic education in Thailand has traditionally revolved around the institution of the *pondok*. *Pondok* schools have a long tradition in Malay history. The *pondok* assumes an integral role in the Malay society of the southern provinces of Thailand and performs the key task of providing religious instruction. Moreover, *pondok* are closely associated with Malay-Muslim identity and often act as the centre of gravity for everyday Malay social life. Beyond that, *pondok* are also important repositories for and progenitors of Malay language, history, and culture. As mentioned earlier, by the nineteenth century the southern kingdom of Patani had become a prominent regional centre for Islamic learning. Muslim students from both archipelagic and mainland Southeast Asia (primarily Cambodia) would sojourn in any of the several hundred *pondok* schools here before moving on to the Middle East and North Africa for further Islamic education.[33] Patani was renowned for its religious teachers and scholars. Patani Muslims were prominent educators in major Islamic institutions throughout the Arab-Muslim world. Such was their prominence that in the nineteenth and early twentieth centuries scholars such as Ahmad Patani, Zayn al-Abidin Patani, and Da'ud ibn Abd-Allah Patani congregated in the Masjid Al-Haram in Mecca and taught in the Malay *halaqah* (study circle), where they were popularly known as "*ulama Jawi*".[34] Back home, *tok guru* (*pondok* religious teachers) were instrumental in translating religious commentaries and sermons from Arabic to Jawi (the modified classical Malay script that includes, among others, Arabic and Khmer influences). Snouck Hugronje, the Dutch bureaucrat and scholar of Islam in the Dutch East Indies, noted the influence of the Patani *ulama* in Mecca:

> During his visit to Mecca in the 1880s, Snouck Hugronje had occasion to have extensive contacts with the Malay community there, and to observe who were the most influential writers living in the community at the time. One of his interesting observations was that the writings of scholars originating from the Patani area were significant, as measured

by the regularity of their publication by Meccan presses. Thus those
Patani thinkers who made a mark in Mecca must have left a legacy
throughout the Malay world via returning students.[35]

The prominence that Patani enjoyed as a regional centre *par excellence* of
Islamic education may have eroded over the decades, yet its historical legacy
continues to inform the identity of the Malay-Muslim population in the
southern provinces and remains a factor that must frame any assessment of
contemporary Islamic education in southern Thailand.

REGULATING KNOWLEDGE AND DISSEMINATION

Malay-Muslim education institutions have traditionally had tenuous relations
with the central government in Siam, and the *pondok* has been, and continues
to be, viewed with a great deal of suspicion and mistrust. Concomitantly, a
major policy challenge for Bangkok, not only from the perspective of education
and regional development in the south but also for security and conflict
management, has been the question of how to integrate Islamic education
into mainstream Thai society in a non-threatening manner. In order to
understand the tense relationship that exists today between the Thai state and
Islamic education institutions, particularly those located in the south, an
appreciation of historical developments is required.

The genesis of the strained centre-periphery relations between Bangkok
and the southern provinces may be traced to the modernization policies
initiated in the early twentieth century. At the heart of this was the state's
attempt to monopolize the means and articulate the ends of education. For
instance, the National Education Plan of 1936 declared that "the government
has the authority to control the institutes, to administer examinations to the
teachers and award them diplomas, to administer examinations to students at
the completion of Primary General Education, Junior Secondary Education,
and Senior Secondary Education".[36] The outcome of this process was to be
the creation of persons "considered to have the knowledge which a Siamese
citizen should have ... he is a citizen who is able to earn his living by having
an occupation; he knows the rights and duties of the citizen, he will prove
himself to be useful for his country by means of his occupation".[37] It was in
this respect that the government was especially concerned about the *pondok*
in the Malay-Muslim southern provinces. Given that these traditional
institutions, being essentially religious schools, did not offer academic courses,
they were not construed to contribute positively to national development.
Moreover, because the *tok guru* of the *pondok* never taught in Thai and the

students never used the Thai language, this institution was considered to have a fractious influence on the broader objectives of fostering national identity and cohesion.

The early 1920s witnessed the onset of more than eighty years of government-sanctioned attempts to integrate, if not assimilate, the Muslim education system of southern Thailand into the national mainstream. It was a process that had a tremendously corrosive impact on center-periphery relations. Early policies enforced integration through the introduction of government schools into the southern provinces and by enactments such as the 1921 Compulsory Education Act that legislated four years of compulsory primary education for all children. These national schools, however, were greeted with suspicion in the Malay-Muslim community. Many parents were not swayed by the provision by legislation of two hours of Islamic studies per week in these institutions — a policy that remains in place to this day. In fact, many Malay-Muslim parents saw the government schools as Buddhist institutions — part of a government agenda to stymie the practice of Islam, undermine the Islamic faith, and convert southern Muslims to Buddhism.[38] Furthermore, the policy of placing Muslim children in Thai schools where Buddhism and secular subjects were taught was also viewed with consternation by the religious elite in the south, as it threatened to undermine their leadership position within the community and imperil long-standing cultural identities. Predictably, Malay-Muslim parents shunned the national schools, which eventually were attended only by a small minority of children of Malay civil servants and aristocrats. The fact that government authorities attempted to strictly enforce the Act only meant greater resentment on the part of the Malay-Muslim community towards the central authorities.

In response to the failure of the government-school integration project, Bangkok contemplated the blanket closing-down of the *pondok*. Eventually, Thai political leaders, no doubt cognizant of the possible ramifications of such a policy, settled for a more cautiously calibrated approach of easing Thai language instruction into the *pondok* through the dispatch of Thai teachers and educational materials to the south. However, the blanket closure of the *pondok* has never really been taken off the table.

Although it was never colonized, Thailand experienced unsettled periods of military dictatorship after constitutional monarchy was established in 1932. Over the years, the various military administrations put forward a range of disingenuous policies that were aimed at bringing Islamic schools under the control of the central government. The National Education System and National Education Plan, formulated in 1932 and 1936 respectively, places strong emphasis on the spread of national culture, history and language.

A series of textbooks for use in government schools throughout the kingdom was prepared by the Ministry of Education. No other languages, religions, or historical narratives were accommodated in the curriculum.[39] Not surprisingly, from the Malay-Muslim vantage, these initiatives were once again viewed as attempts to impose Thai values in a way that threatened Malay culture, religion, and heritage. The end of the Pacific War, during which Thailand had found itself aligned with the Japanese, offered a fresh opportunity for reconciliation. The democratic administration of Pridi Panomyong (1946–47) was viewed as sympathetic to the independent and assertive identity of Thailand's Malay-Muslim minorities. A subsequent spirit of compromise found expression in the not-insignificant concessions that were made to the Malay-Muslim community under the broad rubric of the Patronage of Islam Act already discussed.[40] The return of Field Marshall Phibun Songgkram and military administration, however, saw a return to policies of forced assimilation. Phibun, who served two terms as premier, had already under his earlier administration overseen the introduction of a new education system in 1932 that sought to streamline the cultures, identities, and languages of Thailand's disparate ethnic groups into pillars for a Thai national identity. In the south, this nationalist transformation of education entailed the replacement of Malay textbooks and study aids with Thai vernacular material. Broader policies concerning the expression of Malay-Muslim cultural identity were also promulgated. These included policies and legislation that circumscribed the wearing of the Muslim headscarf in public and that rescinded *shari'a* law. It has been alleged that during Phibun's administration turbans worn by *hajis* were snatched by the police and trampled on, and women wearing Muslim clothing and headscarves were "kicked and jabbed by Siamese police".[41] Even more drastic was his administration's attempt to force all schools to adopt Buddhist ethics, a move that inevitably antagonized the Muslim minority, fuelling further resentment against Bangkok.

In 1958, the Ministry of Education mooted the issue of *pondok* registration. Again, the *raison d'être* of this initiative was two-fold: the integration of *pondok* graduates into the mainstream economy and society on the one hand, and on the other, the monitoring and management of the "threat" arising from suspicions that *pondok* education perpetuated Malay-Muslim narratives of resistance and separatism. The latter imperative has since been elaborated upon by Thanet, whose investigations of archival material led him to conclude that:

> According to the classified memoir of Pattani's governor, the practice in the 1950s was a strict control of the *pondok* under the local administrative officials and the police. They closely 'watched and observed all activities

and movements of the *pondok* especially *tok guru* were under special observations of the district officers and the police chief; (we) must find ways to use them as tools to bring peace to the national state and find ways to prevent any incitement and mobilization (of the people).[42]

Added to this was the larger subterranean problem of how the *pondok* and its students were viewed in mainstream Thai society. Prior to these initiatives to restructure Islamic education, *pondok* were viewed not as educational but religious institutions.[43] The profile of the typical *pondok* graduate — well-versed in religious knowledge but lacking an understanding of Thai national history, not conversant in the Thai language, and lacking technical skills was a matter of consequential concern for the central government.

By 1960, the policy of registration was refined with the following objectives: namely, the much-needed improvement of *pondok* infrastructure and facilities, improvement of the curriculum and pedagogy of Islamic education, and the creation of a proper system of assessment and evaluation that would be in line with national standards. Registration required *pondoks* to provide information about their schools and, in particular, their curriculum and to abide by instructions from the Ministry of Education regarding the restructuring of the latter. In return, these schools would be provided access to government funds for infrastructural development.

Attempts to integrate, assimilate, and transform Islamic education reached a watershed in 1961 with the *Pondok* Educational Improvement Programme (PEIP), which codified the suggestions made by the Ministry of Education regarding the restructuring of Islamic education. The PEIP aimed to persuade traditional *pondoks* to register in exchange for financial support and to introduce academic and vocational subjects with the Thai language as the medium of instruction. Within a year of its introduction, 197 *pondok* registered, either swayed by the instrumentalist imperative or by an interpretation of the policy as a *fait accompli*. In 1965, it was decided that *pondok* that registered and received government aid would be re-classified as private religious schools. By the final year of registration in 1971, more than 400 *pondok* had registered, even though it had not been made compulsory.[44] Several reasons accounted for the initial popularity of the registration programme and the support it garnered from the community. First, unlike some previous policies, the PEIP was not an overt attempt to circumscribe the teaching of Islam in the Malay-Muslim provinces, at least not at first glance. To be sure, the spread of Islamic knowledge would be allowed to continue, but with the evident caveat of greater scrutiny by the state. Second, registration was voluntary and not compulsory. Again, this differed markedly from the more coercive policies of previous administrations that did not proffer choices for the Malay-Muslim community. Third, registration came with much-needed subsidies in terms of financial support, teachers (for academic and vocational subjects), teaching aids, and other necessary equipment and facilities.

Predictably, the PEIP was not without its drawbacks. To be sure, there were several controversial facets to the programme. Though the PEIP was couched in terms of government support for the modernization and advancement of Muslim education, it nonetheless represented a powerful penetration of the state into a formerly closed system of education. In 1949, the Thai government had as part of its larger "Thai-nization" assimilation program promulgated the Private School Act, which required all private schools to register with the education ministry and to bring their curricula into conformity with government guidelines. But because *pondok* schools were classified as religious institutions and *not* as private schools at the time, they fell outside the remit of the Act. In light of this, the 1961 PEIP can be viewed as a political machination to achieve, at least in theory, what the Private School Act had failed to achieve in 1949 — state penetration into and control over the *pondok*. The consequence of this was not lost on some at least in the community. No doubt the PEIP facilitated the gradual modernization of Muslim education, but it also meant that education could now function as a medium of integration as patronage gave way to overt control — a fact that further eroded relations with the state.[45] In response, as more than 400 *pondoks* registered, another 100 or so closed down and went underground in protest against the policy. Likewise, just as the government's policy on the *pondok* was at heart driven by political considerations, so it elicited a highly political response from the Malay-Muslim community. Indeed, as Uthai Dulyakasem has noted, the status of the traditional *pondok* was another issue of contention that was mobilized by Malay-Muslim separatists operating in the southern provinces. In view of this, the following citation extracted from separatist propaganda material is worth reproducing here:

> *Pondok* schools are the only institutions of the Malay people which teach Malay language to serve the community's needs. *Pondok* schools are not a disguised organization for political purposes. Nor are they educationally and economically wasteful. The conversion of the *pondok* schools to the private schools is to introduce an undesirable culture to the people. The use of Siamese language as a medium of instruction, the teaching of Siamese history, the teaching of Buddhist principles in the schools mean the obstruction of learning Islam and Malay language. These subjects are

not only irrelevant to our needs but they will also destroy the intent and aim of the *pondok* schools, and hence Islam will disappear from Siam.[46]

Pivotal to the resistance was the perception that the central government's emphasis on a national Thai curriculum was in fact an implicit enforcement of Buddhist ideology and philosophy, couched in the language of national unity and pluralism.

It is clear that the spectrum of government policies had a significant, consolidated impact on Islamic education in southern Thailand. The piecemeal dismantling since 1961 of the *pondok* structure of religious education had disrupted "the process by which the Malay-Muslim community used to produce its intellectuals", by compelling them to adopt aspects of secularism and Thai culture (including Buddhism), thereby diminishing Patani's status as a centre for Islamic education.[47] In other words, the policy facilitated government penetration of the *pondok*. The net effect of this was the erosion of the tradition of excellence in the standards of Islamic education, as *pondok* schools became instruments and institutions for the expression of broader resistance to perceived Thai colonialism in the Malay-Muslim southern provinces. In the process, large numbers of religious leaders and students were politicized to the extent that Islamic education has for the past four decades been the front line of the contest for identity between Bangkok and the southern provinces. Another inadvertent effect of these policies was the outflow of Muslim students abroad, a phenomenon that will be mapped out in greater detail in following chapters.

The drive to regulate Islamic education continued in earnest into the 1980s under the Private School Act of 1982, which, among other things, sought to improve the management and administration of Islamic private schools. With particular reference to Islamic education (the Act was meant to regulate private schools in general and not just Islamic schools), the government had proposed under the Act to develop Islamic private schools by elevating standards of curriculum, improving administration, and improving facilities (including teaching materials).

Insofar as issues of curriculum are concerned, Islamic education has been subject to constant re-calibration through the years under the auspices of various government directives. Having said that, these efforts to improve the curriculum have mostly entailed adjustments to the number of hours per week devoted to academic and religious studies subjects respectively. They have done little by way of improving the content of religious knowledge, which in any case is something that the Ministry of Education does not appear equipped to do.[48]

EDUCATION DEVELOPMENT PLAN OF THE PROVINCES ALONG THE SOUTHERN BORDER

Released in 2006, the *Education Development Plan of the Provinces along the Southern Border* is the latest and most comprehensive articulation of the Thai government's policies and objectives towards education, in particular religious education, in the three southern provinces. In this respect (and also because there is currently no English version of the document), it is worth close scrutiny here.

Written in Thai, Jawi, and Malay, the policy paper essentially sets out the vision of the Thai government with regard to improving the structure of education in the southern provinces. The beginning of the document essentially acknowledges a number of challenges that confront Islamic education in the south. This includes the observations that current standards and processes of administration have not been effective; that drop-out rates among Malay-Muslim students from the formal education system remain high; that there is lack of an accommodative spirit as well as of a systematic curriculum; and that the current curriculum is unable to impart the "right values" in its students.[49] Because of this, students in the Islamic school system have not obtained an education that brings with it opportunities for advancement and employment.[50] On the other hand, the current state of government schools does not sufficiently recognize the culture, lifestyle, and needs of the local (Malay-Muslim) community. The challenge, then, is identified as that which required the crafting of "cohesive educational policies" that allow for the "merger of Islamic laws with general knowledge and knowledge towards employment that would provide a stepping stone for students and the community" to advance in society.[51] In terms of objectives, the report highlights issues such as the provision of right conditions for effective education, the creation of opportunities for students of all backgrounds, and, ultimately, a proper balance of "secular and religious" education. Noticeably, the report also stresses the importance of language training, not only in Thai and Malay but also in English and Mandarin. It emphasizes in particular the primacy of the Malay language and, without further elaboration, "the correct knowledge of local history".[52]

From here, the report looks specifically at various aspects of education that require attention. These include teacher training and education curriculum development, development of educational facilities in government institutions, development and improvement of private education, career development and public education, and development of higher education. The report lists the following specific areas of focus:[53]

Teacher Training and Education Curriculum Development:
–   To combine compulsory and basic education in every educational institution according to the specific needs of Buddhist and Muslim students;
–   To adapt education and teaching curricula in order to facilitate instruction in the fields of religious studies, Thai language, local history, and foreign languages, in particular English, Mandarin, official Malay, as well as the Malay dialect (Jawi);
–   To accelerate the pace of the usage of combined education mentioned above so as to assess its utility in both religious and secular studies in the education system;
–   To encourage primary schools to adopt a dual-language system (Thai and Malay) in the implementation of the curriculum and the development of teaching aids that are appropriate to the local context;
–   To recognize the educational certificates and diplomas of students who have studied overseas and who have not received recognition for these qualifications so that they can be assessed and can further their education either locally or in foreign institutions;
–   To encourage students to further their education in institutes of higher learning.

Development of Educational Facilities of Government Institutions:
–   To improve the quality of schools that have already developed a reputation for excellence;
–   To encourage Islamic models of education management and teaching in government institutions at every level in accordance to the needs of students;
–   To provide opportunities for degree-holders as well as qualified and well-known religious teachers to be instructors in government schools;
–   To build and develop a range of special schools, such as boarding schools for orphans, children of the poor and disadvantaged, as well as schools that focus on science for students who possess advanced qualifications in sciences in the three provinces and Songkhla (Education District Three);
–   To encourage government education institutions to get involved in community activities in order to provide opportunities for these communities to take an active interest in the development of their children. This echoes the advice of the government motto of "intimate understanding and progress";
–   To raise the standard of religious education in public schools to a level equal to that in private religious schools.

Development and Improvement of Private Educational Institutions:
-   To develop the qualification/standard of foundation committees, school committees, administrators, and teachers in Islamic private schools so as to raise the quality of education for all students, to foster the "correct" knowledge and understanding of the religion and history of the area (the three southern provinces);
-   To encourage the study of academic and vocational skills such as agriculture, finance, and accounting. With the help of private schools, educational centres, and vocational institutes in the three provinces, these subjects should be gradually introduced in Islamic private schools and *pondok*;
-   To strengthen the supervision of private schools so as to enable smooth administration;
-   To provide encouragement and support for Islamic studies in *tadika* (Islamic kindergartens) by providing the opportunity for local religious leaders and experts to get involved in matters of curriculum, administration, organization, and selection of textbooks in these schools.

Career Development and Public Education
-   To create opportunities for public education for students who did not complete twelve years of compulsory education;
-   To upgrade the management of education administration in youth education with the cooperation of relevant working groups;
-   To manage and coordinate the process of assessing knowledge and experience of students and faculty;
-   To coordinate the teaching of the Malay language to government officials, soldiers, police, and others;
-   To coordinate vocational training and tuition according to the needs of the community, such as, among others, the production of *halal* (permissible in Islam) food, production of local products in each district, and support for small businesses.

Development of Higher Education
-   To brand Prince of Songkhla University, Pattani Campus, a free university and its College of Islamic Studies as an international institute;
-   To strengthen the capability of Narathiwatrachanakharin University and links between its faculty of Islamic studies and other departments of modern sciences with the Muslim world through cooperation with Al-Azhar University, Egypt;
-   To construct, strengthen, and expand the standards of the acceptance of students in the educational community;

- To encourage universities in the south to provide skills upgrading training for teachers in government and private schools;
- To encourage and support the management of education with the aim to overcome problems and foster success for education policy in the provinces;
- To encourage and support monks in advanced education in order to produce good and competent Buddhist graduates in the surrounding regions.

Development of Skilled Labour
- The Skill Development Centres operating in Yala, Pattani, and Narathiwat will continue to work with schools to provide vocational courses for students in the south;
- The current coterie of courses that comprise training in computers, needlework, batik production, dress-making, English language, culinary skills, etc. will be expanded.

Though an important blueprint for the advancement of Islamic education in southern Thailand and, more broadly, of relations between the central government and the population of the southern provinces, this latest policy paper arguably raises more questions than it answers. Several in particular stand out. For instance, there is little information on what practical initiatives are envisaged that might fulfil the lofty objectives set forth. Moreover, while the policy paper's recognition of the need for a transformation of content in Islamic education is encouraging, there is little information on how and where this transformation is expected to take place. This is a particularly salient consideration given that the curriculum of Islamic schools has always been a highly sensitive arena. Finally, there is an acknowledgement of the importance of "local history" which should be lauded, if only because this reads on the surface to be a major concession on the part of the state. Yet given the mutual suspicion and distrust between the Thai state and the Malay-Muslim community, which has undoubtedly been further aggravated by recent events, without any articulation of concrete measures it is difficult to envisage how either party may be prepared to compromise on their seemingly obdurate positions on questions of history and identity.

EDUCATION AND THE NARRATIVE OF SEPARATISM

At the heart of the Thai government's perceptions informing the formulation of policy towards Islamic schools was the belief that, because these schools were firmly established in the region prior to the creation of the modern Thai nation-state, they are to be seen as a barrier to attempts at assimilating the Malay-Muslim minorities. On their part, the Malay-Muslim religious elite came to comprehend the educational policies emanating from Bangkok, in particular the emphasis on secular and academic education based on the Thai language, as a strong threat to the Malay-Muslim identity, prompting them to spearhead resistance movements.[54]

The secular and academic educational policies of various Bangkok administrations disrupted traditional forms of Islamic education and precipitated resistance on the part of Malay-Muslim elites who had gained a significant amount of symbolic capital in their local communities through their position as religious teachers. Subsequently, Islamic schools were instrumental in prompting a separatist insurgency and in providing the institutional structures and leadership for separatist organizations. *Barisan Revolusi Nasional* (BRN or National Revolutionary Movement) emerged in the early 1960s, largely in response to educational policies such as the PEIP. Its founder, Karim Hassan, was a religious teacher from Narathiwat who taught at a famous *pondok* in Yala, and who was known to have tapped students from *pondok* schools and later Islamic private schools for the organization's support base. Similarly, another separatist organization, *Barisan Nasional Pembebasan Patani* (BNPP or Patani National Liberation Movement), also relied primarily on religious teachers to recruit students for organized militant activities. In 1968, the Patani United Liberation Organization (PULO) was established and gained the support of disillusioned Muslim intellectuals who shared the perception that the government's education policies constituted a threat to the very institutions that preserved Malay-Muslim heritage, not to mention the social prestige and status of the feudal elite in the community.[55] On the back of material support from Syria and Libya and ideological support from Malaysia and Saudi Arabia, and, to no small extent, an active recruitment process among Malay-Muslim students sojourning in the Middle East, PULO would eventually emerge as the strongest and most organized separatist organization in the south. In fact, the recruitment processes that took place overseas, primarily among southern Thai students attending religious schools in these countries, continues to this day.[56] In his exploration of the historical dimension of separatism and its links with Thailand's Malay-Muslim diaspora, Wan Kadir Che Man estimated that as many as 30,000 Malay-Muslims lived in Saudi Arabia during the 1960s and 1970s, and during the late 1980s at least 10,000 lived there, with most of them "involved in activities of separatist groups".[57]

The emergence of separatist groups out of Islamic schools in the southern provinces should not however be taken to imply widespread and formal support from these educational institutions for the movement. Indeed, just as many Malay-Muslims chose to take up arms, so many more recognized the necessity of gaining the skills and accreditation facilitated by the Thai state's transformation of traditional schools. Uthai notes that most Malay-Muslims came to believe that education grounded on academic and vocational skills not only allowed them to protect their rights against government authorities, but also permitted upward socio-economic mobility.[58] Even separatists came to recognize the importance of assimilating into Thai society. This was exemplified in the following quotation from a PULO member when asked for his views on the importance of gaining a Thai education:

> I am a Malay Muslim. I must stay with my people. The Thai government does not respect us. The villagers are treated with contempt and the educated Muslims are regarded with suspicion. We have a right to self-determination, to remain Malay Muslim. On the other hand, it is a long and difficult struggle. Maybe it is better to stay with Thailand and take as much advantage of the educational and economic opportunities as we can — at least until the movement comes stronger.[59]

Calculated compliance, if not outright assimilation, on the part of Malay-Muslims towards educational changes was even more apparent by the early 1980s. Forbes, for instance, surmised that "a degree of cultural assimilation is acceptable to many Thai Malays" and many are "anxious to learn Thai" and enter higher education.[60] Clearly, the importance of advancement up the socio-economic ladder was not lost on many Malay-Muslims, even as the impetus to resist Thai hegemony and preserve religio-cultural identity weighed heavily on the community. In any case, broader policies of a conciliatory nature towards the Malay-Muslim community in the south were enacted from the early 1980s and encompassed a more assuaging approach to Islamic schools. These marked a gradual but discernible shift in the tenor of the relationship between the Thai state and Islamic education institutions, not to mention the Malay-Muslim religio-political elite. Be that as it may, this progress ultimately proved insufficient and subterranean mutual distrust continued to linger. Consequently, when violence erupted again at the turn of the century, attention shifted once more to the Islamic schools of southern Thailand.

ISLAMIC SCHOOLS AND CONTEMPORARY VIOLENCE

A major consideration that links Islamic schools and the ongoing violence in southern Thailand today pertains to the role of religion in the contemporary conflict. Since 4 January 2004, when suspected militants mounted an audacious raid of an army camp in Narathiwat, violence has become an almost daily affair in southern Thailand claiming more than 2,000 lives, the vast majority being Malay-Muslims killed at the hands of state security forces as well as of militants who are also believed to be Malay-Muslims. According to a recent report, by February 2005 an estimated 875 out of 1,574 villages in the southern border provinces had been infiltrated by militants.[61] The alarming casualty toll clearly indicates that violence has intensified since January 2004, even as the perpetrators' identities remain for the large part frustratingly clouded in mystery, notwithstanding the efforts of many both in the government and in the terrorism and conflict studies community to uncover them.

There are indications that what is being witnessed today heralds the emergence of a new phenomenon in the southern Thai conflict. For one, the almost routine targeting of civilians was unheard of in the 1970s, when separatist violence had hit its previous peak. More disconcerting is the fact that, while a large number of civilian casualties in recent years may have come about as "collateral damage" during bombings, a not-insignificant number have been deliberately targeted. Tactics have also been transformed from rural-based guerrilla skirmishes to bombings in urban centres, though the explosive devices used have yet to demonstrate high degrees of sophistication. Finally, while traditionally confined to the Malay-Muslim provinces of Pattani, Yala, and Narathiwat, the violence has gradually expanded northwards, prompting the Thai government to extend controversial emergency legislation into Songkhla as well.[62] While these are important topics that demand rigorous academic and analytical scrutiny, the details of the conflict and counter-insurgency measures need not pre-occupy us here.[63] Of immediate relevance is the fact that recent attempts to explain this resurgence of violence have, on the part of certain quarters within the Thai government as well as of the academic community, increasingly pointed to Islam as a source of ideological inspiration for a call to arms — and to the institution of the *pondok* as a conduit for the call and as a conveyor belt for militants and foot-soldiers.

At first glance, the fixation with Islamic schools as the first place to "look" for militancy is perhaps not without reason. Bearing in mind the difficult historical relationship that southern Thailand's Islamic education institutions have had with the Thai state, the attention that schools have garnered is to be expected, given some measure of precedence for the purported nexus between these schools and separatist violence. It has already been illustrated that, since the recent emergence of separatism and armed resistance in southern Thailand, insurgents have attempted to penetrate the region's *pondok* schools in order to find recruits in their struggle for a separate Patani state.[64] Today, it is widely believed that recruitment is taking place in a clandestine fashion and, while drawing from the enrolments of religious schools, it is also suspected to be occurring through a highly decentralized and opaque process involving small, unofficial study groups.[65] This was affirmed in the International Crisis Group's study on southern Thailand, which described the following *modus operandi*:

> Recruitment agents, often religious teachers, reportedly select youths who display three key characteristics: piety, impressionability, and agility. Agents recruit these youths into small groups, initially by befriending and inviting them to join discussion or prayer groups. Candidates are sounded out in conversations about Patani history. Those who seem receptive to liberationist ideology are invited to join the movement. [66]

In the course of a typical day at a private Islamic school in southern Thailand, lessons are divided into three sessions of instruction: formal religious classes in the morning, academic and vocational lessons in the afternoon, and unofficial "study groups" in the evening. If mobilization indeed takes place through the school system, it is likely that the unofficial "study groups" provide ready avenues and mechanisms.[67] That said, this implies that (1) school administrations may not be directly involved violence, nor are they necessarily complicit in militant activities, as the Thai government has been wont to assume, and (2) effectively monitoring the activities of such elusive groups has proven, and will continue to prove, an arduous prospect, not just for state security officials, but even for members of the Malay-Muslim community itself. Beyond indoctrination, these religious schools have according to some reports figured prominently as avenues for paramilitary training in the guise of extra-curricular sporting activities, though such speculation have thus far been proven by and large to be unfounded.[68]

Repeated references to the role of religious schools in the contemporary conflict draw on their tradition of involvement in sustaining narratives of victimization and in imparting the ideological impetus of ethno-nationalism to a younger generation. As a result of this, these institutions have commanded the attention of the Thai security apparatus and of politicians, some of whom view the *pondok* as a bastion of radical and militant Islam and who have gone so far as to call for its eradication.[69] In August 2004, for example, the Intelligence Division of the Fourth Army, under whose command Thailand's southern provinces fall, estimated that at least thirty religious schools were suspected to be active in the ongoing insurgency.[70] Recently, several high profile attacks have featured militants who can purportedly be traced back to Islamic schools where they were either students or teachers. In particular, a number of cases have revolved around Yala-based Thamma Witthaya, a prestigious Islamic private school with approximately 3,000 students. Local education foundations have also at some point been accused of funding militancy in the south.

Thamma Witthaya

Thamma Witthaya Islamic Private School was formed in 1951 as a traditional *pondok*. Its founder, Haji Haran Surong, was a locally trained *tok guru* known to have been a member of the BRN. In 1984, the school registered with the education ministry and became an Islamic private school. Today, it is the largest Islamic private school in southern Thailand, operating six programmes under the Islam Witthaya Foundation including a school for girls and two kindergartens. The school owns a fleet of more than 100 school buses — a common gauge for the wealth of an Islamic school in southern Thailand.

On 16 December 2004 four individuals were arrested, all teachers in Thamma Witthaya Islamic Private School. They were alleged to have connections to BRN-Coordinate, a revamped separatist organization suspected of orchestrating much of the recent violence and of involvement in a raid on an army camp in Narathiwat on 4 January 2004. These four were Yusof Waeduramae, a former teacher and supervisor at the school and alleged chief of BRN military affairs; Mohammad Kanafi Doleh, a teacher at Satri Tham Witthaya, the female campus of Thamma Witthaya; Ahama Bula, assistant headmaster of Thamma Witthaya; and Abdul Razak Dolo, a religious teacher at the school. The headmaster of Thamma Witthaya, Sapa-ing Basoe, was accused of being a major leader of BRN but had evidently escaped the dragnet. In particular, he was accused of masterminding the 4 January 2004 incident which is widely seen to have triggered a new cycle of violence in southern Thailand. Masae Useng, a former Thamma Witthaya teacher and secretary of an education foundation in Narathiwat, was alleged to have been Sapa-ing's lieutenant and stood accused of planning a series of attacks on security forces and security installations in the south. At the height of the crackdown, up to twenty-one teachers from Thamma Witthaya were shortlisted as suspects by Thai authorities, and eight continue to be "wanted" for suspected involvement in the ongoing violence, including Sapa-ing and Masae.[71] According to government sources, several of the school's students were identified among casualties from the 28 April coordinated insurgent assault on twelve government buildings and police outposts across Pattani,

Yala, and Songkhla. Apart from this incident, several teachers have also been killed, as has the chief administrator, while some others remain in custody in Bangkok. A large number of teachers have been incarcerated for questioning and interrogation, nineteen on one occasion, though most have been released without having charges brought against them. Until recently, the Thamma Witthaya campus in Yala had also been subjected to regular searches by Thai security forces. As a consequence, by end of 2005 1,000 students had dropped out of Thamma Witthaya.

To be sure, suspicions of Thamma Witthaya are not entirely without basis. The school itself is known to be a bastion of BRN activism. Lately, it has come to attention that certain study groups had in fact been formed in Thamma Witthaya for the purpose of instilling a deeper consciousness of Malay identity and history, though it was unclear if the lessons taking place had moved on beyond "history" to the incitement of violence.[72]

Pusaka

Another matter drawing the attention of security officials were the alleged links that Pusaka, an Islamic education foundation, had with militants.[73] The immediate connection was Masae Useng, a senior administrator at the foundation who is alleged to have links with BRN-Coordinate.

Pusaka was formed as an Islamic education foundation in 1994 in Narathiwat by Najmuddin Umar, until recently a member of parliament and leader of the Wadah faction of Muslim parliamentarians.[74] The foundation sponsors up to 100 Islamic kindergartens or *tadika* in southern Thailand (fifty-six alone in Narathiwat). Despite the fact that it was a legitimate organization, intelligence officials allegedly only came to know of its existence after documents surfaced during a raid on the home of Masae Useng in 2003. Authorities have consequently articulated concerns that Pusaka may be working in tandem with BRN-Coordinate to perpetuate violence. This cooperation is believed possibly to be behind larger scale attacks that require sophisticated levels of skill and coordination such as the 4 January 2004 arms heist.[75] Thus far no evidence has surfaced to substantiate this speculation. Masae Useng remains at large, and the prosecution's case against Najmuddin Umar has been dismissed for lack of substantial evidence.

Revelations of this nature, often grounded on little more than conjecture, have nevertheless fed the view in certain quarters of the Thai political establishment that harsh policies towards Islamic schools — including the blanket shutting down of all *pondoks* — are necessary to solve the ongoing crisis.

UNDERSTANDING THE ROLE OF ISLAMIC SCHOOLS
IN ITS PROPER CONTEXT

There are three considerations that are critical in analysing the specific role that schools might be playing in the contemporary southern Thai separatist conflict. First, while it is probably true that religious teachers from certain schools have been involved in violence, it would be a cardinal mistake to extrapolate from this a causal relationship between Islamic education and violence that implicates all religious schools. This was a major policy *faux pas* of previous administrations (including the recently deposed Thaksin administration). The misinformed policies that resulted did little more than to disrupt traditional forms of Islamic education, aggravate disenchantment towards central authority, ignite resistance on the part of prominent Malay-Muslim religious leaders, and fan flames of separatism. Religious schools, it needs to be stressed again, are more than educational institutions in the eyes of local communities. As earlier described, for the Malay-Muslims of southern Thailand they are a bastion of history and identity. Hence, even if elements within the system are complicit in the insurgency, policy-makers have to tread carefully to avoid targeting the entire system of Islamic education.

Second, since the militants seem to be capitalizing on the infrastructure of the Islam school system, it is important to consider what legitimizations of militancy might be perpetuated through schools. At an abstract level, schools may well be very efficient vehicles of Islamization, since social and political crises may easily be framed in terms of religion for impressionable young minds. Yet in the context of southern Thailand, the nexus between religious schools and separatist conflict has taken a somewhat different form. For instance, as Chapter Four will discuss in greater detail, while the concept of *jihad* is indeed taught and studied, it has not been articulated by most Islamic teachers with any notable frequency, especially in relation to the ongoing violence. On the contrary, evidence suggests that it is more likely subversive "liberationist ideology", as alluded to in the earlier quotation from the ICG report, that has features most prominently; the very fact that the nationalist song *Bumi Patani* continues to be sung widely in schools across the region testifies to this. Furthermore, local schools, as alleged of the study groups at Thamma Witthaya, do emphasize local narratives of Malay history that teach of unjust subjugation of Malay-Muslim lands by Siam regardless of the accuracy of such accounts. The proliferation of the "local" version of the Patani historical narrative is not confined solely to southern Thai religious schools. Elsewhere across the Malay world where many from southern Thailand have flocked, Malay-Muslims are being exposed not to the sanitized version of Patani history promulgated by Thai education authorities but to this "authentic" local history.[76] Curiously though, contrary to what some analysts might suggest, this unwavering belief in Patani's proud Islamic heritage has had the extenuating effect of denying foreign actors, including elements of the international *jihadi* movement, an ideological foothold in southern Thailand.[77]

Finally, the role that Islamic schools is believed to have assumed in the contemporary conflict is all the more striking because of a prevailing belief that the Bangkok government has enjoyed at least some success in integrating the *pondok*, which until recently fell outside its purview. Indeed, if one were to scrutinize the Islamic education institutions on the Thai government's "blacklist", one would be struck by the fact that the vast majority are likely to be state-funded Islamic schools that should have been integrated into the mainstream national academic system through the introduction of academic and vocational subjects, not to mention the Thai language, into their curriculum. This is telling on two counts. First, confidence that the Thai state had "successfully" integrated the Malay-Muslim community and managed the southern conflict over the period of the 1980s–1990s would seem at least to some extent to have been misplaced. Second, local narratives of identity and victimization are patently more resilient than some would have expected, and these narratives continue to feed the Malay-Muslim community's understanding of self and other vis-à-vis the relationship with Bangkok.

It has already been argued that Islamic schools in southern Thailand are not merely institutions of religious knowledge like the *madrasah* in Pakistan or the *pesantren* in Indonesia but also repositories and bastions of Malay ethnic identity and historical memory. The link between Islamic schools and violence may arise more from the role of these schools as defenders of ethnic Malay identity than as producers of "radical" religious ideology. Indeed, the last may function as a meta-ideology of sorts that lends further meaning and intelligibility to the ethno-nationalist narrative rather than anchoring it.[78] This is an important observation considering the interest in religious extremism and militancy of some who closely follow the ongoing violence. In their attempts to unravel the links between Islamic schools and violence in southern Thailand, most observers have approached the question from a distance and bandied about terms such as "Wahhabi" and "Salafi" without properly understanding what these terms mean in the specific context of Islam in Thailand. In order to better understand the convoluted plot involving schools, religion, separatism, and violence in southern Thailand, and to go beyond the already well-documented surfeit of antagonism between the Malay-Muslim community and the Thai state, it is necessary first to understand the dynamics of the Malay-Muslim community itself — and notably, the increasingly intense contestation for legitimacy and authenticity that is taking place within this community and which is captured in its system of religious education. It is to this objective that the book now turns.

Notes

1   In Malay, the area is known simply as *Tiga Wilayah* or the three provinces.
2   Omar Farouk Bajunid, "The Muslims of Thailand: A Survey", in *The Muslims of Thailand: Historical and Cultural Studies*, edited by Andrew Forbes (Bihar, India: Centre for Southeast Asian Studies, 1988), p. 25.
3   This is evident in how Malay-Muslim families of villages surrounding Pattani Bay continue to retain traditional methods of fishing despite the fact that this local industry is becoming increasingly untenable with commercial firms now monopolizing fishing in the bay.
4   See Ibrahim Syukri, *Sejarah Kerajaan Melayu Patani* [History of the Malay Kingdom of Patani]. Translated by Connor Bailey and John Miksic (Athens OH: Ohio State University Press, 1985) for a Malay account of the arrival of Islam; and David Wyatt and Andries Teeuw, *Hikayat Patani* [The History of Patani] (The Hague: Martinus Nijhoff, 1970).
5   Ibrahim Syukri, *Kerajaan Melayu Patani* [The Malay Kingdom of Patani] (Pasir Puteh, 1958); A. Bangnara, *Fatani Dahulu dan Sekarang* [Patani: Yesterday and Today]. (Selangor: Penal Penyelidikan, 1977); Ahmad Fathi, *Ulama Besar dari Fatani* [Patani's Revered *Ulama*] (Kelantan: Pustaka Aman, 2001).
6   See Imtiyaz Yusuf, "Islam and Democracy in Thailand: Reforming the Office of Chularajmontri/Shaikh Al-Islam", *Journal of Islamic Studies* 9, no. 2 (1998): 285.
7   Ibid., p. 284.
8   The National Reconciliation Commission was an *ad hoc* body consisting of fifty scholars, officials, and policy-makers. It was formed in February 2005 by the Thaksin administration with the endorsement of the king. Tasked to investigate the security problems of the south, the NRC came up with a set of recommendations at the end of its year-long tenure. Thus far, no action has been taken on these recommendations, either by the previous Thaksin administration or the current military government of Prime Minister Surayud Chulanont.
9   See for example, Angela Burr, "Religious Institutional Diversity — Social Structural and Conceptual Unity: Islam and Buddhism in a Southern Thai Coastal Fishing Village", *Journal of the Siam Society* 60, no. 2 (1972): 183–216; Roger Albritton, "Political Diversity Among Muslims in Thailand", *Asian Studies Review* 23, no. 2 (1994): 233–46.
10   The allusion to "Jawi" or "Yawi" as a Malay dialect is problematic as Jawi is more accurately described as a written script rather than a spoken dialect. Scholars

refer to the spoken dialect as either Kelantanese or simply the Pattani dialect or language.

11 Omar Farouk Bajunid, "Islam, Nationalism, and the Thai State", in *Dynamic Diversity in Southern Thailand*, edited by Wattana Sugunnasil (Chiang Mai: Silkworm Books, 2005) p. 10.

12 Thanet Aphornsuvan, "Nation-State and the Muslim Identity in the Southern Unrest and Violence", in *Understanding Conflict and Approaching Peace in Southern Thailand*, edited by Imtiyaz Yusuf and Lars Peter Schmidt (Bangkok: Konrad-Adenauer-Stiftung, 2006), p. 116.

13 "Thai coup confounds battle-scarred south", *The Age*, 20 October 2006.

14 See Wan Kadir Che Man, "The Thai Government and Islamic Institutions in the Four Southern Muslim Provinces of Thailand", *Sojourn* 5, no. 2 (1990): 263.

15 Raymond Scupin, "Education and Development for Muslims in Thailand", in *Aspects of Development: Islamic Education in Thailand and Malaysia*, edited by Raymond Scupin (Bangi: Institut Bahasa Kesusasteraan dan Budayaan Melayu, Universiti Kebangsaan Malaysia, 1989), p. 107.

16 See Thanet Aphornsuvan, *Origins of Malay Muslim "Separatism" in Southern Thailand*, Working Paper Series No. 32. (Singapore: Asia Research Institute, 2004).

17 For instance, Bangkok brought the Muslim legal code, built on the *shari'a* and *adat* and adjudicated by the local *qadi*, under the influence and control of Thai Buddhist officials. Such policies provoked conflict not only between the Thai politico-bureaucratic elite and the feudal Malay leadership, but also with the *ulama*, thereby bringing the religious leadership into the slowly burgeoning resistance movement.

18 For a detailed discussion on the impact of the Islamic resurgence on political consciousness in the Malay world, see William Roff, *The Origins of Malay Nationalism* (Oxford: Oxford University Press, 1967).

19 Craig Reynolds, *National Identity and its Defenders: Thailand Today* (Chiang Mai: Silkworm Books, 2003).

20 Raymond Scupin, "Muslim Accommodation in Thai Society", *Journal of Islamic Studies* 9, no. 2, (1998): 230.

21 Surin Pitsuwan, *Islam and Malay Nationalism: A Case Study of the Malay-Muslims of Southern Thailand* (Bangkok: Thai Khadi Research Institute, Thammasat University, 1985), p. 69.

22 For a discussion on the legal history of Thailand, see Tamara Loos, *Subject Siam: Family, Law, and Colonial Modernity in Thailand* (Ithaca, NY: Cornell University Press, 2006).

23 Scupin, "Muslim Accommodation in Thai Society", p. 236.

24 Peter Gowing, "Moro and Khaek: the Position of Muslim Minorities in the Philippines and Thailand", *Southeast Asian Affairs 1975* (Singapore: Institute of Southeast Asian Studies, 1975), p. 35.

25 The office of the Chularajmontri had been dissolved following the 1932

revolution. The first Chularajmontri of the post-revolution milieu was Haji Shamsalladin Mustapi (Cham Promyong), who was a government official from Bangkok and schooled in Islamic studies in Egypt.

[26] For instance, Andrew Holt, "Thailand's Troubled Border: Islamic Insurgency or Criminal Playground?", *Terrorism Monitor* (Jamestown Foundation) 2, no. 10 (20 May 2004). Holt writes that "The Thai provinces of Pattani, Narathiwat, Yala and Satun have long acted as a zone of Islamist discontent and violence".

[27] A number of scholars have documented this historical fact. See Astri Suhrke, "The Muslims of Southern Thailand", in *The Muslims of Thailand, Vol. 2: Politics of the Malay Speaking South*, edited by Andrew D.W. Forbes (Bihar: Centre for South East Asian Studies, 1989); Uthai Dulyakasem, "Education and Ethnic Nationalism: The Case of the Muslim-Malays in Southern Thailand", in *Reshaping Local Worlds: Formal Education and Cultural Change in Rural Southeast Asia*, edited by Charles F. Keyes (New Haven: Yale University, 1991); Andrew Cornish, *Whose Place is This?: Malay Rubber Producers and Thai Government Officials in Yala* (Bangkok: White Lotus, 1997).

[28] See Joseph Chinyong Liow, "International Jihad and Muslim Radicalism in Thailand? Toward an Alternative Interpretation", *Asia Policy* 2 (July 2006).

[29] A similar dynamic was observed by Olli-Pekka Ruohomaki who studied Muslim fishing communities in the southern Islands such as Phangnga. See Olli-Pekka Ruohomaki, *Fishermen No More: Livelihood and Environment in Southern Thai Maritime Village* (Bangkok: White Lotus, 1999).

[30] Ruth McVey, "Identity and Rebellion among Southern Thai Muslims", in *The Muslims of Thailand, Vol. 2: Politics of the Malay-Speaking South*, edited by Andrew D.W. Forbes (Bihar, India: Centre for Southeast Asian Studies, 1989), p. 52.

[31] These sentiments were expressed to me by members of a wide spectrum of Malay society, including religious elite and teachers, politicians, as well as academics and researchers, over the course of several visits to southern Thailand in 2004–2005.

[32] See David K. Wyatt, *Thailand: A Short History* (New Haven, CT: Yale University Press, 1984), pp. 209–20.

[33] William R. Roff, *The Origins of Malay Nationalism* (Kuala Lumpur: Oxford University Press, 1994), pp. 43–45.

[34] Numan Hayimasae, "Hj Sulong Abdul Kadir (1895–1954): Perjuangan dan Sumbangan Beliau Kepada Masyarakat Melayu Patani" [Haji Sulong Abdul Kadir (1895–1954): His Struggle and Contributions to the Malay Community of Patani] (M.Sc. dissertation, University Sains Malaysia, 2002), p. 85.

[35] This observation was recorded in Peter Riddell, *Islam and the Malay-Indonesian World: Transmission and Responses* (Singapore: Horizon Books, 2001), p. 198.

[36] Cited in Uthai Dulyakasem, "Education and Ethnic Nationalism: A Study of the Muslim-Malays in Southern Siam" (Ph.D. dissertation, Stanford University, 1981), p. 83.

37 Ibid., p. 82.

38 It certainly did not help that many of these "national schools" were in fact located within the compounds of Buddhist temples.

39 Dulyakasem, *Education and Ethnic Nationalism*, p. 183.

40 Critics, however, opine that this spirit of compromise served only to embolden the Malay-Muslim community and culminated in Haji Sulong's seven demands, to be discussed later.

41 Syukri, *Sejarah Kerajaan Melayu Patani*, p. 88.

42 Thanet Aphornsuvan, "Nation-State and the Muslim Identity in the Southern Unrest and Violence" in *Understanding Conflict and Approaching Peace in Southern Thailand*, edited by Imtiyaz Yusuf and Lars Peter Schmidt (Bangkok: Konrad-Adenauer-Stiftung, 2006), p. 114.

43 M. Ladd Thomas, *Social-Economic Approach to the Integration of Thai Islam: An Appraisal* (Urbana-Champaign, IL: Center for Southeast Asian Studies, Northern Illinois University, 1967), p. 86.

44 Surin Pitsuwan, *Islam and Malay Nationalism: A Case Study of the Malay-Muslims of Southern Thailand* (Bangkok: Thai Khadi Research Institute, 1985), p. 122.

45 Carool Kersten, "The Predicament of Thailand's Southern Muslims", *American Journal of Islamic Social Sciences* 21, no. 4 (Fall 2004): 18–20.

46 Dulyakasem, *Education and Ethnic Nationalism*, p. 85.

47 Pitsuwan, *Islam and Malay Nationalism*, p. 194.

48 Because these initiatives to "improve" the religious studies curriculum are mostly impressionistic in nature, I have decided not to dwell on them here. For information on how curriculum hours were adjusted in accordance with new directives, see Ibrahim Narongraksakhet, "Pondoks and their Roles in Preserving Muslim Identity in Southern Border Provinces of Thailand", in *Knowledge and Conflict Resolution: The Crisis of the Border Region of Southern Thailand*, edited by Uthai Dulyakasem and Lertchai Sirichai (Bangkok: The Asia Foundation, 2005), pp. 98–105.

49 See Ministry of Education — Thailand, *Perancangan Pembangunan Pendidikan Wilayah — Wilayah Sempadan Thailand Selatan* [Education Development Plan of the Provinces along the Southern Border] (Bangkok: Ministry of Education, 2006), p. 21.

50 Ibid., p. 22.

51 Ibid.

52 Ibid., p. 23.

53 The following is a translation and summary of Ministry of Education — Thailand, *Perancangan Pembangunan Pendidikan Wilayah — Wilayah Sempadan Thailand Selatan* [Education Development Plan of the Provinces along the Southern Border] (Bangkok: Ministry of Education, 2006).

54 A sample of the literature that deals with this mutual antagonism would include Uthai Dulyakasem, *Education and Ethnic Nationalism*, 1981; Kanniga Sachakul,

"Education as a Means for National Integration: Historical and Comparative Study of Chinese and Muslim Assimilation in Thailand" (Ph.D. dissertation, University of Michigan–Ann Arbor, 1984); Surin Pitsuwan, *Islam and Malay Nationalism* (Bangkok: Thammasat University, Thai Khadi Research Institute, 1985); Andrew D.W. Forbes, *The Muslims of Thailand* (Bihar: Centre for Southeast Asian Studies, 1989) (2 volumes); Raymond Scupin, ed., *Aspects of Development: Islamic Education in Thailand and Malaysia* (Bangi: Institut Bahasa Kesusasteraan dan Kebudayaan Melayu, Universiti Kebangsaan Malaysia, 1989); Mohd. Zamberi A. Malek, *Umat Islam Patani: Sejarah dan Politik* [Muslim Politics in Patani: History and Politics] (Shah Alam: HIZBI, 1993); Ahmad Omar Capakia, *Politik dan Perjuangan Masyarakat Islam di Selatan Thailand, 1902–2002* [Politics and Struggle of the Islamic Community in Southern Thailand, 1902–2002] (Bangi: Universiti Kebangsaan Malaysia, 2002).

55   Pitsuwan, *Islam and Malay Nationalism*, p. 193.

56   Discussion with Thai military intelligence officials, Singapore, 23 December 2004. This was confirmed in an interview with a PULO leader in Gothenburg, Sweden, 11 September 2006.

57   Wan Kadir Che Man, "The Thai Government and Islamic Institutions in the Four Southern Muslim Provinces of Thailand", *Sojourn* 5, no. 2 (1990): 110. He did not, however, elaborate on what form this involvement took.

58   Dulyakasem, *Education and Ethnic Nationalism*, p. 86.

59   Astri Suhrke, "Loyalists and Separatists: The Muslims in Southern Thailand", *Asian Survey* 17, no. 3 (1977): 243.

60   Andrew D.W. Forbes, "Thailand's Muslim Minorities: Assimilation, Secession, or Coexistence?", *Asian Survey* 22, no. 11 (1982): 1066.

61   See Human Rights Watch, "No One Is Safe: Insurgent Attacks on Civilians in Thailand's Southern Border Provinces", *Human Rights Watch* 19, no. 13(C) (August 2007): 26.

62   "Thai districts impose martial law", *BBC News*, 3 November 2005.

63   For highly informative and rigorous investigations into the ongoing conflict, see Duncan McCargo, ed., *Rethinking Southern Thailand's Violence* (Singapore: National University Press, 2007); Marc Askew, *Conspiracy, Politics, and a Disorderly Border: The Struggle to Comprehend Insurgency in Thailand's Deep South* (Washington, D.C.: East-West Center Washington, 2007).

64   Che Man, "The Thai Government and Islamic Institutions", p. 113.

65   Interview with Thai Special Branch, Bangkok, 13 July 2005.

66   International Crisis Group, *Southern Thailand: Insurgency, Not Jihad*. ICG Asia Report 98, 2005, p. 26.

67   Indeed, exiled militants I interviewed re-affirmed that this was indeed the recruitment process of the current groups active in southern Thailand. Interview with PULO officials, Gothenburg, Sweden, 11 September 2006.

68   Anthony Davis, "Thailand faces up to southern extremist threat", *Jane's Intelligence Review*, 1 October 2003.

69 "TRT MPs propose shutting down *Pondok* schools", *The Nation*, 14 September 2005.

70 Interview with Fourth Army intelligence, Pattani, 15 August 2004. No clear reasons were provided for why these schools were "blacklisted".

71 At the time of writing there was a 10 million baht reward for the capture of Sapa-ing Basoe.

72 Email interview with a Thai media source, 12 November 2005. The Thai journalist obtained this information from an *ustaz* teaching in Thamma Witthaya.

73 Pusaka is an abbreviation for *Pusat Persatuan Tadika Narathiwat* or the Centre for the Narathiwat Kindergarten Associations.

74 Wadah was a faction formed by Muslim members of parliament in Thailand.

75 Interview with Thai military intelligence, Bangkok, 24 January 2005.

76 I was informed of this peculiar development by a journalist contact in Singapore (22 March 2005) who is following the southern Thailand situation closely, and who had noticed this during a trip to Bandung, Indonesia.

77 This was told to me by three religious teachers during the course of an interview in Pattani on 21 January 2005.

78 I have made this argument more substantively elsewhere. See Joseph Chinyong Liow, *Muslim Resistance in Southern Thailand and Southern Philippines: Religion, Ideology, and Politics* (Washington, D.C.: East-West Center, Washington, 2006).

2

THE STRUCTURE OF ISLAMIC EDUCATION IN SOUTHERN THAILAND

According to the National Education Act (2542/1999) the government of Thailand is responsible for the provision of nine years of compulsory education and twelve years of free education — six years at elementary (Arabic: *ibtidai*, Thai: *prathom* 1–6), three years at middle (Arabic: *mutawassit*, Thai: *mathayom* 1–3), and three years at secondary (Arabic: *thanawi*, Thai: *matayom* 4–6) levels. The move to increase the number of years of compulsory education from six to nine years was welcomed in some circles but also met with reservation by others. The Malay-Muslim community, in particular harboured concerns that increasing the number of years of compulsory education meant that their children would have to spend more time in government schools before they could transfer to Islamic education institutions. Since 2006, the Ministry of Education has worked to align the standard of Islamic studies by bringing its various levels on par with those of government schools. Correspondingly, *ibtidai* has been standardized with primary schools (six years), *mutawassit* with secondary schools (three years), and *thanawi* with upper secondary school/high school (three years).

Despite the fact that southern Thailand has a mix of Islamic and secular national schools, it has been estimated that as much as 85 per cent of Malay-Muslim students attend Islamic schools.[1] This figure is striking and makes abundantly clear that, despite the overwhelming forces of modernization and secularization, and years of pressure to assimilate, Islamic education and

Islamic teachers continue to have pride of place in the collective socio-cultural consciousness and historical memory of Malay-Muslims in southern Thailand. The figures in Table 2.1 and 2.2 illustrate the continued popularity of Islamic schools in the southern border provinces (see Table 2.1 and 2.2).

While marginally different from the estimate of 85 per cent highlighted above, the following figures compiled by the Ministry of Education for the southern provinces of Yala, Narathiwat, and Pattani, along with Satun and Songkhla, of Muslim students and the types of schools they were enrolled in for the year 2000, nevertheless indicate the considerable popularity of Islamic schools (Table 2.3 and 2.4).[2]

On the other hand, it is glaringly obvious that national schools in the southern provinces have among the lowest attendance rates of any in the country.[3] Insofar as the local communities are concerned, while no recent quantitative studies have been undertaken to ascertain the reasons behind this phenomenon, it can be reasonably surmised that, in accordance with historical trends, Malay-Muslim parents tend to equate national schools with the Buddhist religion.[4]

TYPOLOGY OF SCHOOLS

There are six levels of formal Islamic education in Thailand:

1) *Sekolah Anubahn* (nursery)
2) *Raudah* (pre-primary)
3) *Tadika* (*Taman Didikan Kanak-kanak* or primary)[5]
4) *Pondok*
5) Islamic Private Schools or Private Schools Teaching Islam, also known as *Madrasah* (Arabic), *Sekolah Agama Rakyat* or *Sekolah Agama Swasta* (Malay), and *Rongrian Ekachon Sorn Sasna Islam* (Thai)
6) *Institut Pengajian Tinggi* (Universities and tertiary education institutions)

Sekolah Anubahn, Raudah, and Tadika

Religious education for Muslims in Thailand traditionally begins at home, with lessons concentrating on the recitation of the Qur'an. In more recent times however, *sekolah anubahn*, *raudah*, and *tadika* schools have been established in mosques and have mostly taken over the role of early religious education instruction. *Sekolah anubahn*, which are essentially Muslim childcare facilities for infants and toddlers, are a recent phenomenon in southern Thailand. Their popularity is at least partly a result of the transformation of

TABLE 2.1

Total Number of Muslim and Buddhist Students in the Three Southern Provinces, 2004

Level	Total				Percentage			
	Buddhist	Muslim	Others	Total	Buddhist	Muslim	Others	Total
Kindergarten	3,657	47,942	399	51,998	7.0	92.2	0.8	100.0
Primary School	15,070	162,327	7,699	185,096	8.1	87.7	4.2	100.0
Secondary School	11,514	11,527	216	23,257	49.5	49.6	0.9	100.0
High School	5,604	4,794	22	10,420	53.8	46.0	0.2	100.0
Total	35,845	226,590	8,336	270,771	13.2	83.7	3.1	100.0

Source: National Reconciliation Commission, Education Sub-Committee, 2005

TABLE 2.2
Total Number of Students Attending Government Schools and Private Islamic
Schools in the Three Southern Provinces, 2004

Class/Level	Government School	Private Islamic School
Kindergarten	51,998	262
Primary School	185,096	976
Secondary School	23,257	57,947
High School	10,420	30,020
Total	270,771	89,205

Source: National Reconciliation Commission, Education Sub-Committee, 2005

TABLE 2.3
Lower Secondary Level

Province	Private Schools	Islamic Private Schools	Public Schools
Yala	146	6,450	2,094
Pattani	N.A.	6,183	2,409
Narathiwat	20	4,483	2,421
Satun	N.A.	1,465	2,119
Songkhla	2,156	2,157	10,533

Source: Islamic Private School Association, 2006

TABLE 2.4
Upper Secondary Level

Province	Private Schools	Islamic Private Schools	Public Schools
Yala	N.A.	3,952	1,317
Pattani	N.A.	3,722	1,656
Narathiwat	N.A.	2,421	1,680
Satun	N.A.	692	1,735
Songkhla	585	637	6,754

Source: Islamic Private School Association, 2006

traditional gender roles in southern Thailand that has witnessed women becoming increasingly active and engaged in the workforce. *Tadika* primary schools are run by, and located in, mosques or the *balaisoh* (*balai surau* or prayer halls, usually smaller in size than mosques) that are strewn throughout the southern provinces as well as throughout Bangkok, Chiang Mai, and their vicinities. *Tadika* are especially popular in the south and can be found in almost every village. It is estimated that there are 1,343 *tadika* in the three Malay-Muslim provinces in the south (Table 2.5).

TABLE 2.5

Province	Number of Tadika (as of May 2004)
Yala	384
Pattani	412
Narathiwat	547
Satun	40

Source: Islamic Private School Association, 2006

Tadika schools obtain financial assistance from the state and provide integrated primary education combining religious and secular subjects. Some receive additional funds via private charities. *Tadika* students range in age from three to sixteen years old, with those in the upper age range usually also registered either in *pondok* or Islamic private schools; most of the remaining students are in government schools fulfilling the requirements of compulsory education. Students are mostly sent to *tadika* by their parents to take additional Islam classes. There is no standard curriculum in the *tadika* and what is taught varies depending on the schools and individual teachers. *Tadika* usually operate either in the evenings or over the weekends. While some of the teachers in *anubahn* and *tadika* schools are respected religious leaders, the vast majority are themselves students of traditional *pondok* and Islamic private schools.

Traditional Pondok

Traditional Islamic education in Thailand has been built around the institution of the *pondok*. Some sources trace the establishment of the first *pondok* in

Thailand to 1624 in Talok Manok, located in present-day Narathiwat province, though the authenticity of this claim continues to be debated.[6] Notwithstanding the uncertainty surrounding the genesis of the *pondok* in southern Thailand, few would deny that it has become a trademark institution and represents the Islamic character of the southern provinces in popular imagination. As a testament to its popularity, by 1960 there were reportedly over 500 *pondok* schools strewn across the southern provinces.[7]

By far the most popular symbol of Islamic education in southern Thailand, the *pondok* provides traditional religious instruction for the Muslim community. The structure of *pondok* education pivots around the *tok guru*, the traditional religious teacher who is venerated as a knowledgeable and pious man, not only by his students for whom he is a role model, but often by residents in his village as well. Indeed, some have suggested that the *tok guru* ranks among the most important of the religious elite in southern Thailand.[8] *Pondok* schools are often established by Muslim scholars who return from the *hajj* (pilgrimage to Mecca) and who have spent time in Middle Eastern institutions of learning.[9] Because of their informal nature, *pondok* can easily be established in any *kampung* (village) and have as few as three students on their rosters. Typical *pondok* operate as boarding houses, not unlike the *pesantren* of Indonesia, and students live in accommodation within the school compound which they either build on their own or inherit from graduating seniors.

As mentioned above, the curriculum of *pondok* schools revolves solely around religious education — academic and vocational subjects are not part of the syllabus.[10] Islamic studies at the *pondok* can be broadly categorized into three streams: *tauhid* (oneness of God; divinity), *shari'a* (Islamic way of life, including Islamic law) and *akhlak* (ethics). *Tauhid* includes *usul-addin* (principles of Islam) and *aqidah* (belief in the articles of faith); the focus for *shari'a* is *fiqh* (Islamic jurisprudence) and *fara'id* (Islamic law on succession/ inheritance), while *akhlak* is mostly centred on *tassawuf* (spirituality), a discipline typical of, but not exclusive to, Sufi movements. Beyond these topics the curriculum also includes Islamic history, local history, Arabic language, and *falak* (astronomy/astrology). Insofar as pedagogy is concerned, Hasan Madmarn has contended that "the methodology of *pondok* education in Southern Thailand was and is … similar to the widely recognized system of the intellectual learning process among the institutions in medieval Islam."[11] In other words, *pondok* pedagogy essentially centres on rote learning, recitation, and memory. Typically, a *tok guru* expounds on religious texts and scriptures while students transcribe copious notes (usually in the form of interlinear notes scribbled in Jawi texts) and memorize lessons.

No proper accreditation system exists, certainly none that meets the requirements of national standards set by the education ministry, or even formal requirements set by certain Middle Eastern institutions of learning; nor do *pondok* students qualify for entry into tertiary educational institutions. Assessment depends solely on the judgement of the *tok guru*, who confers an *ijazah* (certification) after the student has sufficiently mastered a particular text or subject. As there is no standard age limit, students range from those in their early teens to adults and elderly folk, almost always male, who retire to the *pondok* to engage in meditation and spiritual reflection.[12] In the main, however, most *pondok* students are in their late teens and early twenties who join after completing several years of compulsory secondary education. Given that the popularity of a *pondok* is usually determined by the reputation of its *tok guru*, it is often the case that Muslim students will move from one *pondok* to another to study under specialists in specific fields such as *fiqh*, *hadith* (Prophetic tradition), *tafsir* (exegesis), *tassawuf*, and *kalam* (theology). In other instances, favoured students might spend years learning at the feet of a particular *tok guru*. In this manner, students are initiated into the intense master-disciple relationship which in the system of Islamic education is believed to mirror the close bonds that existed between the Prophet and his companions. *Pondok* graduates reinforce this system of education by either becoming assistant teachers to respected *tok guru* or, in the case of those with sufficient standing and knowledge, by establishing their own *pondok* and becoming *tok guru* themselves. Oftentimes, favoured students will take over the *pondok* from their *tok guru* upon the latter's retirement or passing. Those deemed to possess sufficient *ilmu* (knowledge) will often also inherit the *tok guru*'s usually extensive collection of scholarship and literature.

The historically tenuous relationship between the institution of the *pondok* and the central government of Thailand has already been documented in the previous chapter. Notwithstanding intermittent attempts to regulate, transform, and even close down the institution, the *pondok* system has proven remarkably resilient. As of January 2006, there were an estimated 321 *pondok* in the three southern provinces and Satun that had registered with the government in response to Bangkok's policy of registration-for-aid, enunciated in May 2004. Of these, 62 are in Yala, 210 in Pattani, 47 in Narathiwat, and 2 in Satun.[13] At the time of writing some of these schools were being considered as candidate institutions for transformation into Islamic private schools and *madrasah*, which would entail the introduction of academic and vocational subjects into their syllabus. Of these, a total of 212 have already received some form of funding from the Thai government (43 in Narathiwat, 33 in Yala, 136 in Pattani), with the other cases pending.[14] Approximately

100 remain unregistered, however, at the time of writing.[15] When queried about their reluctance to register, the most common reason cited by *tok guru* from these schools was their concern that the emphasis on religion would be diluted if they were to accept the curriculum stipulated by the state. One might surmise that these *tok guru* feel a sense of responsibility for preserving the Islamic tradition of the *pondok*, which remains crucial to the history and identity of the Malay-Muslim provinces (Table 2.6).[16]

TABLE 2.6

Province	Number of Pondok (as of May 2004)
Yala	62
Pattani	210
Narathiwat	47
Satun	2

Source: Islamic Private School Association, 2006

What is more striking than the continued existence of the *pondok* is the fact that their numbers have evidently increased over the past couple of years. Indeed, notwithstanding the most recent initiatives by the Thai government — which among other things included a commitment to fully fund all *pondok* which made the transformation to Islamic private school status by registering with the government and introducing academic and vocational subjects — according to Nidae Waba, President of the Islamic Private School Association, the number of traditional *pondok* in southern Thailand actually increased from approximately 270 at the end of 2004 to almost 330 in early 2006.[17] Several reasons can be postulated for this increase. First, while the government had introduced a policy of full funding for *pondok* which registered and were transformed into Islamic private schools, it had also undertaken to fund up to 60 per cent of the budget for *pondok* schools that opted to retain their traditional status after registration. Previously, government funds were allotted only to registered Islamic private schools, while *pondok* were financed through *waqf* (Islamic endowments), *zakat* (tithes), and proceeds from small-scale local commercial activities such as the sale of agricultural produce harvested from the compound of the school.[18] Since 2004 the government has begun to make funds available for *pondok* development, though these funds are disbursed annually on a "project" basis and are usually used for infrastructure repairs and construction in the *pondok* compound, rather than for improving the content and curriculum of *pondok* education through either the purchase of books or training of teachers.[19] Second, several *tok guru* explained their reluctance to transform their *pondok* into Islamic private schools by alluding to concerns about excessive government intrusion into this much-revered education system in southern Thailand. Third, not a few *tok guru* and Malay-Muslims in general also opined that the *pondok* continues to play a vital role precisely because of a perceived need to balance Thai society's fixation with modern secular education, which in their view has opened the way for social ills to creep into the community. Indeed, several *tok guru* interviewed opined that their students had had enough exposure to secular academic instruction after nine to twelve years of compulsory schooling under the national education system, and hence what was urgently required was precisely the opportunity for focused and intense spiritual and religious development that the exclusive emphasis on religious studies at the *pondok* offered. Finally, several *tok guru* also expressed their feeling that the survival of the *pondok* was critical to the preservation of southern Thailand's vaunted reputation as a historical centre of Islamic learning in Southeast Asia. The memory of Patani's historical status as a hub of Islamic education was alluded to by a *tok guru* from the famous Pondok Dalor, who explained that the school's reluctance to convert itself to an Islamic private school owed precisely to the fact that "Pondok Dalor wants to strive for excellence in Islamic teachings and maintain the historical standing of Pattani in the Islamic World".[20]

The recent proliferation of *pondok*, however, does not in itself indicate that the number of Malay-Muslim students who attend Islamic private schools and national schools has declined. On the contrary, a common practice is for Malay-Muslim parents to send their children to Islamic private schools or national schools during the weekdays, and to the *pondok* for evening or weekend instruction in religion. In other words, students are often enrolled in more than one educational institution, whether exclusively religious or religious and secular, at any one time.

Another facet of the *pondok* that has been a matter of vibrant academic and policy debate is its seemingly political character. According to Surin Pitsuwan, politics is integral to the outlook of the *pondok*, and *tok guru* view one of their primary responsibilities as "necessarily the sporadic outbursts of political opposition to the central government in their quest for a higher degree of self-rule".[21] Raymond Scupin, however, suggests otherwise, and has contended that "there was no explicit political purpose within the *pondok*".[22]

Inherent in intimations such as Pitsuwan's is a tension that arises from the question of whether politics is inherent in the structure and *raison d'être* of *pondok*, many of which remain faithful to their essential character as conservative Muslim institutions, or, whether it is an inevitable consequence of the struggle of the *pondok* to maintain its autonomy against pressures of modernization, integration, and assimilation.

Islamic Private Schools (Sekolah Agama Rakyat/ Sekolah Agama Swasta)/*Madrasah* and Institute of Learning — *Pondok*

Despite the historical reputation enjoyed by Thailand's *pondok* schools and the romanticism with which it has been imbued by the Muslim communities in the south, and despite the fact that their numbers have increased in recent years despite government attempts to ensure otherwise, the fact of the matter is that at present it is believed that only about five per cent of the Malay-Muslim student population attend only the traditional *pondok* for their education.[23] The vast majority of Malay-Muslim students have chosen to attend Islamic private schools. While there are compelling reasons why *pondok* schools continue to proliferate in the southern provinces, there are equally persuasive reasons why the popularity of the institution appears to be declining in the Malay-Muslim community when it comes to actual enrolment. Several in particular are worth highlighting. First, *pondok* have been placed under constant pressure by the central government to revamp their education structure so as to adopt a more systematic and bureaucratic model of governance and administration, as well as to introduce vocational and academic subjects for their students. This recalibration of Islamic education is undertaken in order to align curricula in Islamic schools with the requirements of the national education system. The message from the state that Islamic schools need more structure appears to resonate with at least some parents and guardians, notwithstanding their overall misgivings towards Bangkok's intrusion into local matters. Second, there is an instrumentalist realization within the Muslim community as a whole that the traditional *pondok* is simply not equipped to prepare Muslim youths for the challenges of modernity — and this includes the question of employability. As Madmarn has observed, "in the village there is no preparation for religious training among the people and the parents do not encourage their children to study in independent *pondok*. Because many of these villagers are poor farmers and fishermen, their economic problems may inhibit them from their obligatory Islamic duty to educate their children (in independent *pondok*)".[24] To a great extent, the creation of the Islamic private school was as much an outgrowth of the Muslim community's own attempt to bridge the moral and instrumental role of Islamic education in southern Thailand as it was the outcome of state policies to streamline and transform traditionalist educational institutions deemed too parochial and ineffective for the realization of national objectives.

The primary point of departure between the *pondok* and the Islamic private school is the curriculum. Unlike that of the *pondok*, the curriculum of the Islamic private school includes academic and vocational subjects alongside religious studies. Moreover, the compulsory academic/vocational component of the syllabus has to be approved by the Ministry of Education. Herein lies another subtle distinction, this time between the Islamic private school and the *madrasah*, two institutions which otherwise share similar points of origin, motivation, and objective.

Like Islamic private schools, *madrasahs* in Thailand sprang from the move by the Muslim community to reform Islamic education with the introduction of an academic curriculum. However, while in Islamic private schools the academic/vocational track is formulated in consultation with the state, in the *madrasah* the introduction of academic subjects is taken solely at the initiative of Malay-Muslim community leaders and the school's committee or foundation; it does not involve the state, nor does it require formal endorsement on the part of the state. In terms of the historiography of Islamic schools in southern Thailand, the *madrasah* has been described by some as the precursor to the Islamic private school.[25] This is because *madrasahs* had already appeared on the southern Thai landscape by the 1930s, when reformist Islamic scholars returning from the Middle East saw a need to reform Islamic education and introduced academic subjects such as mathematics and sciences into the traditional curriculum. In this way the *madrasah* in effect provided the historical reference point for Muslim scholars and educators when they were later both coaxed and compelled by the state to consider the transformation of traditional Islamic education. Much in the same vein, we find today that some traditional *pondok* have started gradually to integrate academic and vocational subjects into their curriculum, without either subscribing to the school structure and curriculum established by the education ministry or subjecting their revamped curriculum for scrutiny by the Ministry of Education. These schools are sometimes also referred to as *madrasah* in the local community.

On balance, however, the institutions of the Islamic private school and the *madrasah* are more alike than different, notwithstanding the distinctions flagged above. Both institutions view traditional *pondok* education as insufficient to meet either the moral or instrumental needs of Muslim students;

they also recognize the urgent need to supplement the curriculum with practical education. Because of this, the terms Islamic private school and *madrasah* are often conflated and in southern Thailand today are used interchangeably. Indeed, it is often the case that the only distinction found is in the language in which a school is referred — in Arabic it is a *madrasah*, in Thai or Malay it is an Islamic private school.[26]

In Islamic private schools (including *madrasahs*) the general practice is for religious studies to take place in the morning and evening, with the latter being usually through informal study groups, while the afternoons are reserved for academic and vocational subjects taught by both Muslim and Buddhist instructors in the Thai language. Insofar as the religious component of the curriculum is concerned, there is much that is similar between the Islamic private school and the *pondok*. Both place emphasis on traditional Islamic subjects such as *fiqh, tafsir, hadith,* Islamic history, etc. There are, however, several noteworthy points of departure. A major difference is the way the syllabus is structured as a whole. As noted earlier, in the case of the *pondok* much of the syllabus is arbitrary, dictated as it were by the proclivities and knowledge of individual *tok guru*. Though some *pondok* have coalesced together informally to share expertise and to achieve a degree of coherence and uniformity across their curricula, the *pondok* system has mostly been a decentralized one. In the Islamic private school, however, the syllabus must be aligned with national practices. Hence, the curriculum of the Islamic private school accords with the structure of national schools, where it is broken down into elementary (*ibtidai*), middle (*mutawassit*), and secondary (*thanawi*) levels.

Moreover, unlike the traditional *pondok*, Islamic private schools confer on their students the requisite, nationally recognized qualifications that enable them to pursue further studies in the national tertiary education system. While their counterparts at the *pondok* are known in the local parlance as *tok guru*, religious teachers in Islamic private schools and *madrasah* are known as *ustaz* or *babo*. Islamic private schools are also staffed by instructors of academic and vocational subjects such as science, mathematics, English, and computer studies.

The creation of Islamic private schools began in 1961 with government efforts to officially register *pondok* schools under the Pondok Educational Improvement Programme. Later, in 1970, the Ministry of Education formulated the Education Promotion Project to develop a stream of education for these registered *pondok*, one that entailed the teaching of academic and vocational courses alongside religious studies. These objectives came under the purview of the Private Islamic Schools Improvement Committee, created by the Ministry of Education in 1973, whose role was to advise the ministry on matters pertaining to Islamic education and to harmonize the curriculum in Islamic schools with those established for national schools. In 1982, the Islamic private school was officially created as an educational institution and placed under the supervisory authority of the Private Education Committee at the education ministry. In what appears to be the harbinger of yet another policy shift, education authorities have lately been contemplating a change in the nomenclature of Islamic private schools to Institute of Learning — *Pondok* in order to recognize the fact that the Islamic private school is an outgrowth of the old *pondok* tradition.

There are currently some 327 Islamic private schools in southern Thailand (including Satun) that are supervised by the Educational Region Two Office (Yala) in conjunction with the Islamic Private School Association. Of the 298 from the three southern provinces of Pattani, Yala, and Narathiwat, 125 schools enjoy 100 per cent funding from the government, while the remaining 173 currently have 80 per cent of their budget covered by government funding (the discrepancy is largely procedural and this figure will eventually be 100 per cent as well) (Table 2.7).[27]

As noted earlier, the offer for a transfer of status from *pondok* to Islamic private school in exchange for a greater sum of government aid has been made to some 321 *pondok* that have registered with the government since May 2004. In terms of the academic success of these Islamic private schools, according to some Muslim educators an estimated 80 per cent of Muslim students who successfully passed the government university entrance examinations have come from Islamic private schools, though this figure is difficult to authenticate and may at best be informed speculation.[28] Indeed, these figures appear optimistic, given that elsewhere it has been contended that only 60–70 per cent of Malay-Muslim students actually complete

TABLE 2.7

Province	Number of Islamic Private Schools (as of May 2004)
Yala	72
Pattani	168
Narathiwat	58
Satun	29

Source: Islamic Private School Association, 2006

elementary education, while only 25–30 per cent of them go on to complete secondary school. Less than 10 per cent of the Malay-Muslim student cohort actually makes it to the university, and even fewer proceed to obtain post-graduate qualifications.[29] Even if the more impressive figures are true, they may reflect nothing more than that the vast majority of Muslim students come from the Islamic private school system in the first place. On the matter of student performance, Table 2.8 and 2.9 illustrates the performance of secondary school students from the three southern provinces (both Islamic private schools and government schools) as compared to students from other regions in Thailand, and of Islamic private school students as compared to those from government schools (see Table 2.8 and 2.9).

TABLE 2.8
Average Results of Secondary School Students According to
Geographical Regions

Institutions	Subject	Thai Language	Mathematics	Science	English Language
Three southern provinces		47.51%	32.98%	35.47%	37.81%
Southern provinces (besides Pattani, Yala, and Narathiwat)		54.78%	35.26%	38.30%	37.86%
Beyond the south (excluding Bangkok)		53.42%	34.35%	37.64%	36.70%

Source: National Reconciliation Commission, Education Sub-Committee, 2004

TABLE 2.9
Average Results of Secondary School Students (Government Schools and Islamic
Private Schools) in the Three Provinces

Institutions	Subject	Thai Language	Mathematics	Science	English Language
Government schools		45.58%	32.62%	34.44%	35.20%
Islamic private schools		43.45%	31.78%	33.67%	37.23%

Source: National Reconciliation Commission, Education Sub-Committee, 2004

Notwithstanding the changes that the Islamic education system has undergone over the past few decades, many quarters within the Muslim community, while cognizant of the challenges of modernization, still believe that the *pondok* should continue to play an important role in Muslim education as an informal component that supplements Islamic private schools. This explains why the community is reluctant to dispense with the institution even as parents prefer to send their children to Islamic private schools for their main source of education. Consequently, calls continue to be made for the Thai government to preserve *pondok* education as an additional source of evening and/or weekend religious education.[30] The continued relevance of the traditional *pondok* is apparent in the fact that while a majority of Malay-Muslim students are officially registered with Islamic private schools, a significant number of them concurrently attend traditional *pondok* schools in the evening or weekends in pursuit of religious education.

Institut Pengajian Tinggi *(Tertiary Education Institutions)*

Tertiary Islamic education in southern Thailand currently revolves around two institutions — the College of Islamic Studies at Prince of Songkhla University in Pattani, and Yala Islamic University (which was upgraded from a college in July 2007) in Yala and Pattani. A third university, Princess of Narathiwatrajnakarin University, has just been opened. This university is governed by an advisory committee consisting of prominent Muslim academics and scholars from Thailand, and external advisors from Al-Azhar University.

Tertiary Islamic education in southern Thailand owes its genesis to the Department of Philosophy and Religion at the Prince of Songkhla University, which introduced an Islamic studies component to its programme in 1982, in the wake of the global resurgence of Islamic consciousness that significantly impacted Thailand's Muslim minority communities. The rationale of this programme, however, which subsequently evolved into a full-fledged College of Islamic Studies in accordance with the 5th National Economic and Social Development Plan (1982–1986), was decidedly political. Rather than being an initiative of the education ministry, as one might expect, the change was tellingly mooted by the National Security Council. Consequently, it is not surprising that the initiative has been characterized as an outgrowth of "efforts to solve the problems of the southern border provinces".[31] Beyond that, it can also be surmised by the timing of the move that there was a concern to manage the impact of the Islamic resurgence among Thailand's Muslims by stemming the outflow of students to the Middle East. By this time, the Middle East was in the throes of Islamist activism (which at times verged on radicalism) as a result of the Iranian Revolution, the Afghan Mujahideen struggle in Afghanistan, and widespread disenchantment over Israel's occupation of Lebanon. The College was envisaged to fulfil this role in two ways. First, by providing the means for tertiary education in religious studies for Islamic private school graduates, the founding of the College served as a gesture to the Muslim community of the government's consideration for their interests and aspirations. Second, through its short-term programmes catering to non-Muslim government officials posted to the south, it was also an attempt to facilitate interaction and mutual understanding between Muslims and non-Muslims in southern Thailand.[32] Instruction at the College is in three languages — English, Arabic, and Thai. The Islamic studies programme consists of two streams, one in Arabic and the other in Thai.

Yala Islamic University was formed as a college in 1998 in Tambun Budi, Yala province, with a faculty of religious studies housing departments in *shari'a* and *usul-addin*. A second campus was established at Bukit Datu in Kampung Serong, Pattani, in 2003. According to its administrators, the rationale behind the formation of Yala Islamic College flowed from the observation that, while the Islamic private school system had seen many Muslim students attain secondary education, very few entered public universities and even fewer had the opportunity to pursue tertiary studies abroad if financial support was not readily available.[33] The initiative that gave birth to Yala Islamic College essentially arose from within the community, with Malay-Muslim academics being the primary drivers of the process. Yala Islamic College was established under the Southern Higher Education Foundation and continues to be supervised by the Committee of Higher Education Institutions at the Ministry of Education.

While Yala Islamic University centres its syllabus on religious studies, it has also begun integrating a parallel curriculum in general education. For instance, in 2004 the University introduced departments of public administration and information technology under a faculty of science, as well as a department of Islamic banking and finance.[34] Courses in the Islamic studies faculty (towards the degree in *shari'a*, for instance) are taught in Arabic, those in public administration and Islamic finance are taught in Thai, while information technology training is conducted in English. The Yala campus also has an international language academy that teaches Arabic, English, Chinese, Malay, and Thai. It caters both to students without the requisite language skills for specific programmes and those with a broader interest in languages (as elective courses). At present, the university offers bachelor of arts degrees and diplomas. The University is currently awaiting government approval for an M.A. programme in Islamic civilization as well as an M.A. programmes in education and *dakwah*.[35] For all degrees, students are required to take basic courses in Islam. For example, all students have to take a core introductory course on Islam, taught in English, Thai, and Arabic. Moreover, all students, including those taking programmes in Thai and English as well as non-religious courses, have to commit two chapters of the Qur'an to memory before they are permitted to graduate. Notably however, being Muslim is not a requirement for acceptance in Yala Islamic University, and the University is envisaged not only as an institution of tertiary education but also as an avenue for *dakwah* to Muslims as well as non-Muslims.[36]

The philosophy behind this initiative of reforming, modernizing, and Islamizing education for Thailand's Muslim community will be discussed further in the following chapters when the ideas of the University rector, Ismail Lutfi Japakiya, are studied more closely. For now, several core principles have been articulated by the University administration to ensure that faculty and instructors are equipped to carry out the school's mission. According to these principles, faculty are expected to:

1. Comprehend and internalize the Islamic value system which is based on the *tauhidic* world-view;
2. Understand the philosophical and historical development of knowledge and education within the Islamic and Western traditions;
3. Understand the relationship between knowledge, education, religion and society;
4. Have a command in great depth of particular areas of knowledge, whether revealed or acquired, in order to teach and guide the youth;
5. Possess psychological and pedagogical knowledge and skills to teach effectively;
6. Be morally excellent and intellectually sound to act as role model (*uswah hasanah*);
7. Be critical, creative, reflective, and sensitive to social demands and problems;
8. Observe the pursuit and dissemination of knowledge as an act of worship.[37]

Public Schools

While the vast majority of Malay-Muslim students attend either the *pondok* or Islamic private school (or both), there are a minority who remain enrolled in the government or public school system throughout their years of formal schooling. Public schools are required under the statutes of the Ministry of Education to provide religious education for a minimum of two hours a week. Because this is seen as insufficient for a good grounding in Islam, parents who enrol their children in public schools usually also send them to *pondok* and/or *tadika* for weekend instruction in Islam. Currently in the three southern provinces there are a total of eighty-seven national primary schools and thirty-one national secondary schools that provide religious education as described above.

Following the typology of Islamic education institutions charted above, the table below serves as a consolidation of figures on the types and number of educational institutions that are attended by Muslim students in the three Malay-Muslim-dominated southern provinces (see Table 2.10).

TABLE 2.10

Educational Institution	Number
Tadika	1,343
Registered Traditional *Pondok*	319
Unregistered Traditional *Pondok*	100 (approximate)
Islamic Private School	298
Public Schools with religious studies (Primary and Secondary)	118
Tertiary Institutions	2 (plus 1 pending)

Informal Institutions

Aside from these formal institutions, there is another category of informal, parallel Islamic education that augments this system. In this category are schools such as *diploma aliy*, *kuliyyah*, and *qira'atiy*. *Diploma aliy* and *kuliyyah* are integrated into Islamic private schools, where they operate as associate programmes that supplement the religious curriculum for students intending to proceed overseas for tertiary education in Islamic studies. *Qira'atiy* provides instruction in the memory and recitation of the Qur'an, and while functioning independently (as compared to *diploma aliy* and *kuliyyah*) they are run as one-hour classes that take place between *magrib* (sunset daily prayer) and *isha* (evening daily prayer).

The following table illustrates the structure of and options for religious education in southern Thailand for Muslims and, for comparison, Buddhists (see Table 2.11).

TABLE 2.11
Structure of Religious Education (Islamic Studies and Buddhist Studies)

| Pengajian Dunyawi | Religious Studies | | | |
| | Islam | | Buddhism | |
Level/Class and curriculum	Level/Class	Institution	Level/Class	Institution
Kindergarten	Qira-atiy	Raudah	No	No
Primary School	Ibtidai (1–6)	Tadika	Dharma scholar (third grade-second grade-first grade)	Buddhists studies of Sunday
Secondary School	Mutawassit (1–3)	Pondok/ Islamic private school	Pali Dharma (1–9)	Dharma to be studied (study of the
High School	High School (4–6)			Buddhist scripture)
Tertiary/University	Islamic Studies (B.A. & M.A. Degree)	Yala Islamic College/ College of Islamic Studies, Prince of Songkhla University	B.A. & M.A. Degree	University of Chulalongkorn Ratjawitayali/ University of Maha Mongkut Ratjawitayalai

Source: National Reconciliation Commission, Education Sub-Committee Report, 2005.

FINANCING ISLAMIC EDUCATION

In evaluating the nature and pace of education reforms, the fairly considerable financial and resource constraints under which most Islamic schools operate must be borne in mind. For a long time *pondok* education in Thailand was funded primarily by *zakat* and *waqf* as students were often not charged for their education. As a matter of fact, some *pondok*, like Pondok Alfatah Papao in Kabang, Yala, even provide stipends of several hundred baht per week to their students. *Zakat* and *waqf* funds were at times supplemented by small-scale agricultural activities that *pondok* students and *tok guru* engaged in. While some of these traditional practices remain, Islamic schools currently enjoy funding from a variety of sources including the Thai government as well as external sources such as foreign Muslim governments and charities.[38] Prominent members of Thailand's Muslim community, including parliamentarians and politicians, also make regular private contributions to schools.

Because of the government's concerns over the recent influx of foreign funding, which falls outside its purview and is difficult to monitor or regulate with any precision, Bangkok has consistently prodded Islamic schools to accept government-regulated funding in the hope of discouraging schools from turning to outside sources of assistance. Since passing legislation for the registration of *pondok* on 4 January 2004, the Thai government has been committed to providing registered *pondok* that transformed themselves into Islamic private schools, with 5 million baht of aid per year for every 500 pupils. In most schools, these finances are received and managed by a school foundation.[39] This compares to just 100,000–200,000 baht for registered *pondok* that insist on retaining traditional *pondok* status. For Islamic private schools, these subsidies account for 100 per cent of the school budget, as compared to a decade ago when the government subsidized only 60 per cent of their budget. The trade-off, however, is that the government takes on an active role, at least in theory, in developing the school, both in terms of infrastructure and curriculum. Under the 4 January 2004 scheme, the traditional *pondok* also receive subsidies, though with a ceiling of 60 per cent of their budget. Though Islamic private schools and *pondoks* are recipients of government funding, they are free to receive donations from private interests either from within Thailand or abroad, despite the Thai government's reservations about the latter.[40]

As explained earlier, the government's most recent attempt to encourage registration in exchange for aid has generally been welcomed, if only for instrumental reasons.[41] The hundred or so traditional *pondok* that have chosen to remain independent are under pressure to register in order to obtain the much-needed subsidies. However, education ministry regulations do not permit registration without the fulfilling of basic requirements such as the provision of proper rooms and facilities, regulation of the location, class size, and the need for *tok guru* to possess teaching certificates. Many of the remaining independent *pondok* currently do not meet these logistical requirements.[42] As a matter of fact, while the situation appears on the surface to be improving for these traditional Islamic educational institutions, a number of challenges remain.[43] First, the quality of *pondok* infrastructure continues to lag far behind that of Islamic private schools and national schools. Significant improvements are required in terms of simple amenities such as paved roads, regular supply of electricity and clean water, and general condition of the *balai* (huts) which house boarding students. The schools located farther out in the rural areas are in particularly urgent need of upgrading. Second, *pondok* administration still lacks the level of professionalism as compared to their counterparts in national schools and even Islamic private schools. The *tok guru*, who serves not only as the chief (and at times sole) instructor but also principal and chief administrator, usually does not possess the requisite certification, knowledge, and skills required for the administration of a modern and structured organization, as the "modern" registered *pondok* or Islamic private school is envisaged to be. Third, insofar as the maintenance of traditional practices in curriculum design is concerned, some *tok guru* have expressed a desire to retain the oral tradition of *pondok* education against pressures to introduce a more structured curriculum and pedagogy. A key challenge in this respect is striking a balance between retaining that tradition and creating a system where academic achievement can be quantified, so that students may have opportunities for educational advancement either in Islamic private schools or at universities in Thailand and abroad. A more pressing problem though, remains the need to balance government funding on the one hand with the desire to remain autonomous on the other.

By comparison, the situation of Islamic tertiary education institutions is considerably less onerous and vexing. While the College of Islamic Studies has benefited from its association with Prince of Songkhla University in terms of funding, Yala Islamic University has been funded primarily by private and external interests. The World Assembly of Muslim Youth (WAMY), Islamic Development Bank, and International Islamic Relief Organization have been instrumental in bankrolling the formation of the Yala Islamic University, as have the governments of Saudi Arabia, Kuwait, and Qatar.[44] While the University does receive some measure of government funding, it is only for the conduct of extra-curricular activities.[45] Interestingly, it is also attempting to obtain funding from the Asia Foundation in Thailand for a number of their programs and activities.

Though the exact amounts are impossible to determine with any accuracy, foreign Islamic charities and governments have undoubtedly played an active role in funding Islamic education in Thailand since the 1970s. A large portion of this aid has taken the form of scholarships. Because education policies in the 1960s were viewed as thinly veiled projects of assimilation, numerous *ustaz* and *tok guru* had chosen to pursue their education overseas.[46] The question of external influences on the religious education of Thailand's

Malay-Muslim students will be taken up in greater detail in the following chapters. For now, it is enough to note that some sources estimate that pre-September 2001, roughly up to 300 Thai Muslims annually received foreign scholarships from institutions in Saudi Arabia, Egypt, Jordan, and elsewhere in the Middle East, while another 200 were funded by institutions in Indonesia, Malaysia, Brunei, and Sudan.[47] Other sources state that up to 1,700 Thai students may currently be studying in Egypt, while another several hundred are in Saudi Arabia, though it is unclear if the source of their scholarships is foreign or local (i.e., *zakat* or *waqf* money).[48] Scholarships for these students mostly cover tuition, books, and accommodation. In other instances, as in the case of Saudi financial assistance, monthly stipends are also provided of around 8,000 baht per student on top of coverage for necessary expenses (tuition and accommodation).[49] Since September 2001, however, funding from Saudi Arabia has declined sharply. This is the result of a conscious policy of the Saudi government to reduce funds for Islamic education, against the backdrop of widespread international concern that these funds were somehow being channelled to finance terrorists and jihadists. Consequently, according to figures provided by the Thai Students' Association in Saudi Arabia, the number of Thai recipients of scholarships from the kingdom fell from twenty-two in 2000 to only four in 2006.[50] For 2007 the figure has returned to approximately 20.[51]

While the majority of scholarships has been offered by host governments, the Thai government has in recent times provided a small number to Thai Muslim students planning to further their tertiary Islamic education overseas. For instance, Hasan Madmarn has noted that there are currently ten scholarships offered by the Ministry of Foreign Affairs to Thai Muslim students pursuing tertiary Islamic studies in Egypt and Morocco.[52] These scholarships are administered by the College of Islamic Studies, Prince of Songkhla University.

CURRICULUM MANAGEMENT

To monitor the curriculum of Islamic schools in the Malay-Muslim provinces, the Ministry of Education created the Office of Local District Education Region (OLDER) under the National Education Act (2542/1999). The previous departments and offices that were tasked to oversee education policy in the southern provinces, such as the Office of Education Region Two and the Provincial and District Education Offices, were brought within the operational boundaries of this Office.[53] The OLDER works closely with individual Islamic private schools, Islamic private school foundations, and the Islamic Private School Association to coordinate the curriculum at elementary, middle, and secondary levels. The curriculum itself is divided relatively evenly between religious and academic/vocational subjects, though certain schools have instituted a breakdown consisting of 18–22 hours per week for religious education and 22–28 hours a week for general academic/ vocational subjects.[54]

At local levels, the curriculum of formal Islamic education comes under the jurisdiction of the Islamic Private School Association and is devised to accord with the framework and standards of academic institutions in the Middle East. This is so that Thai Islamic schools "are of the same quality and character and providing the same levels of study (to) be recognized by those universities and authorities".[55] This indicates the centrality of the Middle East in prevailing perceptions of Islamic knowledge, and again suggests the erosion of Patani's erstwhile popularity and tradition of academic excellence in Islamic studies.

A long-standing concern of state officials is the need for the Islamic education curriculum to address the socio-political challenges confronting Thailand's Malay-Muslim minority. This concern finds expression in the state's generally circumspect response to the use of imported Islamic studies texts in Islamic schools. In this regard, Hasan Madmarn offers two explanations for the government's concerns. First, he observes that imported textbooks "may not fully serve the needs" of Thailand's Muslim-minority community and might in fact attract Thai students away from local schools to foreign institutions.[56] Second, Madmarn also notes that reproduced imported texts are more expensive compared to locally written and produced literature.[57] While both these concerns are valid, there is a third issue that Madmarn skirts — namely that the Thai government has in recent years become increasingly alarmed at the influx of radical ideology through the introduction of foreign educational material.[58] Consequently, the education ministry has made some effort to encourage and monitor the production of local material, primarily Jawi texts and to a lesser extent Arabic texts with Jawi explanatory notes.[59]

Nevertheless, in order to balance these security concerns with sensitivity towards the norms of Islamic religious education, provisions have been made for upper secondary-level students in Islamic private schools to use certain texts published in the Middle East that advance students' understanding and usage of Arabic — seen by many orthodox Muslims as the "authentic" language of Islam — and to prepare students who intend eventually to pursue further education in the Middle East.[60] The result is an approximate balance of 80 per cent–20 per cent between locally-written and imported textbooks.[61] Aside from printed texts, the internet has played an increasingly important role in Muslim education, and websites such as www.sasnupatam.com and www.muslimthai.com are regularly cited as popular internet resources by religious teachers.

While the process of modernizing and developing Islamic education in southern Thailand is proving to be a challenging task for both the state and the Malay-Muslim community, some distinct positives have accrued. Notably, the creation of modern secondary education in the form of the Islamic private school has facilitated an increase in the number of Muslim students gaining entry into universities throughout Thailand, even if this number has remained small in comparison to other minority groups. This has resulted from the introduction of examinations for the higher secondary certificate of Thai education that has allowed Muslim students to compete with their non-Muslim counterparts from national schools for tertiary education positions. To be sure, their task has been assisted by the implementation of a quota system for Muslim students entering national universities under the auspices of the Ministry of the Interior.

The preceding two chapters have dwelled substantively on how Islamic education has come to reflect the difficult relationship between the state and Malay-Muslim society in Thailand. Notwithstanding the salience of this issue, there is another parallel concern which has thus far eluded careful scrutiny and analysis, and which falls outside the state-centric framework that oftentimes defines the analytical parameters of the study of the Malay-Muslim community in southern Thailand, sometimes to the extent that the latter is mistakenly assumed to be a homogeneous entity juxtaposed against the hegemonic Thai state. This issue pertains to the rise of tensions and contestations within the Malay-Muslim community itself as a result of the emergence and, to some extent, resurgence of reformist and modernist trends within the community and the impact this has had on patterns of Islamic education in the region and beyond.

Notes

[1] Interview with an independent Malay-Muslim researcher, Pattani, 17 January 2005. It should be noted that attending an Islamic school does not preclude attending a non-Islamic state school. In fact, while the numbers would be difficult to ascertain, I do know of instances where Muslim students attend both Islamic and non-Islamic state schools at the same time.

[2] Ministry of Education — Thailand, *A Brief Report on Development of the Islamic Private Schools in Regions 2, 3, and 4 in the Fiscal Year 2000* (Bangkok: Office of Private Education Committee, Ministry of Education, undated). Also found in Hasan Madmarn, "Secular Education, Values and Development in the Context

of Islam in Thailand: An Outlook on Muslim Attitudes toward Thai Educational Policy", in *Asian Interfaith Dialogue: Perspectives on Religion, Education, and Social Cohesion*, edited by Syed Farid Alatas, Lim Teck Ghee, and Kazuhide Kurada (Singapore and Washington, D.C.: RIMA and The World Bank, 2003), pp. 75–76.

3   Charles F. Keyes, *Thailand: Buddhist Kingdom as Modern Nation-State* (Boulder and London: Westview Press, 1987), p. 131. Having said that, it is possible that there is a class dynamic at work, where Malay-Muslims from the urban area prefer national schools while those in the rural areas opt for religious schools.

4   Interview with a senior administrator, College of Islamic Studies, Prince of Songkhla University (interview was conducted in Yala), 17 January 2005.

5   It should be noted that the *tadika* of southern Thailand differs from that in Malaysia. While the Malaysian *tadika* is essentially a pre-school, in southern Thailand the term refers to primary schools.

6   Reference to this *pondok* can be found in Abdul Haleem Bashah, *Raja dan Dinasti Jembal dalam Patani Besar* [King and Jembal Dynasty in Patani] (Kelantan: Pustaka Reka, 1994).

7   Uthai Dulyakasem, "Education and Ethnic Nationalism: A Study of the Muslim-Malays in Southern Siam" (Ph.D. dissertation, Stanford University, 1981), p. 84.

8   See Wan Kadir Che Man, *Muslim Elites and Politics in Southern Thailand* (Penang: Universiti Sains Malaysia, 1983).

9   Most congregate at Malay-speaking *halaqah* (scholastic circles) in Mecca's holy mosque as well as Medina University.

10 This makes for interesting comparison with the traditional Indonesian equivalent, the *pondok-pesantren*, which though primarily focused on Islamic education, did also provide instruction in mathematics.

11 Hasan Madmarn, *The Pondok and Madrasah in Pattani* (Bangi: Penerbit Universiti Kebangsaan Malaysia, 1999), p. 66.

12 Joseph Liow, "The *Pondok* School of Southern Thailand: Bastion of Islamic Education or Hotbed of Militancy?", *IDSS Commentaries* (August 2004).

13 Figures obtained from the *Persatuan Sekolah Agama Rakyat* or Islamic Private School Association, 22 July 2006.

14 Beyond that, thirty-seven *pondok* from Yala, thirty-six from Pattani, and three from Narathiwat are scheduled to obtain further government assistance in the financial year of 2006. Information obtained from the *Pondok* Association, 23 February 2006.

15 Interview with officials at the *Pondok* Association, Pattani, 18 January 2006.

16 See the discussion in Supara Janchitfah, *Violence in the Mist: Reporting on the Presence of Pain in Southern Thailand* (Bangkok: Kobfai Publishing Project, 2005), pp. 53–65.

17 Interview with Nidae Waba, President, Islamic Private School Association, Pattani, 14 January 2006.

[18] In many *pondok* schools, students are encouraged to grow vegetables for their own sustenance as well as for sale at the local markets to cover their education expenses.

[19] For example, *pondok* schools such as Pondok Samala and Pondok Islamhudin in Klongmaning (Pattani), Pondok Darusalem (Pattani), Annasiriyah Islamiyah in Yaring (Pattani), and Suksawinai in Beneng Seri (Yala) interviewed in the course of research revealed that they received between 200,000–280,000 Baht for sanitation projects, roof repairs, construction of roads, plumbing, signage, etc. That said, there are still *pondok* schools that apparently do not receive support from the government. One such example is Attaufikiah Islamiah in Sri-Sakorn (Narathiwat). Attaufikiah Islamiah currently has an enrolment of 250.

[20] Interview at Pondok Dalor, Pattani, 2 February 2006.

[21] Surin Pitsuwan, *Islam and Malay Nationalism: A Case Study of the Malay-Muslims of Southern Thailand* (Bangkok: Thai Khadi Research Institute, Thammasat University, 1985), p. 179.

[22] Raymond Scupin, "Education and Development for Muslims in Thailand", in *Aspects of Development: Islamic Education in Thailand and Malaysia*, edited by Raymond Scupin (Bangi: Institut Bahasa Kesusasteraan dan Kebudayaan Melayu, University Kebangsaan Malaysia, 1989), p. 104.

[23] Interview with a local Malay-Muslim journalist at the Issara News Centre, Pattani, 17 January 2005.

[24] Madmarn, "The Pondok and Change in South Thailand", in *Aspects of Development*, edited by Scupin, p. 65.

[25] See Madmarn, *The Pondok and Madrasah in Pattani*.

[26] Hence, for instance, the Islamic private school Sekolah Darusat Witthaya Islam (Malay) would be known in Arabic as Madrasah Islamiah al-Aliah.

[27] These figures were obtained from the Association of Private Islamic Schools. I was unable to obtain the breakdown for schools in Satun.

[28] Interview conducted in Yala with a senior administrator of the College of Islamic Studies, Prince of Songkhla University, 17 January 2005.

[29] Darwish Moawad, "Southernmost Thailand Violence: Illiteracy, Poverty, Politics, Illicit Drugs Trafficking, Smuggling, and Nationalist Separatists — not Religion and Culture — the Issue". Paper presented at UNESCO Conference on "Religion in Peace and Conflict", Melbourne, Australia, 12 April 2005, p. 8.

[30] Interview with Pakorn Priyakorn, Islamic Center of Thailand, Bangkok, 23 January 2005.

[31] Madmarn, *The Pondok and Madrasah in Patani*, pp. 115–16.

[32] Ibid., p. 117.

[33] Interview with Kariya Langputeh, Yala Islamic University, Pattani, 18 January 2005.

[34] The rationale for the creation of a public administration program was described by administrators at YIC as an initiative to address the rampant corruption and

general lack of ethics among Thai bureaucrats operating both in southern Thailand and more generally across the country.

[35] *Dakwah* refers to the duty of Muslims to "call" or "invite", implying proselytization.

[36] Interview with Kariya Langputeh, Yala Islamic University, Pattani, 18 January 2005.

[37] Sukree Langputeh, "The Islamization of the Discipline of Public Administration in a Thai Higher Education Institution: The Experience of Yala Islamic College" (paper presented at the International Workshop on Voices of Islam in Europe and Southeast Asia, Nakhon Si Thammarat, 20–22 January 2006). In turn, Sukree cited these principles from Rosnani Hashim, "The Construction of an Islamic-based Teacher Education Program", *Muslim Education Quarterly* 14, no. 2 (1997): 59.

[38] One Islamic private school in Ranget, Narathiwat, Rahmaniah, is partially funded by the Arrahmah Islamic Foundation in the United Kingdom. Interview at Rahmaniah School, Narathiwat, 27 February 2005.

[39] The purpose for creating the in-house foundation is to officially manage the administration, including finances, of the school.

[40] For example, new buildings at the Attarkiah Islamiah Institute, a large Islamic private school in Narathiwat, was funded by King Faisal of Saudi Arabia, Iqraa Charitable Society, and the Islamic Development Bank. Interview at Attarkiah Islamiah Institute, Narathiwat, 24 February 2005.

[41] This exercise involved not only the registration of schools, but also of all teachers and students, who had their family and personal backgrounds scrutinized. Interview at Saiburi Islam Wittaya School, Pattani, 24 February 2005.

[42] Interview conducted in Yala with a senior administrator, College of Islamic Studies, Prince of Songkhla University, 17 January 2005.

[43] See Ibrahim Narongraksakhet, "Pondoks and their Roles in Preserving Muslim Identity in Southern Border Provinces in Thailand", in *Knowledge and Conflict Resolution: The Crisis of the Border Region of Southern Thailand*, edited by Uthai Dulyakasem and Lertchai Sirichai (Nakhon Si Thammarat: School of Liberal Arts, Walailak University, 2005), pp. 96–97.

[44] For example, the new campus in Pattani was recently given a donation of 30 million baht for the construction of two new buildings from the Kuwaiti government, while Sheikh Hamad bin Khalifa al-Thani of Qatar personally donated 43 million baht to the University for the construction of a new building and dormitory. Interview with Kariya Langputeh, Yala Islamic University, Pattani, 18 January 2005.

[45] "Crown Prince to open Islamic college headquarters in Pattani", *The Nation*, 6 March 2004.

[46] Madmarn, *The Pondok and Madrasah in Patani*, pp. 80–81. It should be noted that the reason for the exodus of Muslim students taking place since the 1960s revolved primarily around oppressive state policies on Muslim education in

Thailand and differed substantially from earlier movements of students to the Arab world, which were less a reaction to state policies than a desire among some students to study in the heart of early twentieth-century Islamic reformism.

47   Interview with Pakorn Priyakorn, Central Islamic Committee of Thailand, Bangkok, 25 January 2005.

48   Correspondence with Hasan Madmarn, 2 April 2005.

49   "Students Come Home to Suspicion", *The Nation*, 31 October 2006.

50   Ibid.

51   Email interview with Saudi alumnus, 24 September 2007.

52   Correspondence with Hasan Madmarn, 2 April 2005.

53   Ibrahim Narongraksakhet, "Developing Local-based Curriculum Guidelines for Islamic Private Schools in Southern Thailand" (Ph.D. dissertation, Universiti Malaya, July 2003), pp. 9–14.

54   These figures were determined over a range of interviews in the southern provinces from January to April 2005.

55   Madmarn, *The Pondok and Madrasah in Pattani*, p. 83.

56   Ibid., pp. 95–96. Hasan goes on to elaborate that "to have the curricula and related text introduced effectively, the executive personnel of the Office of Educational Region Two recommended that the textbooks be produced in a form relating to the local situation to properly serve the levels of learning in an Islamic private school."

57   Ibid., p. 96.

58   Interview with a senior intelligence officer, Armed Forces Security Center, Bangkok, 24 January 2005. That said, from my own observations it seems that writings of known radicals such as Sayyid Qutb (not just his popular *Tafsir al-Quran* but *Signposts*) have been more accessible to the public in places such as Kuala Lumpur and Jakarta than in Pattani. In the course of visits to Islamic bookstores in the former two cities I have come across versions of these writers' publications; I have yet to find them in Pattani.

59   This stems from earlier attempts by previous Thai governments to "correct" and introduce uniformity to *kitabs* or local Islamic texts. See Pitsuwan, *Islam and Malay Nationalism*, p. 131.

60   Madmarn, *The Pondok and Madrasah in Pattani*, p. 98.

61   This breakdown is based on interviews conducted with various religious teachers during the course of fieldwork from January to April 2005.

3

THE CHALLENGE OF ISLAMIC REFORMISM

The impetus to preserve and sustain religious and communal identities against the backdrop of a wider Buddhist culture has traditionally led Muslims in southern Thailand to look to independent religious education as an alternative to Buddhist and secular national education. Consequently, much of the extant literature portrays such separate forms of education as a symbolic struggle to gain recognition for Muslims. This tendency has been most evident in the case of the Malay-Muslims concentrated in the three southern border provinces. Less visibly, however, Islamic education has recently emerged as an arena where tension and contestations within the Muslim community itself have come to be captured and expressed. This trend now operates parallel to, and to a great extent independently of, structural pressures posed by state education policies which had previously defined the parameters of the politics of Islamic education. At the heart of these contestations is the advent of the Islamic reformist movement in Thailand, with its implications for Islamic thought and praxis in a hitherto traditionalist environment.

As was the case throughout Muslim Southeast Asia, Islam in Thailand has enjoyed a long tradition of syncretism, coexisting with earlier Hinduistic and Malay religio-spiritual and supernatural beliefs and practices. In this way, both the transcendental and mundane concerns of rural communities were addressed.[1] Particularly pronounced was the imprint of Sufism, which sought to harmonize mysticism with orthodoxy and which rejected rigid, ritualistic adherence to the *shari'a*. The resulting brand of Islam was pliable enough to reconcile all manner of local beliefs and customs with the monotheistic faith at its base. This syncretic nature of so-called folk Islam in Southeast Asia, though, would soon come under pressure from Islamic reform movements to abandon this characteristic elasticity for a more pristine, fundamentalist creed.

In thinking about the emergence of the Islamic reform movement in Thailand, two of its conceptual pillars – Salafism and Wahhabism — should be examined, for two main purposes. First, as the following chapters will show, Salafism and Wahhabism are seen as the intellectual and ideological foundations of reform, by virtue of the fact that they oppose traditional Islamic orthodoxy. Indeed, local scholars and educators tend to apply these terms interchangeably when describing reformist patterns in the configuration of Islamic knowledge and education in southern Thailand. Second, these concepts are often treated in popular Western parlance in a pejorative fashion. Such treatments are for the most part impressionistic caricatures that show no proper appreciation of the complex meanings of these concepts. Indeed, when *Salatism* and Wahhabism are used as reductionist labels, significant differences among thinkers within these two traditions tend to be obscured. In more sophisticated and nuanced readings, it is often the case that continuities and discontinuities will emerge within these fundamentalist positions on different issues.

Salafism should not be conflated with Wahhabism, for while they share some basic premises, there are also, as noted above, significant points of departure. And while in the minds of Western foreign-policy-makers these concepts form the ideological and intellectual basis of extremism, neither tradition is in and of itself a monolithic phenomenon.

In the historiography of Islam, reformists such as Muhammad Abduh (1825–1905), a teacher at Al-Azhar and later Grand Mufti of Egypt, and his prodigy Rashid Rida believed that the "golden age" of Islam was the period that accorded with the activism of the early *ummah* and its Salaf, the three generations of the community of elders and companions of the Prophet. Indeed, there is a clear creedal injunction in which the Prophet himself pronounced the special status of the Salaf. In other words, Salaf includes the companions of the Prophet (the *Sahabah*), *their* students the "successors" (the *Taabi'een*), and their students (the *Atbaa Taabi'een*).

Since the time of the illustrious companions, *imam* and scholars have been seen to be the righteous successors to this legacy of piety, and as such the term *Salafus-Saaleh*, the "Pious Predecessors", has commonly been used to describe them. To the reformists, the Salaf represented the spiritual and epistemological core of Sunni Islam which was developed by the great theologians and thinkers of the third and fourth Islamic centuries. It is in this context that these reformists are known in Islamic studies parlance as Salafi — in the manner of their subscription to the ways of the Salaf in their comprehension of *aqidah, manhaj* and *fiqh*. In Islamic studies in the Malay world, the reformist nature of the Salafi movement has been captured in the concept of the "*Kaum Muda*" or "New Generation". This term essentially refers to Salafis who attempt to reform Islam by taking it away from its traditional syncretism and re-orienting it towards scripturalism. Describing the objectives of these reformists in the Malay world, William Roff has argued that, to them, "the traditional practice of Islam ... adulterated by impurities of custom and belief derived from *adat* and from other religions, and inimical to progress, must be cleansed of these elements, and the *ulama* who transmit the imperfections brought to a sense of their errors and obligations".[2]

Wahhabism, on the other hand, refers to a particular brand of Salafism rooted in the historical evolution of Islamic thought and praxis in the Arabian Peninsula. This is not the place to launch into a detailed elucidation of the doctrinal underpinnings of Wahhabism, but it is worth emphasizing that Wahhabism drinks from the same epistemological well as Salafism in its objective of a return to the tradition of the Prophet and his companions. Wahhabism is grounded principally in the religious thought of Muhammad ibn Abd Al-Wahab, a Salafi thinker who was trained in the Hanbali school of Islamic jurisprudence and was influenced by the writings of Ibn Taymiyyah (1263 to 1328). Abd Al-Wahab had openly condemned *ulama* for what he saw as laxity in the practice of Islam and as deviations from the pristine faith of *tauhid* (monotheism). He condemned the Sufis for indulging in the practice of *shirk* (syntheism) and *bid'a* (innovation). Here, we must take note of Wahhabism's political undertones, by way of its historical association with the seat of Arab government. Beyond merely articulating the need for a return to the God-centred model of Islamic life and society associated with Salafism, Wahhabism sought to give political expression to these objectives in its condemnation of such acts as the intercession of *imam* and *ulama*, the veneration of saints, the commemoration of holidays (including religious holidays), and any manner of devotion to the Prophet. In the history of the Arabian Peninsula, this translated to outlawing of cultural rituals and customs, and in certain instances, violence and militancy in the name of purifying faith and religion. Explaining Wahhabism's political mien, Azzam Tamimi contends:

> Although the ideas of Ibn Abd Al-Wahhab were purely religious in nature, it was inevitable by virtue of the nature of Islam itself as a faith and a worldview comprising a frame of reference, a standard of preference

and a code of morality that many influential individuals and circles perceived these ideas as posing a serious threat to their authority. It might have been possible that had Ibn Abd Al-Wahhab's ideas not been censored and every effort made to curtail free discussion of what he was proposing or promoting he might not have been compelled to seek political empowerment and his followers might not have engaged in *jihad* and conquest.[3]

The political character of Wahhabism was demonstrated most profoundly with the capture of Mecca in the nineteenth century by supporters of Abd Al-Wahab. The movement subsequently expanded across West Africa and South Asia and was halted only with the intervention of the Ottoman Empire. The political nature of Wahhabism was codified in 1744 when Wahab entered into an alliance with Muhammad bin Saud, a local Arab emir. Today, the House of Saud enforces a state-sanctioned Wahhabism in Saudi Arabia at the same time as the Wahhabi clerics endorse its political authority.

The traditional schools of Islamic jurisprudence or *fiqh* — also known as the four Mazhab — that anchor much of traditional Islam were established in fact after this "golden age" that the Salafis identify. In other words, according to the historiography of Islam, the four *imam* who founded these schools were not authentic Salaf themselves, but merely followers of the Salaf. Hence, reformists see the Mazhab as evolving outside the context of the *hadith* and as a digression from the traditions of Salaf. Moreover, the reformists see *taqlid*, the uncritical acceptance of textual sources that typifies traditionalist Islamic pedagogy, as an ultimately fallible mode for the transmission of religious truths.

As in the rest of the region, reformist Islam in Thailand was rooted in the late nineteenth-century intellectual reformism of the Salafiyya movement led by Muhammad Abduh.[4] Abduh's reformist ideas of authenticity based solely on the Qur'an and *hadith* were popularized through his student Rashid Rida's journal *Al-Manar*, which proved the standard-bearer for Muslim students from the region who were studying in the Middle East. *Al-Manar* spawned several regional journals such as the *Al-Imam*, a journal of the Salafiyya movement that began publishing out of Singapore in 1906 and that served as a source of inspiration for early Islamist and anti-colonial organizations across the Indo-Malay world such as Muhammadiyah and Sarekat Islam. Notably, the first stirrings of the reform movement in Thailand were felt not in the southern provinces but in Bangkok. This reformist tradition was brought to Thailand by Ahmad Wahab (not to be confused with Muhammad ibn Abd Al-Wahab, the founder of the Wahhabi movement), a Sumatran member of the Indonesian modernist organization Muhammadiyah who had studied in Mecca and was subsequently exiled by the Dutch colonial authorities for his political views.[5] After settling in Taman Tok, Bangkok, Wahab slowly expanded his following and established *Ansorisunnah*, the first Islamic reformist organization in Thailand. His followers included Direk Kulsiriswasd (Ibrahim Qureyshi), who would eventually translate the Qur'an into the Thai language. Under Wahab's leadership, Bangkok soon became the centre of reformist thinking among the Muslim intelligentsia and middle class. Additionally, a South Asian variant of reformist influence soon found its way to Thailand with the formation by Pakistani migrant workers of the *Jami-yatul Islam*. Modelled along the lines of the Pakistani *Jamaat-I-Islami*, *Jami-yatul* was organized along ethnic lines in its early years (catering to the South Asian diaspora), but gradually opened its doors to all Muslims in Thailand. *Jami-yatul* was later to play an instrumental role in the formation in 1967 of the YMAT or Young Muslims Association of Thailand, which had a membership that comprised mostly reform-minded youths and intellectuals.

At the time of its inception, Islamic reformism in Southeast Asia differed from that in the rest of the Muslim world in a number of respects. In particular, reformism in the region was primarily a reaction to folk traditions, seen as the decadent and indulgent practices of the *jahiliyya* (the age of pre-Islamic ignorance), and was aimed more at "purifying" Southeast Asian Islam through the exercise of *ijtihad* (independent judgement) than at rejecting the classical commentaries of Qur'an and *hadith*.[6] These early reformers also rejected the uncritical acceptance of textual sources and prevailing religious authorities. Rather, they advocated a return to the true and authentic sources of Islam — the Qur'an and *hadith* — in their emphasis on *tauhid*, the oneness of God, as the foundation for all knowledge. The reformists translated the Qur'an into the vernacular languages (Thai in Bangkok and Malay in the southern provinces) in order to make it accessible to ordinary Muslims and they also had the *khutbah* (Friday sermons) delivered in Thai so that the public could comprehend them.[7] The reformists were highly sceptical of Islamic education in Thailand, with its uncritical acceptance of authority and reliance on the rote learning of the Qur'an and *hadith*, and they saw it as a system on the verge of decline.

In the southern border provinces, the reform movement was viewed by the traditional religious elite of Thailand as a challenge to the premises of *taqlid*, which formed the cornerstone of their dissemination of Islamic knowledge. In addition, it was a challenge to their authority and status as the religious commissars of Thailand's Muslim communities. In response, the traditional Muslim leadership launched an attack on the reformists, prevailing upon local and state authorities to clamp down on their activism. While the influence of reformist Islam was on the whole effectively curtailed up until the 1970s through the combined efforts of the traditional religious establishment and the authoritarian Thai state, its influence is sustained with the recent establishment of tertiary religious institutions in southern Thailand and with the increasing number of Thais studying in religious schools in the Middle East and South Asia.

In southern Thailand, the early nexus between Islamic reformism and Islamic education was in many ways personified in the life and activism of Haji Sulong bin Haji Abdul Kadir. Haji Sulong is widely viewed as the champion of Malay cultural autonomy in pre-war Thailand and as the *cause célèbre* of the Malay-Muslim separatist cause, even though he himself never publicly advocated separatism. While few would contest this depiction of Haji Sulong's influence, the tendency to focus on his politics detracts from his considerable contributions as a Muslim educator. In fact, though Madmarn traces the transformation of the *pondok* to the early 1960s, it may be argued that Haji Sulong had already set this process in motion by the 1930s.[8]

REFORMISM'S FIRST WAVE: HAJI SULONG BIN HAJI ABDUL KADIR

Haji Sulong was born in 1895 in Kampung Anak Ru (now a thriving commercial district serving as a gateway to Pattani town). He came from a line of eminent *alim*, the most renowned of whom was his grandfather, Syeikh Zainal Abidin bin Ahmad al-Fatani, who is even today fondly remembered by the Malay-Muslims in southern Thailand as "Tok Minal".[9] In the family tradition, Haji Sulong was schooled in Arabic and Islamic texts. Kamal Zaman notes that Haji Sulong was a gifted and intelligent student who had memorized the entire Qur'an by the tender age of eight.[10] Haji Sulong attended Pondok Haji Abdul Rashid in Kampung Sungei Pandang, Patani, for his early education before proceeding to Mecca Ma'ahad Dar al-Ulum, a well-known institution popular among Malay-speaking students in the vicinity of the Holy Ka'abah.[11]

The years which followed were the most consequential and formative for Haji Sulong in terms of his pursuit of Islamic knowledge and his subsequent emergence as the progenitor of reformist and modernist Islamic education and thought in southern Thailand. It was during these early years in Mecca that Haji Sulong established a firm grounding in formal religious studies, particularly in the classical texts. At Ma'ahad Dar al-Ulum, Haji Sulong was trained in the traditional science of *tafsir* (Qur'anic exegesis), *hadith*, *usul al-fiqh* (principles of jurisprudence) and *nahwi* (Arabic grammar).[12] It was also during this time that he began to explore reformist ideas as a result of his encounters with eminent Arab *alim* who were the followers of Muhammad Abduh.

With the outbreak of the First World War (1914–18) and its expansion into the Arab world, Haji Sulong decided to return to Patani towards the end of 1915. On his overland journey home, he made a stopover at Kampung Cham in Cambodia and spent time with the local Muslim community. He was arrested by the French colonial administration in Indochina on suspicions that he was a Turkish spy.[13] Though the charges quickly proved unfounded and he was released a few days later, the incident may well have had a profound effect on his political outlook and probably ignited in him strong anti-colonial sentiments. Such sentiments resonated with his interest in the reformist religio-political thought of Abduh and Rashid Rida, both renowned scholars of Islam and staunch anti-colonialists.

Following his brief arrest, Haji Sulong worked in Cambodia for three months as a religious teacher. He then returned to his native Patani, but made stops along the way in Bangkok, Aceh, and British Malaya. It was during this journey across the Malay world which he undertook as part of his *tabligh* (Islamic missionary effort) as a *musafir* (a traveller) that Haji Sulong acquainted himself with the anti-colonial struggles of his fellow Muslims, especially in Aceh and the Malay Peninsula.[14] This experience had a profound influence on him, especially as Malay nationalism of this era had a strong religious dimension and was dominated by Islamic ideologues with a reformist-modernist intellectual bent.[15] As noted earlier, it was reformist followers of Abduh's teachings who had launched the anti-colonial tabloid *Al-Imam* in colonial Singapore, while in Indonesia several modernist movements merged, such as the Sarekat Islam in 1911 and Muhammadiyah in 1912, which sought to challenge Dutch colonial authority in the archipelago.[16]

Haji Sulong's return to Patani was shortlived and he returned to Mecca in 1916. There he was introduced by Malay *alim* to the Malay-speaking *halaqah* (scholastic circles) in the Masjid Al-Haram. Among the *alim* closest to Haji Sulong were Syeikh Wan Ahmad bin Mohamed Zain al-Fatani, a famous Patani scholar, and Tok Kenali, a renowned Islamic scholar from the northern Malayan state of Kelantan which bordered Patani. Both Syeikh Wan Ahmad and Tok Kenali were known in the circle of Muslim scholars in Mecca as "*Ulama Jawi*", a title that reflected their stature as distinguished scholars of Islam from the Malay world.[17] In 1927, Haji Sulong joined the ranks of his distinguished mentors and became a junior lecturer on the Islamic jurisprudence of the Shafi'i school.

While participating in the Malay *halaqah* circles of Mecca, Haji Sulong also came into contact with Egyptian scholars, many of whom were prominent reformists and modernists. He became interested in the Arab nationalism that was at the time sweeping across the Arabian Peninsula and which was distinctly captured in the Islamist thinking emanating from Egypt. He became intimately acquainted with reformist ideas through exchanges with Egyptian Islamists and intellectuals, and saw on a daily basis how *ulama* led the struggle to bring justice to the *ummah* on the Arab socio-political scene. Haji Sulong began increasingly to see his role extending beyond the mere teaching of religion into the socio-political sphere. He developed an abiding interest in political and social activism that was to pre-occupy him for the rest of his life and that catapulted him to prominence as a leader of southern Thailand's Malay-Muslim community.

As a junior lecturer, Haji Sulong was popular among the Southeast Asian Muslim students and pilgrims. Through them, his reputation and influence spread across the Malay Peninsula.[18] On his return to Patani in late 1927, he was dismayed at what he perceived as a state of ignorance and nonchalance in the Muslim community with regard to spiritual matters. The Malay community was increasingly involved in and committed to animistic rituals and ceremonies and, to Haji Sulong's mind, this undermined the purity of their Islamic faith. He attributed this degeneration of faith among the Patani Muslims to two factors — a parochial and stagnant *pondok* education system on the one hand and excessive government interference in Islamic affairs on the other.[19] In response, Haji Sulong embarked on an ambitious programme to transform the traditional *pondok*. In his view, the *pondok* was steeped in animism and as a result was a narrow, ineffective institution ill-equipped to lead a response to the social and economic challenges confronting the Malay-Muslim community in southern Thailand.[20] To him, it was the *pondok*'s decadent condition that had inadvertently facilitated the Thai government's intervention into the realm of Islamic education.

RELIGIOUS AND POLITICAL ACTIVISM

Haji Sulong's early activism in Patani was focused on guiding the community back to the path of "pristine" Islam from which it had "strayed". To him, Islam was not just a spiritual obligation built around the five pillars of faith but rather a total ideological orientation that encompassed both personal and public spheres, governing every aspect of Muslim life.[21] Haji Sulong apparently saw in the local Muslim community a people who were poor and backward, akin to the *jahiliyya* society in pre-Islamic Arabia.[22] Patani, once the cradle of

Islam in Southeast Asia, was to his mind now plagued with religious decline and (from his perspective) an alarming dilution of faith and piety.

Driven by the Islamic modernist ideals of Middle Eastern reformers, Haji Sulong set about transforming the stagnant *pondok* education system, which he identified as a root cause for the socio-religious backwardness of the Malays in Patani. He observed that the approximately 500 *pondok* that existed at the time (circa 1929) were ineffective by virtue of being enslaved in non-Islamic cultural matrices. Furthermore, the *pondok* curriculum was generally ad hoc in nature and lacked structure and direction. As discussed earlier, the *pondok* model of education relied heavily on the *tok guru* and thus was dictated by his area of expertise. For instance, if a particular *tok guru* was learned in *fiqh*, most likely the *pondok* would focus the majority of its syllabus on the study of *fiqh*. In addition, students were allowed to enrol and leave the *pondok* at will. This meant assessment was a problem, particularly if *pondok* students were to be compared with their counterparts in the national education system for scholastic advancement. Because a proper accreditation system was lacking and excessive reliance was placed on the *tok guru*'s assessment, even a well-established *pondok* could not continue functioning if its *tok guru* did not anoint a successor to replace him on his retirement or death. This effectively meant that the *pondok* either lost its reputation, or the *tok guru*'s successors were ill-equipped to transmit his teachings.

Haji Sulong found such shortcomings an unacceptable impediment to the progress of the community. To him, the study of general academic subjects such as mathematics, geography, and science was a critical facet of Islamic education that had to be taught alongside the religious curriculum. He stressed the need for greater structure and regulation on matters such as the entry age of students, standardized durations of learning, and compulsory annual examinations to assess academic development. As an *alim*, Haji Sulong also felt compelled to engage the community even as he sought to transform the system of Islamic education. He began by teaching Islam as a *tok guru* through *tabligh*, travelling across the Patani region from one village to another. Very soon, his teachings attracted a mass following among Malays.

As might be imagined, the traditional religious elite did not take kindly to veiled charges of incompetence. They viewed Haji Sulong's growing popularity with no small degree of disdain. Haji Sulong's reformist and modernist religious outlook inevitably undermined their religious authority and status within the strictly hierarchical Malay-Muslim community. Furthermore, his ideas were construed as an attempt to undermine the centuries-old tradition of the *pondok*. At the height of this opposition from traditionalist quarters, the *pondok* religious elite accused Haji Sulong of undermining established authority, dividing the Malay-Muslim community, fostering instability, and threatening the peace of the region.[23] They subsequently used their considerable influence to fight the reformist vision of a new Islamic identity. Complaints were registered with local government authorities and Haji Sulong's activities came under intense scrutiny.

Though Haji Sulong was summoned for interrogation, he was released soon after as the charges made against him by the traditional religious elite could not be substantiated. Needless to say, this experience only served to inspire Haji Sulong and convinced him of the need to push through Islamic education reforms. Moreover, at the same time as he had evoked the ire of the traditional religious leadership, Haji Sulong also enjoyed significant popular support from various segments of the local community.[24] With this support, in 1933 Haji Sulong established Madrasah Al-Ma'arif Al-Wattaniah Fatani, Patani's first private Islamic school.[25] Madrasah Al-Ma'arif was a modern Islamic school with a curriculum designed around religious, academic and vocational education. Systematic evaluation replaced the arbitrary assessment of the traditional *pondok*. Under Islamic science, the subjects taught were *qira'at* (recitation of the Qur'an), *tafsir*, *hadith*, *fiqh*, *nahwi* and *sarf* (grammar and conjugation), *tauhid* (theology), *tarikh* (history), and *akhlak* (ethics). The general education syllabus consisted of science, geography, and mathematics.[26]

The opening of Madrasah Al-Ma'arif came at the time when Thailand itself was undergoing a major transformation from absolute monarchy to constitutional government. In a bid to improve its relationship with the Malay-Muslims of the south, the People's Party government relaxed the policies of the preceding administrations that had strained relations with the community through initiatives that later also included the establishment of the Patronage of Islam Act, restoration of the Islamic laws governing private and family affairs, and the reinstatement of the office of the Chularajmontri. At the time, Prime Minister Phyara Phahol also made a personal donation to Haji Sulong's Islamic School building project and even attended its inauguration ceremony as a gesture of the government's support.[27] Such demonstrations of support were unprecedented, given the suspicion and antagonism that had existed between the Thai state and the Malay-Muslim population. On his part, Haji Sulong was aware that the greatest opposition to his reform initiatives would likely come not so much from the state but from the *tok guru* of the *pondok* schools. Haji Sulong attempted to pre-empt these objections by embarking on a public campaign to persuade *tok guru* of the benefits of his modern conception of Islamic education. These attempts received an initial boost when Haji Sulong's efforts were endorsed by several of Patani's more prominent educators such as Haji Mohd Idris, a widely respected scholar of Islam in the southern border provinces.[28]

Support for Haji Sulong's education reform initiative was, however, short-lived. As anticipated, his efforts were undone not by elements from within the state but by members of the very community he sought to uplift. In the same way that Ahmad Wahab's reformist initiatives failed to make much headway in Bangkok, Haji Sulong's efforts in Patani were resisted by the traditional religious elite. The reservations of the *tok guru* towards Haji Sulong's reformist agenda persisted despite his attempts to win them over and they continued to view his initiatives not only as a threat to the status quo, but also as an attempt to undermine their long-standing authority and influence over the local community.[29] The response was another round of concerted attempts to discredit Haji Sulong in the eyes of the Thai state by calling into question his loyalty. Vivid depictions of Haji Sulong's "megalomania" were made to government officials. Thanet Aphornsuvan describes one such attempt: "the followers [of Haji Sulong] even knelt down to take off Haji Sulong's shoes and clean his feet for him before entering a *masjid*. Others were ready to carry the umbrellas to protect the sun when he visited the Muslim communities in the four southern provinces including some districts in Songkhla".[30] Given that Haji Sulong had become a prominent scholar with a wide following and had a political base as Chairman of the Pattani Provincial Islamic Council, a whispering campaign of this nature easily resonated with his detractors.

Haji Sulong's *madrasah* was closed down in 1935 on suspicions that it was operating as a political organization. This act of closing down the modernist school served only to confirm the *madrasah* as a symbol of the Malay-Muslim struggle around which resistance would later mobilize. Soon after its closure, the *madrasah* premises did indeed become the covert base for meetings and assemblies among Haji Sulong's supporters in the Malay political leadership. The most significant of such events was the meeting of Malay elders convened by Haji Sulong to chart the future of Greater Patani. It culminated in the historic seven-point demand for autonomy presented by the Malay leadership to the government in July 1947. Among other things, this document called for the appointment of local Malays as governors of the Malay-Muslim provinces, the reservation for Malays of up to 80 per cent of government administrative positions in the region, and the creation of a Muslim board to govern religious affairs. While not originally intended as a centre for subversive activity, Madrasah Al-Ma'arif nevertheless became an important symbol of resistance, as did its founder Haji Sulong.

Despite the closure of Madrasah Al-Ma'arif and the cautious reaction towards Haji Sulong's attempts at reform, the momentum of change had already been to certain extents set in motion. Gradually, more and more *pondok* began to introduce the reform curriculum conceptualized by Haji Sulong, thereby transforming the *pondok* into an institution of systematic education. This, however, has not been captured in Hasan Madmarn's study on the transformation of *pondok* education. In "Pondok and Madrasah in Pattani", Madmarn attributes the transformation to government policies began in the 1960s and that gained momentum in the 1970s. He reasons that *pondok* were compelled to change or face the threat of irrelevance and extinction — even demonization — when new legislation mandated the teaching of general and academic subjects in all Islamic education institutions. Though legislative pressure was undoubtedly one catalyst of change, Madmarn fails to appreciate Haji Sulong's contributions in generating the subterranean momentum for change well before the advent of state legislation to regulate education in the southern provinces with the creation of the Islamic private school.

Notwithstanding the (halting) progress of his reformist project, Haji Sulong's demise in 1952 — when he mysteriously disappeared after being arrested by the Thai government-led to its swift deceleration. With Haji Sulong removed from the religio-cultural scene, it certainly appeared at the time that the reformist movement in southern Thailand had run its course.

THE CONTEMPORARY REFORMIST MOVEMENT

The tension between traditionalists and reformists that echoes the *Kaum Tua-Kaum Muda* contestations of the pre-war Malay world — and which was expressed in Haji Sulong's attempt to transform Islamic education — has since resurfaced in southern Thailand.[31] This time, it is expressed in the form of the "threat" posed by Salafi reformists to mainstream, traditionalist Islamic education. Specifically, the challenge recalls Haji Sulong's attempts to transform Islamic education and reflects a desire on the part of reformists to embrace modernist approaches to Islamic education through the introduction of academic and general subjects into the curriculum, *yet with a distinct emphasis on the need to "Islamize" epistemology and pedagogy.* This could be accomplished by combining Islamic knowledge with Western scholarship in the sciences, while advocating a return to a Salafist interpretation of pristine Islam.[32]

To the reformists, this effort stems at least in part from the realization that traditional institutions of Islamic learning require reform. Additionally, the traditionalists and secularists from the Islamic education establishment are perceived to have failed to meet the demands of an Islamic community that is increasingly conscious of the challenge posed by Western intellectual tradition and politico-strategic hegemony.[33] Hence, while the austere and literalist translations of the Qur'an commonly associated with Salafism anchor these transformational ideas, in the realm of education they are also distinctly "reformist" and "modernist" in the sense that they challenge traditional models of religious education — models that among other things are premised primarily on the authority of the *tok guru*, the use of *Jawi* (as opposed to Arabic) literature, and resistance to the teaching of science and other general academic and vocational subjects. Beyond its attempt to restructure Islamic education, the contemporary reformist movement also aims to contest the ideational and cultural matrices associated with the Malay-Muslim community which they deem to be either *shirk* or *bid'a*.

This movement is led by Ismail Lutfi Japakiya, who graduated in 1986 from Islamic University of Imam Muhammad bin Saud with a doctorate in *shari'a*. Ismail Lutfi is widely seen as the leading Salafi reformist Muslim educator in Thailand today. It would not be an exaggeration to say that he has charted the course of the contemporary reformist movement in southern Thailand. Summarizing the impact of Ismail Lutfi and his brand of reformist Islam on Islamic education in the Malay-Muslim south, Alexander Horstmann writes categorically that "Lutfi's scholarship challenges the authority of the traditional *ulama*".[34] A popular reformist scholar who recalls Haji Sulong in his heyday, Lutfi's appeal has undoubtedly been facilitated by generous financial support from the Saudi government and Saudi-linked charities that have overseen the establishment of a number of mosques and Islamic schools modelled on the *madrasah*.

REFORMISM'S SECOND WAVE: ISMAIL LUTFI JAPAKIYA (ISMAIL LUTFI AL-FATANI)

Ismail Lutfi is currently the rector of the Yala Islamic University, which boasts modern educational facilities in both its campuses in Pattani and Yala. Lutfi is also principal of Bamrung Islam Mukim Pujud, an Islamic private school in Muang, Pattani, where he conducts weekly lectures for the general public from the school's mosque, often to audiences of more than a thousand people.[35] In addition to his profile as an *ulama* and educator, Lutfi holds a number of prominent positions, serving as the Chairman of the Consultative Committee of the Foundation for Islamic Education in Southern Thailand, a Member of Parliament under the Surayud administration, and current Amir al-Haj for Thailand's Muslim population (where he oversees Thai pilgrimages during Haj). Lutfi is a popular speaker in Islamic scholarly circles in northern Malaysia, though he notes that since September 11 his speaking engagements in Malaysia have been markedly reduced.[36] The intensity of his preaching and forcefulness of his personality, not to mention his personal charisma, have ensured that while certain aspects of Lutfi's reformist dogma are met with caution by the traditionalist custodians of the faith, he has emerged as one of the most popular religious scholars in Thailand. His competence in Arabic is clearly his forte for it allows him to demonstrate a deep knowledge of the "authentic" scripture that few among Thailand's Islamic intelligentsia can match. Lutfi is viewed as a scholar who has the ability to simplify complex concepts of Islamic thought, a factor which has no doubt contributed to his appeal.

Ismail Lutfi's popularity is enhanced by his embrace of technology. He uses communication devices such as microphones, cassette recorders, and CDs, that clearly distinguish him from traditional teachers. Lutfi's popularity is further augmented by his access to substantial Saudi financial support, which he manages and disburses through Islamic charities in each of the three Malay-Muslim provinces. As mentioned earlier, the Saudi government was instrumental in setting up the Yala Islamic University. That said, while Ismail Lutfi is no doubt an immensely popular and respected *ulama* in Thailand, his pool of committed followers — those who imbibe his reformist ideas to the extent that they are prepared to challenge their traditional religious leaders — is significantly rather small, probably because most Muslims in southern Thailand remain respectful followers of long-held practices.

There is no question that Ismail Lutfi views his reformist agenda as part of the advancement of Islamic knowledge in the region. Be that as it may, his vision has also been a source of some disquiet to mainstream, traditionalist Islamic circles. As in the case of Haji Sulong decades earlier, the traditionalist religious establishment fears the appeal of Lutfi's charisma and of his brand of Islam among the younger generation. The disquiet can perhaps be traced to his perspective of Patani's place in the history of Islamic knowledge in Southeast Asia. Contrary to the conventional view of Patani as a centre of excellence in Islamic studies, Lutfi argues controversially that earlier epochs of Islam in Thailand (by which he means periods prior to the advent of the current wave of reformist thinking) were in fact marked by a lack of *ilmu* (knowledge).[37] To his mind, the advent of reformist Islam was both a basis and consequence of an increase in *ilmu*. In Lutfi's own words, "Islamic knowledge in Thailand used to be weak, and traditional Islam was based on this lack of knowledge. But it (*ilmu*) has improved over time. This leads to a deeper understanding of Islam".[38]

Despite his preaching on the need to transform Islamic knowledge, a message that would no doubt resonate well with government authorities who have always viewed resistance to change on the part of Islamic schools in the south as a constant source of provocation, Ismail Lutfi has been demonized in some (primarily Western) media and counter-terrorism circles as a "hardline Wahhabi cleric". His agenda for the transformation of Islamic education in Thailand has been dismissed as nothing but a cover for a more insidious programme to radicalize the Muslim population of southern Thailand.[39] Many of these allegations come from sceptics who equate Salafism with Wahhabism, the highly politicized, fundamentalist offshoot of broader Salafi dogma which has had a chequered history both as a reform and militant Muslim movement, and which has captured the attention of the terrorism studies community since September 11, 2001. Ismail Lutfi's training in Saudi Arabia (where he obtained his bachelor and doctoral degrees) and his ties with both government and private interests in the kingdom have been used by detractors against him. Underlying these suspicions is an ideological reading of Wahhabism not only as an austere and strict genre within Salafism, a reading which enjoys widespread consensus, but as a militant and uncompromising brand of Islam. However, under careful interrogation, Lutfi emerges as a considerably more ambivalent figure than the conventional analysis implies.

Though Ismail Lutfi studied at the Islamic University of Imam Muhammad bin Saud, a university with known Wahhabi links, those who exercised the most influence on his intellectual and religio-ideological development were not in fact conventional Wahhabi ideologues or educators at all. Rather, his tutor and supervisor was Shaykh Said Hawwa, a Syrian lecturer and member of the *Ikhwanul Muslimin* (Muslim Brotherhood) who taught in Saudi Arabia during Lutfi's stay there.[40] Lutfi's own ideas offer up intriguing discontinuities insofar as the complexities surrounding his doctrinal inclinations are concerned. For instance, in his dissertation on *shari'a* (discussed in the next chapter) Lutfi argued for the importance of time, space, and context when applying the precepts of Islamic law. In this way, his views certainly appear to echo those of "progressive" Muslim scholars on the question of rigidity in the application of Islamic law, though the actual substance of Ismail Lutfi's understanding of jurisprudence may depart fundamentally from the views of liberal-progressive Islamic scholars.[41] Given the perception of Lutfi's Wahhabi credentials, it is worth noting that while many have criticized Wahhabism for its doctrinal conservatism and rigidity, the appreciation of context is also a typical trait of Wahhabi thought, which believes, at least in theory, that the doors of *ijtihad* remain open.[42] Whether Lutfi is indeed the scripturalist, literalist Muslim scholar that he is often made out to be, his emphasis on context speaks to his appreciation of the complex and multifaceted nature both of the challenges confronting Islam and the avenues of response available to the Muslim community.

Some of Ismail Lutfi's other activities place in further question his "Wahhabi" credentials. For instance, while mainstream Wahhabism rejects *Mawlid* (the celebration of the Prophet Muhammad's birthday), in the past two years Lutfi has contributed to an annual collection of essays marking the Prophet's birthday, compiled by Thai Muslim scholars and published by the Islamic Centre of Thailand to "propagate the valuable teachings of the great Prophet Muhammad ... to all human beings".[43] Lutfi's contribution to the 2006 volume is entitled "Status and Roles of Ulama in the Holy Qur'an and Sunna", and is remarkable both for its reiteration of distinctively Salafi beliefs and practices and its departure from patently orthodox Wahhabi perspectives. In his discussion on the role and status of *alim* in Muslim society, for instance, while acknowledging that they are to be respected and sought out for their wisdom, Lutfi also cautions, in characteristic Salafi fashion, that "esteem and respect from any society for *alim* should not be frenetic and indulgent. The love and respect has to be based on the foundation of the Qur'an and *sunna* and in accordance with the level of his *imam* to Allah and His Messengers".[44] He goes on to elaborate that this is because "however high the status of an *alim*, he is also a human being who will have defects and errors".[45] Lutfi's view here accords with the practice of Salafi teachings in cautioning against the excessive celebration of human capabilities, even those of noted religious scholars. On the other hand, compared to some Wahhabi and Salafi scholars, Lutfi appears to demonstrate a sophisticated appreciation of nuances in the Islamic faith; his approach to Shi'ism provides a further point of departure from conventional Wahhabism. While more orthodox Salafi and Wahhabi scholars tend to make sweeping characterizations of Shi'ism as apostasy, and of Shi'a Muslims as heretics, in his discussion of "bad" and "wicked" *ulama* and the act of *fitnah* where he alludes to key events in Islamic history associated with the rise of Shi'ism, Lutfi reserves harshest criticism for the Kharawij as well as those who rejected the peace treaty between Ali, whom Shi'a Muslims believe to be the fourth "Rightly Guided Caliph", and Muawiyyah:

> They try to propagate the errors of *alim*, try to dramatize small errors and amplify them. They further try to destroy the dignity and fame of the *alim* in vicious ways. This is a root of catastrophes and *fitnah* (disbelief) that is traceable to the past such as *fitnah* from those who disagreed with Ali in the armistice with Muawiyyah, *fitnah* from the

group of Kharawij (the group that protested both Ali and Muawiyyah
and their respective supporters), and others because the attitude and
positions of these two groups is not based on knowledge and justice, but
on ignorance and bigotry, which cause extremism.[46]

While Islamic scholars continue to discuss the impact of the Battle of Siffin
(from which the armistice between Ali and Muawiyyah arose) on the evolution
of the office of Caliph, it appears that embedded in Lutfi's message is an
expression of concern for the unity of the *ummah* rather than the polemics
and hubris that is sometimes found in Islamic historiography.

Finally, while much is made of the financial support that Ismail Lutfi's
Yala Islamic University has received from the governments of Saudi Arabia
and Kuwait, little attention is paid to vast contributions from the government
of Qatar, not normally known for its scripturalist position on matters of
religion.[47] Even more astonishing is the fact that the University has applied to
the U.S.-linked Asia Foundation for a grant in support of English language
training for its faculty and study trips to Malaysia.[48]

This is not the place for a detailed discussion of Wahhabi ideology, but
if Ismail Lutfi is indeed a Wahhabi (and not just a Salafi, as he himself
claims), there are clearly aspects to his brand and practice of Islam that
deviate from the commonly understood dictates of Wahhabism. It may be
worth recalling here how Islam had adjusted itself to suit local cultures and
belief systems when it arrived on Southeast Asian shores, thereby giving rise
to the syncretic Islam that has become the trademark of the region. Perhaps
what we see in Lutfi is somewhat analogous to that — his brand of
"Wahhabism" might have undergone a similar process of "localization" so
that some of its features differ from mainstream Wahhabi thought and praxis.
It should be noted that Lutfi himself refuses to acknowledge the term
"Wahhabi", but has welcomed the label of Salafi. Yet Lutfi's Islamic thought
is not entirely devoid of explicit connections to Wahhabism, for he has on
other occasions defended the teachings of Ibn Abd al-Wahhab, and he shares
in the traditional Wahhabi apprehension about Sufi practices.[49]

A key facet of Ismail Lutfi's reformist agenda is his belief that a major
component of *ilmu* is the ability to make Islamic studies speak to modern
science in a manner that emphasizes the Qur'anic roots of modern knowledge,
and for that matter, of modernity itself. As a self-proclaimed Salafi, Lutfi's
project stresses the adoption of an exclusively Islamic vocabulary, and rests on
the twin concerns for the moral health of the Muslim community and the
dangers of excessive rationalism, which, to his mind, lures Muslims away
from *tauhid* in its attempt to conquer nature.[50] To Lutfi and his reformist

colleagues, the modernization of Islamic education through the introduction of general academic subjects, anchored on Islamic principles, is in line with the teachings of Islam. Accordingly, deans at the Yala Islamic University have been tasked to expand their curriculum so that it embraces information technology, business, finance, and the social sciences in a manner that incorporates Islamic principles.[51] The vision of how the sacred and the secular may be fused into a modern curriculum is illustrated in the following description of the University's degree programmes:

> The commencement of the initial conception [*sic*] Islamic educational philosophy set forth by the founders of the college is to offer courses like *shari'a*, *usul-addin*, and Arabic language so as to pave the way for the YIC's [Yala Islamic College's] infrastructural platform of *fard'ain*. After four years of its first phase the YIC submitted its proposal for establishing new departments in order to fulfil the *fard kifayah* in its second phase. They are Department of Public Administration, Department of Finance and Banking, and Department of Information Technology. This second phase reminds us of the task of the Prophet's *Madinan* period while the first phase of the college presents a picture of the first period of Islam in *Makkah*. The categories of *fard'ain* and *fard kifayah* are integratively [*sic*] blended into the YIC's curriculum in order to do justice to each individual by respecting one's unique capacities and interests. *Fard'ain* knowledge is religiously obligatory. It is to be studied and mastered by all mature and free Muslims, whereas *fard kifayah* is obligatory not for all, but for a sufficient number of such Muslims in the community.[52]

It is in this manner that the Yala Islamic University is seen by reformists as a microcosm which "reflects the Prophet in knowledge and action in its duty to produce Muslim men and women who reflect the qualities of the Prophet as much as possible according to their respective potentialities and abilities. This is the noble task for every Muslim to uphold the Qur'anic dictum that the Prophet is the best model for Muslims (*Uswah Hasanah*)".[53] Explaining the reformist mission in the field of education, a Saudi-trained, Salafi *ustaz* has expressed that "those who graduated from Islamic studies in Saudi Arabia return to build schools with the aim of giving back to the community in a way that allows them to live a pure Islamic lifestyle that reflects the practices of Muslims during the era of the Prophet in every aspect of their lives".[54]

There are no clearly visible Salafi or reformist "enclaves" beyond the area surrounding Bamrung Islam Mukim Pujud in Bra-o, yet Islamic community leaders interviewed in the course of research estimate that approximately twenty Islamic schools in the southern provinces today may be considered either substantially influenced by or propounding reformist thinking that in their opinion is in line with Salafi ideology.[55] Anecdotal evidence suggests that some of the larger schools include Islam Prachasongkroh (Muang, Yala), Muslim Phattana Sasana (Yaring, Pattani), Islahiyah (Muang, Yala), Udom Sasana (Muang, Yala), Suksawad Wittaya (Yaha, Yala), Sukan Sasana Wittaya (Muang, Narathiwat), Islam Burana Tokno (Muang, Narathiwat), Nuruddin (Tak Bai, Narathiwat), and Thamsetam Wittaya (Bajoh, Narathiwat).[56] Aside from these schools in the south, there are also a number of schools in Songkhla, Satun, Phatalung, Phuket, and Nakhon Si Thammarat who teach the Hanbali school of Islamic law, the jurisprudential well from which Wahhabism is widely believed to have sprung.[57]

In almost every instance, these schools have been beneficiaries of Saudi funds that have been flowing into Thailand's Islamic education system since the early 1980s.[58] This funding by Saudi charities and private interests often translates to active involvement in the schools' curricula through the provision of textbooks and training of teachers. Many of these educational institutions are Salafi-oriented and some are found on the trail from Bra-o in Pattani, where Lutfi's *madrasah* is located, to the Yala campus of Yala Islamic University in Paramitang.[59] These schools are distinguished from others in that they receive assistance from Ismail Lutfi's charity organization in addition to foreign assistance or government funds and hence are generally more affluent. This affluence is discernible from the school buildings and compounds, which are generally much larger and better equipped than those of the average Islamic private school. In return for funding, these schools are obliged to employ Saudi-trained instructors who mostly (though not all) teach Islam from a Salafi perspective.[60]

The schools associated with Ismail Lutfi's reformist agenda in southern Thailand are predominantly run by Saudi-trained teachers who do not subscribe to the traditional emphasis of Shafi'i Mazhab that characterizes the jurisprudential inclinations of the vast majority of Malay-Muslims.[61] Indeed, such has been the deviation of the reformist template from the norms of Sufi and Shafi'i Islamic traditionalism in southern Thailand that it has been suggested that "some of these teachers returning from Saudi Arabia are introducing a new school of *fiqh*".[62] To say however that these reformists reject the Shafi'i school, the dominant legal tradition in Southeast Asia, is not entirely correct, for these schools do provide Mazhab instruction, including Shafi'i jurisprudence. It is more appropriate to say that these reformist scholars do not consider Shafi'i Mazhab, or any of the other traditional schools of Islamic law, to be the blanket authoritative statement of Islam on any given issue.

Aside from Saudi and Kuwaiti-trained instructors, there are also an estimated 100 graduates from the Yala Islamic University who currently teach in Islamic private schools throughout southern Thailand.[63] While this is instructive of trends in Islamic thought and education, it is important not to interpret the relationship between religious training in Saudi Arabia and Wahhabi ideological inclinations in a deterministic and axiomatic fashion, as is often the case in the popular perception. Given its geographic location and symbolism in Islamic history, Saudi Arabia has been the logical location of preference for Malay-Muslims seeking a more authentic religious education experience. Yet while numerous Malay-Muslims from Thailand have over the years studied in noted Salafi and Wahhabi institutions, many among them have also been actively involved and trained in distinctly Malay *halaqah* at the Masjid Al-Haram, where instruction commonly takes place in Jawi, and where lessons are sometimes contextualized with reference to Malay culture and history.[64] Indeed, several prominent "*Ulama Jawi*" from southern Thailand, such as Ismail Sepanjang, continue to teach in these *halaqah* today.

While the presence of these schools is not as provocative as was the case in the 1930s with Haji Sulong's Madrasah al-Maarif al-Wataniyyah, they have been viewed as a challenge to traditional Islamic institutions and ideas and at times have elicited negative responses from religious teachers. One *tok guru* interviewed assailed the reformists as *Kaum Muda* who were "*sangat takbur*" (very arrogant) in their attitude towards more established schools of Islamic thought.[65] Others described the residual tension between the *Kaum Muda* and *Kaum Tua* as that between those who think themselves "faultless" (*yang merasa sempurna*) and traditionalists who resist change.[66] Numerous traditionalist *ustaz* have berated their reformist counterparts who condemn the inclusion of local beliefs and practices in Islamic education. While these reformists justify their attack on tradition as "improving the community's understanding of and adherence to Islam", traditionalists retort that the reformists are, in the words of a *tok guru* from the famed Pondok Dalor, "self-righteous".[67] Others see this influence as "incompatible with local *adat* (customary law)" which remains an important institution in Malay culture.[68] Such is the acrimony that some traditionalist institutions, such as Charoen Witthaya Nusron in Sai Buri (Pattani), make it official policy not to engage reformist Salafi teachers.[69] There are, of course, traditionalists who are more measured in their response to the reformists. The following opinion, for instance, conveys a more conciliatory note: "*fiqh* starts with Qur'an and *sunna*, and then some lean towards Shafi'i but not too much. Traditional practices are left for individuals to decide, especially when they go home. There is no condemning the locals' beliefs and practices".[70]

Notes

1   For instance, traditional Malay society subscribed to beliefs in *jinn* (traditional Islamic spirits) as well as *hantu* (ghosts believed by Malays to be descendants of *iblis*, the Islamic conception of Satan). Likewise, while Malay-Muslims declare their faith in the omnipotent Allah, they also call upon *bomoh* (traditional, pre-Islamic faith healers) to control spirits.

2   William R. Roff, *The Origins of Malay Nationalism*, Second Edition (Kuala Lumpur, Oxford University Press, 1994), p. 58.

3   Azzam Tamimi, *Muhammad Ibn Abd Al-Wahhab dari Pembangunan Semula Abad Ke 18 Aktivisme Abad Ke 21* [Muhammad Ibn Abd Al-Wahab from 18th Century Revivalism to 21st Century Activism] (paper presented at *Seminar Antarabangsa Mengenai Syeikh Muhammad Abdul Wahab* [International Seminar on Syeikh Muhammad Abdul Wahab], Kangar, Perlis, Malaysia, 16–17 March 2006), pp. 3–4.

4   See Nabeel A. Khoury and Abdo I. Baaklini, "Muhammad Abduh: An Ideology of Development", *The Muslim World* 69, no. 1 (1979).

5   Raymond Scupin, "Muslim Accommodation in Thai Society", *Journal of Islamic Studies* 9, no. 2 (1998): 251.

6   Traditionalist Shafi'i teachers and scholars in the Middle East shared similar objectives toward the reform of popular Islam. In Southeast Asia, however, and certainly in Thailand, traditionalist Shafi'i thinkers also embrace certain aspects of Sufism and permit Muslims to partake in traditional practices, especially with regard to *adat*. For example, I interviewed a local Shafi'i *imam* from Pattani who, when discussing *ubudiah* (burial rites), believed in spirits of the dead that roam between the home and the grave for forty days. While this belief is still widely held in Southeast Asia, it is generally shunned by reformists.

7   The traditionalists, however, had insisted that the language of the Qur'an and the *khutbah* remain Arabic, the original language of Islam. The debate over translation and the *khutbah* was won by the reformists. Today, sermons are conducted in the vernacular — Thai in Bangkok and the north, and Malay in the south. Such "victories" for the reformists were rare until more recently. For further discussion, see Scupin, "Muslim Accommodation in Thai Society", pp. 249–54.

8   Abdul Rahim Zakaria, "The Legacy of Haji Sulong in the Contemporary Separatist Struggle in Thailand's Restive South" (M.Sc. dissertation, Nanyang Technological University, Singapore, 2005).

9   Muhammad Kamal K. Zaman, *Fatani 13 Ogos* [Pattani 13 August] (Kota Bahru, 1996), p. 1.

10 Ibid., p. 2.

11 Numan Hayimasae, "*Hj Sulong Abdul Kadir (1895–1954): Perjuangan dan Sumbangan Beliau Kepada Masyarakat Melayu Patani* [Hj Sulong Abdul Kadir: Struggle and Contributions to the Patani Malays]" (M.Sc. dissertation, Universiti Sains Kebangsaan Malaysia, 2002), p. 83.

12   Surin Pitsuwan, *Islam and Malay Nationalism: A Case Study of the Malay-Muslims of Southern Thailand* (Bangkok: Thai Khadi Research Institute, Thammasat University, 1985), p. 115.

13   Hayimasae, *Hj Sulong Abdul Kadir*, p. 84.

14   Ibid., p. 85.

15   See Roff, *The Origins of Malay Nationalism*.

16   Hayimasae, *Hj Sulong Abdul Kadir*, p. 109. See also Roff, *The Origins of Malay Nationalism and Takashi Shiraishi, An Age in Motion: Popular Radicalism in Java, 1912–1916* (Ithaca, NY: Cornell University Press, 1990).

17   Hayimasae, *Hj Sulong Abdul Kadir*, p. 85.

18   Pitsuwan, *Islam and Malay Nationalism*, pp. 147–48.

19   Interview with Senator Den Tomena, son of Haji Sulong, Pattani, 19 December 2004.

20   See Zahidi al-Helmi and Muhammad Jihad, "*Rahsia dan Iktibar disebalik Kejatuhan Pondok*" [Lessons from the Demise of Pondoks], *Imam* 2 (December 1989). Zahidi and Jihad identified some of the problems confronting the *pondok* as a stagnant curriculum, lack of community spirit, and a lack of financial resources.

21   The five tenets are the *syahada* (proclaiming belief in Allah and Muhammad as His messenger), daily prayers, fasting, giving out alms, and performing the pilgrimage.

22   Hayimasae, *Hj Sulong Abdul Kadir*, p. 86.

23   Ibid., p. 118.

24   Thanet Aphornsuvan, *Origins of Malay Muslim "Separatism" in Southern Thailand*, Asia Research Institute Working Paper Series No. 32 (Singapore: Asia Research Institute, 2004), p. 16.

25   Zaman, *Fatani 13 Ogos*, p. 8.

26   Hayimasae, *Hj Sulong Abdul Kadir*, p. 145.

27   Ibid., p. 142.

28   Ibid., p. 146.

29   Ibid., p. 146.

30   Aphornsuvan, *The Origins of Malay Muslim "Separatism"*, p. 22.

31   *Kaum Tua* refers to the traditionalists or "older generation" and *Kaum Muda* to the reformists-modernists or "young turks".

32   Interview at Yala Islamic College, Pattani, 15 January 2006.

33   Interview at Bamrung Islam Mukim Pujud, Pattani, 14 January 2006.

34   Alexander Horstmann, *Class, Culture and Space: The Construction and Shaping of Communal Space in South Thailand* (Tokyo: Research Institute for the Languages and Cultures of Asia and Africa, 2002), p. 80.

35   Interview with Ismail Lutfi, Pattani, 14 January 2006.

36   Ibid.

37   Ibid.

38   Ibid. In the course of my interview I used the term 'traditional Islam' to refer to

the predominant Shafi'i-Sunni as well as Sufi Islam that continues to be widely practised in southern Thailand.

[39] See, for example, John Bradley, "Waking Up to the Terror Threat in Southern Thailand", *Straits Times*, 27 May 2004; Zachary Abuza, "A Conspiracy of Silence: Who is behind the escalating insurgency in southern Thailand?", *Terrorism Monitor* 3, no. 9 (May 2005).

[40] I would like to thank Muhammad Haniff Hassan for alerting me to this fact. For information about Shaykh Said Hawwa, see Al Mustasyar Abdullah al Aqil, *Mengenang Said Hawwa* [Reflection on Said Hawwa] <www.boemi-islam.com> (accessed 27 May 2004). While he was undoubtedly a Salafi, Said Hawwa was also known to be sympathetic towards Sufism, and this put him at loggerheads with Wahhabis under King Fahd, resulting in his expulsion from Saudi Arabia.

[41] Ismail Lutfi Fatani, *Ikhtilaf Ad-Darain wa Atsaruhu fi Ahkam Al-Munakahat wa Al-Muamalat* [The Effect of Two Dars (Dar Al-Islam and Dar Al-Harb) on Islamic Personal and Transaction Laws] (Cairo: Dar As-Salam, Cairo, 1990).

[42] Natana J. Delong-Bas, *Wahhabi Islam: From Revival and Reform to Global Jihad* (London and New York: I.B. Tauris, 2004), pp. 107–8.

[43] See Maulid Klang Organising Committee of Thailand, *Holding Fast to the Ideology of Harmony Among Thais* (Bangkok: Islamic Committee of Thailand, 2006).

[44] Ismail Lutfi Chapakiya, "Status and Roles of Ulama in the Holy Qur'an and Sunna", ibid., p. 21.

[45] Ibid., p. 23.

[46] Ibid., pp. 23–24.

[47] Although Wahhabi Islam played a special role in the establishment of the nation-state of Qatar and the coming to power of its ruling family — Al-Thani — in the early 1970s, it has been used primarily as a legitimizing ideology rather than enforced as a way of life. The Qatar Constitution recognizes Islam as the religion of the state and the *shari'a* as the primary source of law, but also provides underpinnings for the existence and functioning of secular courts. In this regard, Qatar's legal system can be characterized as dual. It recognizes the jurisdiction of both *shari'a* courts and *adlia* courts (secular courts responsible for conflicts/issues in labour, trade, business, criminal law, etc). This dualism is also exemplified by the emergence of a new legal elite — mostly educated abroad either in the West or in Egypt, Lebanon, and Jordan — vis-à-vis the traditional array of *muftis* and *qadis*. Furthermore, though Qatar and Saudi Arabia have Wahhabism in common, Qatar is wary of its powerful neighbour's ambition. Al Jazeera's criticism of the Saudi monarchy has already led to a serious diplomatic spat between the two countries.

[48] Interview at Asia Foundation Thailand Office, Bangkok, 17 January 2006.

[49] See, for example, Ismail Lutfi, *Penyebaran Ilmu Salafi Khususnya Penulis Syeikh Muhammad Abdul Wahab* [The Expansion of Salafi Knowledge in the Writings

of Syeikh Muhammad Abdul Wahab] (paper presented at Seminar Antarabangsa Syeikh Muhammad Abdul Wahab [International Seminar on Syeikh Muhammad Abdul Wahab], Perlis (Malaysia), 16–17 March 2006). Beyond this, Ismail Lutfi has also endorsed a book written in Thai entitled *Wahhabism: Definition and Meaning* by Sufum Usman and Usman Idris.

50   Interview with Ismail Lutfi, Pattani, 14 January 2006.

51   Interview with Sukree Langputeh (Yala Islamic University), Pattani, 15 January 2006.

52   Sukree Langputeh, "The Islamization of the Discipline of Public Administration in a Thai Higher Education Institution: The Experience of Yala Islamic College" (paper presented at the International Workshop on Voices of Islam in Europe and Southeast Asia, Nakhon Si Thammarat, 20–22 January 2006).

53   Ibid.

54   Interview at Suksana Sasana Witthaya, Narathiwat, 19 April 2007. Clearly, the *ustaz* interviewed is of the opinion that most, if not all, scholars trained in Saudi Arabia are of the reformist persuasion.

55   There are obviously no official statistics of "Salafi" or "Wahhabi" schools available. The figure twenty was arrived at on the basis of conjectural approximates provided by religious teachers and scholars interviewed during the course of research.

56   These schools are known to have on staff a majority of teachers of Salafi-reformist persuasion.

57   The instructors at these schools, however, are almost all Malay-Muslims from the southern provinces.

58   A list of institutions in the three southern provinces that are believed to have received funding assistance in some form or other from Saudi Arabia is provided in Chapter Five under the sub-section of "Saudi Arabia".

59   Interview at Chongraksat Witthaya, Pattani, 14 February 2006.

60   Ibid. See also "Planning for a peaceful future in the South", *The Nation*, 28 August 2005. Funding is available from Ismail Lutfi's charity organization for any Islamic school in the region.

61   Interview at Sad Samaki School, Pattani, 16 January 2006.

62   Interview at Chongraksat Witthaya, Pattani, 14 February 2006.

63   Interview with Ismail Lutfi, Pattani, 14 January 2006.

64   Interview with Nidae Waba, Pattani, 14 January 2006; interview with Hasan Madmarn, Pattani, 16 January 2006.

65   Interview at Darunsat Wittaya School, Pattani, 5 February 2005.

66   Interview at Saiburi Islam Wittaya School, Pattani, 24 February 2005.

67   Interview at Pondok Dalor, Pattani, 19 January 2006.

68   Interview at Aliman Foundation, Narathiwat, 18 January 2006.

69   Interview at Charoen Witthaya Nusron, Pattani, 18 January 2006.

70   Interview at Narawi Islam, Narathiwat, 2 August 2006. The *ustaz* interviewed was a retired officer who had served in the Royal Thai Army.

4

PEDAGOGIES, CURRICULA,
AND TEXTS

Islamic education in southern Thailand has traditionally been based on the *Kitab Kuning* or *Kitab Jawi* (classical Malay religious literature written in Jawi script by Patani scholars), and "the ideas passed in these texts and explanation pursued orally by scholars have tremendous impact on their followers: for a simple reason, the widespread [*sic*] of their use and the nature of teacher-student ties in religious circles".[1] These *Kitab*, authored by Patani scholars out of both Mecca and Patani in the nineteenth century, were written to provide instruction in Islamic subjects for students who were not conversant in Arabic. Because the standard of Arabic remains generally weak among the Muslim student population in southern Thailand, these texts remain in circulation today and form critical parts of the curriculum. From the early nineteenth to the mid-twentieth century, Patani was an established centre for the dissemination of Islamic knowledge through the efforts of presses such as Patani and Nahdi Press.[2] While their publishers' output has declined somewhat over the years, some such as the Saudara Press continue to reproduce the writings and publications of prominent Pattani Islamic scholars.

The writings of traditional scholars such as Abu Hamid Muhammad Al-Ghazzali (1058–1111) and Sheikh Nawawi Al-Bantani (1230–1314) have long dominated Patani scholarship and instruction on *fiqh* (jurisprudence), *aqidah* (theology), *tassawuf* (spirituality), and ethics.[3] Correspondingly, Patani *ulama* played an instrumental role in editing, translating, and authenticating these works for use in Islamic schools throughout Southeast Asia.[4] Beyond this, prolific local luminaries such as Sheikh Daud Al-Fatani, Sheikh Ahmad Al-Fatani, and Sheikh Wan Muhammad Ismail Al-Fatani were known also for their own works of Islamic scholarship which continue to be used in Islamic schools across the Malay world today. The more popular works from this genre include *Faridatul-Fara'id* (on Ash'arite theology) by Sheikh Ahmad Al-Fatani, *Aqidatul-Najin* (on Ash'arite theology) by Sheikh Zain al-'Abidin Al-Fatani, and several titles by Sheikh Daud Al-Fatani, namely *Munyatul-Musalli* (on *fiqh* concerning prayer), *Furu' al-Masa'il* (on *fiqh* concerning advanced *fatwa* or legal opinion), *Bughyatu't-Tullab* (*fiqh* on Shafi'i spiritual devotions), and *Kashf al-Litham* (*fiqh* on Shafi'i jurisprudence).

As highlighted in the previous chapter, early reformist influence mostly centred on the works by Muhammad Abduh and Jamaluddin al-Afghani that became popular among the Patani *ulama* and Muslim intelligentsia in the early twentieth century. Haji Sulong, for instance, was profoundly influenced by the teachings of Muhammad Abduh, and he subscribed to the latter's teaching that the selective adoption of Western innovations and technology for the advancement of the Muslim community was not antithetical to Islam.

KAUM TUA-KAUM MUDA REDUX

Attention has already been drawn to the tensions and contestations embedded in southern Thailand's Muslim landscape and which have come to be expressed in Islamic education. Not only have reformists not ingratiated themselves to the traditional religious leadership in southern Thailand with their "new" perspectives on Islamic knowledge and lifestyle, but their ideas on epistemology, methodology, culture, and identity have been greeted with circumspection, if not outright hostility, in some traditionalist quarters. Consequently, debates over authenticity and legitimacy within the Muslim community are beginning to redefine the terrain of Islamic thought and praxis. Describing the impact of the reformists on traditional Islamic education and the challenge they pose to the traditional commissars and custodians of the faith, Horstmann surmised that "the religious style differs from that of the *imam* who is respected for mystical qualities. The new religious style is rule-oriented and anti-esoteric. The *imam* marks special events such as marriage. The new style is sober and puritanical. The *imam* is looking for a mystical relationship. The new style is literalist and *shari'a*-oriented".[5] A major epistemological distinction between the two schools relates to their position on *fiqh*.

The predominant school of jurisprudence taught in the majority of *pondok* and Islamic private schools in southern Thailand remains Mazhab Shafi'i.[6] Schools associated with traditional Shafi'i Islam place much emphasis on *fiqh* and its role for Muslims in the modern world. Traditionalist scholars argue that while the Qur'an and *sunnah* provide general instruction for Muslim conduct in a modern society, it is *fiqh* that provides the necessary guidelines for everyday living (*kehidupan*).[7]

While reformist schools do indeed provide instruction in Mazhab Shafi'i (as in the other three traditional schools of jurisprudential thought), what distinguishes them from their traditionalist counterparts is the markedly different emphasis accorded to *fiqh* in general, and the reluctance to privilege a specific Mazhab in particular. This approach is premised on their belief that the emphasis of Islamic education should be on *tauhid* (the unity of God), from which all else flows, and that the Qur'an and *sunnah* are the only binding sources of law. According to the Manhaj Salafi (Salafi doctrine), adherence to any Mazhab in this respect depends on which stands closest to the Qur'an and *sunnah* on any particular issue. This, alongside the fact that the reformists by and large deny *qiyas* (analogy), has reinforced the perception among certain observers that they are scripturalist, literalist, and puritan. In addition to being fundamentalist in theological and epistemological orientation, they are also reformist in their challenge to the legalist-traditionalist culture of Islam in southern Thailand.

Three factors are commonly cited by reformists in southern Thailand to justify their position on Islamic jurisprudence. First, it has been argued that because *fiqh* is not primarily rooted in the Qur'an (*bukan berasal Qur'an*), it should not command the intellectual and exegetical primacy that should rightly be reserved for the Qur'an and *sunnah*. Second, it has been suggested that *fiqh* is highly contextual, and that the relevance of respective schools of jurisprudence ultimately depends on the specific circumstances that surround any particular situation. It is partly from this intellectual elasticity (i.e., the focus on context) in the realm of Islamic jurisprudence that reformists derive their credentials.[8] Finally, reformists follow epistemological traditions that reject *taqlid*, the unquestioning acceptance of established interpretations that is a feature of conventional Islamic education. They argue for individual interpretation (*ijtihad*) based on a return to the Qur'an and *sunnah*, the scriptural sources of Islam, rather than on classical jurisprudence.[9]

KIFAYAH AL-MUHTADI (PROVISION FOR A PERSON WHO RECEIVES GUIDANCE)

This popular book on *aqidah* was authored by Muhammad Nur bin Muhammad bin Ismail Al-Fatani and is believed to have been written in the 1930s. The book was written as a commentary on *Sullam Al-Mubtadi*

(Beginner's Ladder) by Sheikh Daud Al-Fatani, a prominent Patani-born Malay scholar of Islam who had taught at the Masjid Al-Haram in Saudi Arabia. The book captures some of the intellectual tensions alluded to earlier between Salafi reformists and their traditionalist Sunni and Sufi counterparts. While the book's title is in Arabic (likely because *Sullam Al-Mubtadi* was written in Arabic), its contents are in Jawi.

Kifayah covers two aspects of Islamic studies, namely, *aqidah* and *fiqh*.[10] The Salafi orientation of this reformist text comes across clearly in the characteristic Salafi manner in which it skirts rational and philosophical epistemology in the study of theology. Instead, the book centres its discussion almost exclusively on the Qur'an and *sunnah*. *Kifayah* provides a brief exposition on the pillars of faith with specific elaboration on matters relating to the afterlife and ends with a discussion of apostasy. Another indication of the Salafi orientation in the book is the explicit omission of any discussion on *Sifat 20* (twenty attributes) of God — a dominant feature of traditionalist theology often associated in the Malay world with the *Kaum Tua*. Yet another indication is the explanation offered for the phrase *istiwa' 'ala al-arsy* (God's position on the throne). After mentioning the rational view of the Muktazilite which interpreted the phrase as "God's rule of the universe", the author defends an alternative Salafi explanation of the phrase which takes its meaning literally. At the heart of this distinction between Salafi and rationalist interpretations of holy scripture is the theological doctrine of *tauhid* and whether God operates within the limitations of human reason. Put simply, while rationalists interpret descriptions of God with human features as figurative devices, Salafis reject all symbolic interpretations of the revealed scriptures, claiming that any reference to traits such as God's "face" or "hands", while not meant to be likened to human faces and hands, are nevertheless to be taken literally. In this manner, the author contends that the scriptural assertion of God taking his position on the throne is to be taken literally, yet the manner in which this action (of a divine entity without physical form) takes place is beyond human comprehension.[11] The author, however, skirts any elaboration on how this can be so. Betraying his Salafist orientation, he instead argues that elaboration is in fact unnecessary because it is a temptation to *shirk* (innovation).[12]

Another issue *Kifayah* touches upon, which is again indicative of its Salafi orientation, pertains to the performing of *qunut* (act of standing or special supplications in a standing posture) during dawn prayer.[13] The followers of Imam Shafi'i, the dominant jurisprudential position subscribed to by Muslims in Southeast Asia, are of the opinion that the *qunut* is to be made during the dawn prayer. The author however makes the Salafi argument that the *qunut* is an innovation as, according to him, neither Abu Bakr, Umar, nor Uthman performed the *qunut* during dawn prayer.[14]

The book has a clear Salafist orientation on issues pertaining to knowledge and cultural lifestyle. Yet, in all fairness, the author does in some instances defend the Shafi'i legal tradition as well. This being the case, it is likely that the author was ideologically from a *Kaum Muda* or reformist tradition. This would accord with trends which were emerging when the book was published in 1932, at the time the *Kaum Muda* movement led by Haji Sulong Abdul Kadir was gaining popularity.

The author's emphasis on form in the detailed discussion on the pillars of the faith differs from the Sufi emphasis on inner spirituality, thereby undermining one of the more dominant traditions of local Islam in southern Thailand. A similar distinction is drawn by Ismail Lutfi in his discussion of Al-Anfaal:24, where he defines the injunction "and know that Allah comes in between a person and his heart" as indicating that it is Allah who "prevents an evil person from doing anything (presumably evil acts)".[15] This distinction between the Sufi and Salafi notions of the human heart as human intention is further captured in the different local textual exegeses on the topic of theology. Whereas *Kifayah* represents the reformists' understanding of spirituality and theology (with its emphasis on forms and literal interpretations as described above), Sufi texts such as *Hidayatul Salatin*, a popular traditionalist text on *aqidah* and *tassawuf* written by Syeikh Samad al-Palimbani, a renowned Malay Sufi scholar, stresses the cultivation of the heart and love for the divine. Citing the famous Sufi scholar Imam Ghazali (1058–1111), Samad stresses the theme of gratefulness to God above all else. This is exemplified in Samad's contention that:

> The reality about being grateful to Allah is the acknowledgement that there is no other but God who can provide. At the same time, one must acknowledge that everything that a human being owns, including his life and soul, is from God. Having known this, one would feel gratefulness to God in one's heart for all that He had provided for. As such, one will then focus his life on serving God through prayers and supplications using his tongue, heart, and other parts of his body. The heart will continuously say the *zikr* and acknowledge God as the true giver of everything.[16]

In line with the theme of cultivating the heart, the text also places much emphasis on the human ego, another typical characteristic of Sufism. On this matter, Samad contends that it is important for Muslims to learn *tassawuf* as this will allow them to cleanse their hearts of ego and envy. To substantiate this, Samad quotes Imam Ghazali again, where the imam noted that "envy is the worst sin for a man. Envy is *haram* (unclean) and a person who is envious of another will face God's retribution. One must distance one's self from ego and envy and must conduct one's life with patience".[17]

Syeikh Samad's regular references to Imam Ghazali and his explicit call for Muslims to practise *tassawuf* are not only typical of traditional Sufism; they are also anathema to Muslim scholars of the reformist and Salafi persuasion, some of whom have come to view Imam Ghazali as a heretic and a deviant, and who critique *tassawuf* as an un-Islamic practice.

CULTURE AND PEDAGOGY

Reformist educators seek to purge Islam of mysticism by rejecting those expressions of religious devotion commonly associated with the vibrant Sufi traditions of Malay folk Islam, such as the use of prayer beads and holy water, as well as celebrations commonly associated with Malay culture, such as the *dikir barat* and *wayang kulit*. Reformists are uncompromising in their criticism of these activities, denigrating them as *bid'a* (innovation) and "un-Islamic". The act of smoking, a social and cultural institution among rural Malay males, is also frowned upon by Salafi reformists. Likewise, reformist scholars and teachers express scepticism about traditional beliefs, still held in many rural communities, that certain well-known *tok guru* of popular *pondok* are *berkat* (blessed).

Pedagogy is another area of contestation between traditionalists and reformists. Traditional Islamic schools in southern Thailand still use the methodology of rote learning (*hafiz*), which Raymond Scupin describes as "mnemonic domination", and which lays the basis for "the mastery of the Islamic sciences".[18] Describing this traditional mode of knowledge dissemination in southern Thailand, Michel Gilquin suggests "this way of studying Islam was based on assimilating unchallengeable norms, rather than true acquisition of theological knowledge. Rationality and logic, though central to classical Muslim thought, were annihilated in rigid reading of texts which did not provide a means of facing a changing world".[19] Scupin, however, has correctly warned against taking this as an indication of a static religious tradition, suggesting that there has been an element of fluidity, even within this pedagogical framework as Islamic educators in Thailand observe trends in the Middle East and adjust accordingly.[20]

In the Malay-Muslim tradition of knowledge dissemination, the *tok guru* exercises a considerable amount of influence over his students, and Islamic education in this setting relies entirely on his interpretation and translation of

Qur'anic teachings. Again, however, this tradition appears to be under pressure from reformist scholars, particularly those who were trained in Saudi Arabia and Egypt and who returned to take up teaching positions in Islamic schools across the region. These scholars seek to re-orient the curriculum of Islamic schools by introducing academic subjects such as science and mathematics, albeit with an Islamic focus. Rather than rely on traditional, hierarchical modes of learning, reformists are encouraging a return to the original texts by stressing the use of Arabic sources and *ijtihad*. By contesting tradition and its proponents, reformists in fact follow in the Hanbali tradition of challenging the prevailing structures of authority and power in Muslim intellectual community. In practice, however, the resistance to convention may not be as prevalent or the break from tradition as severe as one would expect, a fact that speaks once again to the ambivalent nature of these trends. This is because, in reality, Thai reformist circles continue to prize the opinions of prominent *ulama* and *mujtahid* such as Ismail Lutfi and Ismail Ali, another popular reformist scholar who is also Director of the College of Islamic Studies, Prince of Songkhla University. *Fatwa* from such religious scholars are still widely sought and accepted without criticism, in effect reinforcing rather than challenging the adherence to the rigid and onerous hierarchical structures of authority and knowledge that the reformists claim to want to transcend. This being the case, it appears that the reformists' stress on *ilmu*, which presumably must be vested in an individual teacher, is in truth little changed from the mode of knowledge transmission of the *tok guru* from a traditionalist and/or Sufi *pondok*.

TEACHING AND LEARNING IDENTITY AND CITIZENSHIP

Issues of identity and citizenship are very much a part of Islamic education today and inform government initiatives towards Islamic schools in southern Thailand. A central theme underlying these initiatives is the question of how the preservation of Malay identity and culture can be reconciled with the objective of nurturing a Thai national identity that will transcend communal allegiances. That relations between the Malay-Muslim community and the Thai state have improved considerably when compared to the situation in the 1960s and 1970s is clearly evident. This lends weight to the claims of some such as Ismail Lutfi that Pattani is in fact a Dar Al-Islam, or Abode of Islam, by virtue of its status as a land ruled by non-Muslims but where Muslims enjoy the freedom to practise and implement aspects of *shari'a*.[21] Notwithstanding Lutfi's endorsement and the improved situation, it should also be patently clear against the backdrop of ongoing violence that the question of how Muslim students relate to the Thai state and nation as minorities still remains a freighted and controversial issue.

A fundamental issue that emerges in Islamic schools is that of religious freedom; the abiding question of whether Malay-Muslims enjoy religious freedom in southern Thailand. Put differently, some of the pivotal issues that Islamic educators are forced to deal with in schools are those pertaining to cultural and religious space. As one *ustaz* put it, "the government has to protect the belief groups and work with them … Muslims and non-Muslims can live together if everything is equal without discrimination".[22] From this, one can extrapolate that it is the question of space to practise *shari'a* in their personal lives as Muslims, and not the desire to challenge the laws of the state, that explains at least in part the approach of Malay-Muslim educators to the teaching of minority rights.

Paradoxically, even as the issue of the freedom to practise Islam is raised by some religious educators, others have suggested that the implementation of the *shari'a* need not be a major goal for Muslims. Some have intimated that the government "need not reconstruct their state or use the *shari'a* system, because the Qur'an calls multi-ethnic people to live in peace and to know each other".[23] Others have called the question of minority status "irrelevant" since Malay-Muslims are not settlers but were born in the region. By this token, the right to practise their own culture, religion, and lifestyle is a "birthright".[24]

The question of identity points to yet another controversial facet of education: language. The "problem" of language and national identity has long informed perceptions of Islamic education on the part of both the Thai state and the Malay-Muslims of the south. At the practical level, Jawi continues generally to be recognized as the language of transmission and interpretation of Islamic knowledge in the Malay world. This is expressed in the popularity of *Kitab Jawi*, which continues to play a major role in laying the foundations of traditional Islamic knowledge in southern Thailand. The stature of Jawi in Islamic education in Southeast Asia is further augmented by the fact that it is accorded the same status as Arabic and Turkish literature in the Islamic centres of Mecca and Cairo.[25] As for the Thai language, while it has become a major feature of Islamic private school education today, its relevance is confined to secular fields of education, and the prevailing opinion among the local community is that "the Thai language will never supersede the Malay language".[26] In recognition of this, the Thai government has attempted to finesse language policy by introducing bilingual textbooks that allow Malay children to learn Thai phrases but with reference to local cultures.[27] It is difficult to gauge at this juncture the success of this new policy.

Notwithstanding the continued importance of Jawi and the increasing relevance of Thai, it is not surprising to find that, as is the case throughout most of the Muslim world, knowledge of and proficiency in the Arabic language is arguably the most highly prized skill in the realm of Islamic education. Correspondingly, while Jawi is accepted as the main language through which Islam is taught at the elementary level, Arabic is expected to supersede it as the medium of instruction at secondary level.[28] This appears particularly to be the case in reformist schools, where one finds that a greater emphasis is placed on Arabic in the belief that this permits access to the authentic texts, an access which in turn equips students for *ijtihad*.

Aside from language, another issue that has generated some degree of tension is the place of history in the curriculum. As discussed in the first chapter, much of the suspicion that Bangkok harbours towards Islamic schools in southern Thailand stems from their role in disseminating narratives that reinforce an identity of "otherness", which in turn makes for fertile conditions for mobilization towards separatism and insurgency. Given the primacy of these concerns, it is surprising that very little is known about how Malay identity is preserved and reinforced through formal education, and how this affects pluralism in the Thai context.

At the heart of these contestations lie competing renditions of Patani history that are easily discernible from a perusal of Thai and Malay historical texts. In the mainstream textbooks used in Thai national schools, students are taught about the struggle of the Sukhothai kingdom against the Khmer Empire in the thirteenth century. The successful struggle for independence led quickly to the consolidation of Sukhothai rule over principalities in the south, where the kingdom's influence is thought to have extended to Melaka and even Temasek (present-day Singapore) at the foot of the Malay Peninsula. According to this version of history, Patani had for some time already been in the Siamese sphere of influence.

This historical premise underlies the belief among many Thais that the separatist agenda in the southern provinces is illegitimate. Unsurprisingly, it has been challenged by local (Patani) histories narrated through texts such as *Sejarah Kerajaan Melayu Patani* and *Sejarah Perjuangan Melayu Patani*.[29] Jawi versions of these texts continue to circulate among the Islamic schools of southern Thailand today. They describe the glory of the sultanate and make the case that Patani was never a part of the kingdom of Siam. In describing the southward expansion of Siam for example, *Sejarah Kerajaan Melayu Patani* stresses that Patani rulers dealt with the "Siam-Thai" of Ayutthaya (it does not mention Sukhothai) as equals and not vassals.[30] Central to both texts is the 1785 invasion of Patani by Siam and its formal annexation in 1902 through "trickery and deceit", which was greeted with antagonism by the

Malay-Muslims of Patani who felt that their culture, language, and religion had been threatened by the imposition of the Siamese way of life and system of governance.[31] These narratives further stress the Malay character of the Patani sultanate. In the vitriolic fashion characteristic of nationalist texts, *Sejarah Kerajaan* decries "the loss of sovereignty of its (Patani's) rajas, the destruction of the right of suzerainty on the Malays in the country of Patani, and the pawning of all rights to liberty and independence to the raja of Siam-Thai".[32]

In many instances, history, and in particular history from the local Pattani perspective, remains a major component of the education system. Consider for instance, the fact that numerous traditional *pondok* and Islamic private schools continue to use the works of noted *ulama* such as Sheikh Ahmad bin Muhammad Zain al-Fatani as key texts in their curriculum. The continued salience of Sheikh Ahmad Fatani's scholarship lies not only in his fame as a religious scholar, but also in his numerous works discussing questions of race and ethnicity among the Malay-Muslims of Patani. These have contributed to the discourses of identity that feature prominently on the intellectual landscape of southern Thailand.[33] In certain circles among educators in southern Thailand today there is also a discourse on *"fikiran Melayuisme"* (roughly translated as Malay Nationalist thought), as an oral tradition that perpetuates what is effectively a local history of Patani. In the words of a sympathizer of *"fikiran Melayuisme"* interviewed, "these *ustaz* teach the history of the state of Melayu Patani that was seized (*dirampas*) by Siam, and many of them explicitly teach separatism under the direction of senior *ustaz* influenced by or involved in BRN, BNPP (*Barisan Nasional Pembebasan Pattani* or National Pattani Liberation Movement) and PULO".[34] These views resonate with the findings of Andrew Cornish who concluded from ethnographic fieldwork of the 1980s that if Malay Muslims thought separating from Thailand was possible and would provide benefits, then most would prefer to become independent from Thailand.[35] While this is not to imply that the vast majority of Malay-Muslims in southern Thailand today favour independence from Thailand (indeed, it is likely that the opposite is true), it does point to the spirit of separatism that exists in the southern provinces today and which is being perpetuated by at least some religious teachers. As if to drive the point home, certain schools continue to sing nationalistic Patani songs such as *"Bumi Patani"* ("Patani Land") along with Thai national songs and anthems. Because these songs are sung in the local Malay dialect, Thai security officials who are not familiar with the language remain oblivious to these "everyday acts of resistance", to borrow a phrase from the anthropologist James C. Scott. The students inevitably imbibe an "indigenous narrative of history" which against the backdrop of ongoing tensions with the

Thai state invariably threatens to set them at odds with "national" history. Drawing attention to this dichotomy, Ismail Lutfi has noted that "the problem did not occur just two or three days ago. It goes back to hundreds of years ago when the kingdom of Patani was annexed. At times, we have managed to reduce tension, but now, the symptoms are emerging again. The problem is related to the governance of the area in which many mistakes have been made. The patience of the local people has eventually run out".[36]

GENDER IN ISLAMIC EDUCATION

For Muslims, it is clear from the Qur'an that men are the leaders in family and the community and they exercise authority over women. That said, it is also true that the Qur'an details the guaranteed rights and protection of women. This dichotomy is perhaps best captured in Khadija, the first wife of the Prophet and a successful businesswoman, and Aisha, the Prophet's third wife who was a sharp and astute observer of politics. Highly capable in their own right, both women also consciously accepted subservient roles in support of their husband and his work.

Muslims in southern Thailand are generally socially conservative and not given to the major re-evaluation of gender roles. Concomitantly, gender issues do not constitute a major component of Islamic education and are not a formal feature of the curriculum in most schools. To the extent that it is formally discussed, gender is framed in relation to Islamic law and *tauhid*. This context is seen by the community as providing sufficient guidelines for the roles and rights of women in the community, the family, and in marriage. Religious teachers mostly take the view that the Qur'an calls for men to assume positions of leadership in society and for women to be subservient. To many educators, "this subservience is a reflection of the conduct and loyalty of Khadijah, wife of the Prophet, to her husband throughout his life, including his period of recluse in the cave of Hira' as well as his emergence as a social and political leader of the nascent Islamic community in Medina".[37] Education for girls, then, serves in the words of an *ustaz* to "teach them to be good wives". More often than not, *shari'a* and Islamic jurisprudence in traditional Malay-Muslim society is weighted against women on a host of issues. Divorce, for instance, is one issue where religious rulings work to the advantage of men. The same can be said of child custody and inheritance laws.

There are, however, some exceptions to the rule and palpable departures from conservative interpretations of the *shari'a* on certain issues. One such issue is that of female employment, where the climate in southern Thailand has been far more liberal than in other places across the Muslim world. Women participate increasingly actively in trade, commerce, and capitalism in southern Thailand. They are widely accepted in the workforce and a woman's right to work is supported by the vast majority of teachers in Islamic schools. Indeed, as elsewhere in the traditional Malay world, in southern Thailand today the marketplace remains a gendered space where women preside over transactions and commercial activity. This is manifestly evident in the *pasar-pasar* (marketplaces) and *gerai-gerai makanan* (food stalls). In fact, the only arena of commerce where women are clearly outnumbered by men is in the compound of the *Markaz Dakwah* (Dakwah Centre) Yala, an enclave of conservatism in the province of Yala. By and large, the Malay-Muslim community seems well aware that the changes wrought by globalization sometimes demand that women leave the confines of home and contribute to the workforce. That said, the decision to work is understood to be for supporting the husband more than for personal ambition or self-satisfaction. Most Malay-Muslims are of the opinion that while women should make positive contributions to the economy, they need to know their "place" and "responsibility", which in traditional contexts remains that of a home-maker and caregiver to children. There are some schools, however, that are very active in promoting the role of women in their teaching. For example, an educator from Tabia Witthaya (an Islamic private school in Benang Seri, Yala) informed us that his school actively stresses the rights of women in Islamic society in its lessons, as well as the need for social mobility among women through education.[38]

Another matter which speaks to the reassessment of gender roles relates to females taking leadership positions in politics and society at large. In general, while Muslim women in Thailand are not dissuaded from taking up leadership positions, they are taught to be "true to Islam and to subscribe to Qur'anic teaching" on this matter. Most Thai Muslims maintain that a woman's calling remains in the home where her duty as a man's wife (*suri rumah tangga*) is her prime responsibility. Be that as it may, women in fact play increasingly prominent roles in both community and political leadership. In the southern provinces, female Thai Muslims have been approached to occupy such offices as *tok pengulu* or *ketua kampung* (village head) as well as other positions in local government. Some have even been approached to run for senate positions. Even so, one *ustazah* was quick to retort that in the three southern provinces "females have never pushed for representation at the upper echelons of local politics".[39]

The increasing visibility of women outside the home is also evident in the enrolment trends of Islamic schools. Female students outnumbered males in almost all of the thirty Islamic private schools researched for this project. The trend appears reversed in traditional *pondok*, where one tends to see more male students. In addition, there are three exclusively female Islamic private schools in southern Thailand. Satri Islam Wittaya Mulniti in Muang and Satri Sasanupatham in Yaha are both in Yala province, while Satri Pattanasuksa is in Tanjungluluk, Pattani. Wittaya Mulniti (also known as Sekolah Haji Harun or the Haji Harun School) is the sister school of the famous Thamma Witthaya and is the largest with an enrolment of more than 2,000 female students, while Satri Pattanasuksa has approximately 1,000. Satri Sasanupatham is the smallest in terms of enrolment, with several hundred students on its roster.

CITIZENSHIP AND PLURALISM

Possibly one of the greatest challenges confronting Muslim educators in southern Thailand today is to explain notions of citizenship and pluralism against the backdrop of an intensifying conflict that appears increasingly (and alarmingly) sectarian in nature, and that has become an everyday reality for both students and teachers. Unsurprisingly, educators are not too forthcoming with their opinions on this matter. While questions of how to preserve Malay identity and culture clearly weigh heavily on the minds of most Malay-Muslims whatever their station in life, less clear (and more controversial) are the questions of how they understand their position as Muslims and minority citizens in Thailand. Amid the tendency to skirt these provocative issues, some of the most detailed articulations of these concerns are contained in the scholarship of Ismail Lutfi. In particular, though they do not address these issues directly, much can be gleaned from Lutfi's works on the classification of holy lands and his treatise on Islam as a religion of peace, which provide an insight into how some Muslim educators and thinkers in southern Thailand navigate these difficult issues. Yet Ismail Lutfi does not enjoy a monopoly of opinion on the situation in the south. Indeed, as the rest of the chapter will show, his ideas on violence, history, peace, and identity stand in marked contrast to those of two other works that circulate (or had been circulating) in Thailand's Islamic schools — *Jihad Fi Sabilillah Pengertian dan Bidang* (The Understanding and Call for Holy Struggle in the Way of Allah) and *Berjihad di Pattani* (The Conduct of a Holy Struggle in Pattani).

IKHTILAF AD-DARAIN WA ATSARUHU FI AHKAM AL-MUNAKAHAT WA AL-MUAMALAT (THE EFFECT OF TWO LANDS [DAR AL-ISLAM AND DAR AL-HARB] ON ISLAMIC PERSONAL AND TRANSACTION LAWS)

This book, originally written as a doctoral dissertation, is Ismail Lutfi's first major published treatise. By and large, the book deals with issues surrounding Islamic law in the realm of marriage and divorce as well as business and property transactions in the context of Islamic and non-Islamic societies. Of immediate interest, however, is his introductory chapter where he lays out the premises for his understanding of the nature and character of Islamic society in various socio-political contexts.

The book's major premise is that in the application of Islamic law (in this case primarily personal and transaction laws), Muslims must be prepared to accommodate different contexts and constraints. In order to establish this case, the book considers the application of Islamic law under the following contexts;

a.   When the status of a territory changes from Dar Al-Islam (House of Islam) to Dar Al-Harb (House of War), or vice versa;
b.   When the status of an invidivual changes from a citizen of Dar Al-Islam to a citizen of Dar Al-Harb, or vice versa;
c.   When citizens of two opposing lands (Dar Al-Islam and Dar Al-Harb) enter into marriage or transactional contracts.[40]

Characterization of Lands (States)

Ismail Lutfi begins his book with a discussion on the characterization of lands provided in classical Islamic studies scholarship. Following the majority of classical Muslim scholars, Lutfi accepts that lands in Islam are broadly categorized into two realms — Dar Al-Islam and Dar Al-Harb.[41] He defines Dar Al-Islam as a land ruled by a Muslim ruler and where the *shari'a* is held as the rule of the land. In contrast, a land is considered a Dar Al-Harb when it is ruled by non-Muslims or when the *shari'a* is not recognized as the law of the land.[42] Lutfi acknowledges that some contemporary scholars suggest Dar As-Sulh (Land of Peace Treaty) as a third category, but he argues that Dar As-Sulh would merely qualify as a sub-category of Dar Al-Islam or Dar Al-Harb because of its transitory nature.[43]

Lutfi proceeds to elaborate on the terms of reference for relations between Muslims and non-Muslims in these various contexts. If a non-Muslim land enters into a peaceful treaty with a Dar Al-Islam with no agreement that it would submit to the authority of the Dar Al-Islam and pay *jizya* (tributary tax), then that land will be regarded as Dar Al-Muwada'ah (Dar Al-Harb in a no-hostility agreement with Dar Al-Islam). However, if a non-Muslim land enters into a peace treaty with conditions — the non-Muslim ruler submits to the authority of Dar Al-Islam and agrees to pay *jizya* — the land is regarded as Dar Al-'Ahd (Dar Al-Islam with autonomous rule by a non-Muslim ruler), and the non-Muslim ruler is allowed to retain his position.[44]

Types of Lands (Territories) in Dar Al-Islam

Lutfi contends that lands under Dar Al-Islam can be divided into three categories:

1.   The Haramain (Two Holy Lands)
     This refers to the holy land of Mecca and its vicinity and the holy land of Medina. Non-Muslims are not allowed to enter Mecca at all. As for the holy land of Medina, non-Muslims are only permitted temporary entry for purposes of trade.
2.   The Land of Hijaz
     Hijaz is the Arabian Peninsula. Non-Muslims are allowed to enter if they possess the proper permits issued from the authorities, but they are not allowed to stay longer than three days.
3.   Other lands of Dar Al-Islam
     Non-Muslims are allowed to stay in these lands as *zimmis* (protected minorities).[45] Citizens of Dar Al-Harb are allowed to enter and stay in the lands if they possess proper permits.[46]

Obligations of Muslims to Dar Al-Islam

Ismail Lutfi asserts that Dar Al-Islam is land for all Muslims. Non-Muslims, however, may be accepted as citizens if they accept *zimmi* status. Insofar as the obligations of Muslims are concerned, all Muslims are called upon to defend any Dar Al-Islam and to fend off all hostile forces. The obligation could become *fardhu ain* (personal obligation) upon all Muslims if the enemy occupies any part of Dar Al-Islam. Also, all Muslims are to support the mission of Dar Al-Islam — to spread Islam and implement the *shari'a* in other lands.[47]

Pedagogies, Curricula and Texts 115

Conversion of Dar Al-Islam to Dar Al-Harb

Lutfi opines that conversion of Dar Al-Islam to Dar Al-Harb could take place under the following circumstances:

1. When Dar Al-Islam is occupied by Dar Al-Harb.
2. When citizens of Dar Al-Islam denounce Islam as their religion, take over the land, and establish a government ruled by legislation other than Islamic law.
3. When non-Muslim citizens (*zimmi*) rebel and take over the land.[48]

Types of Dar Al-Islam and Dar Al-Harb

Lutfi refines his understanding of the nature of Dar Al-Islam by providing a typology of the concept that essentially rests on two categories:

1. Authentic Dar Al-Islam
   An authentic Dar Al-Islam refers to lands that fulfil two key conditions: they must be governed by a Muslim ruler and subject to full implementation of the *shari'a*. When these conditions are met, the land is described by Lutfi as a "juristic Dar Al-Islam".[49]
2. Nominal Dar Al-Islam
   There are three types of territory that are encompassed in this category:
   a. Land that is ruled by non-Muslims (Dar Al-Harb), but where Muslim residents are allowed to practice and implement some aspects of the *shari'a* in their private and communal lives;
   b. Muslim land that has been taken over by non-Muslims or converted to Dar Al-Harb as described above, but where there remains a Muslim population that is permitted to practise some aspects of the *shari'a*;
   c. Land that is ruled by heretics or corrupt Muslims who implement man-made law instead of the *shari'a*.

This typology accommodates the view of classical Muslim scholars that Dar Al-Islam does not become a Dar Al-Harb simply by virtue of the fact that non-Muslims take over positions of leadership. Instead, it suggests a more sophisticated understanding that argues that so long as there are Muslims residing in the land and they are accorded freedom to practise major obligations in Islam such prayer, fasting, and the pilgrimage, the land could still be considered a Dar Al-Islam.[50] Indeed, as will be elaborated later, this has significant implications for how we might judge the status of the Muslim-dominated provinces in southern Thailand under the rule of Bangkok.

As for Dar Al-Harb, Lutfi offers two separate possibilities:

a. Authentic Dar Al-Harb — a land that is literally at war with Islam;
b. Dar Al-Muwada'ah or nominal Dar Al-Harb — land that has entered into a peace treaty with Dar Al-Islam but that remains independent and does not pay *jizya*.[51]

Division of Lands

Ismail Lutfi concedes that the distinction of lands as Dar Al-Islam and Dar Al-Harb is not based on clear injunction from the Qur'an and *hadith*. He does note, however, that there are verses in the Qur'an alluding to this division, such as Surah 59:9.[52] Nevertheless, Lutfi proceeds to offer three reasons that explain the distinction constructed by classical Muslim scholars. First, he suggests that such divisions were necessary for organizing Muslims into a united front that could protect the *ummah* from potential common external enemies, especially during the formative stages of Islam. In this respect, even though there was in reality a variety of rulers and states, Muslim scholars regarded all Muslim lands as one coherent Dar Al-Islam. Second, this division was required in order to determine the appropriate Islamic injunctions, *fatwa*, or laws, since the *shari'a* recognized that the status of political authority (Muslim or non-Muslim) had an effect on the population and how it was to be governed. Finally, it also enabled Islamic jurisprudence to speak to the dichotomous relationship between Muslims and non-Muslims, Dar Al-Islam and Dar Al-Harb. This was necessary for the organization of international relations in accordance with Islamic precepts and principles.[53]

Differentiating the Lands

Because the status of a land has implications for how Islamic law is applied, Lutfi suggests criteria to differentiate one particular land from another. In the opinion of classical Islamic scholars, a land is essentially differentiated from another based on two conditions, namely, the identity of the ruler and its ability to defend itself from external threats. In other words, these conditions involve concepts not unlike the notions of independence and state sovereignty that are central to the modern parlance of international politics.

Lutfi suggests that all Dar Al-Islam may be considered as one undifferentiated category. Although in reality Muslim lands could be divided into several sovereign and independent political entities, such differentiation is only in form and does not accord with the purposes of Islamic jurisprudence. A land is regarded as Dar Al-Islam and is differentiated from Dar Al-Harb if it possesses the above-mentioned traits of sovereignty and independence. Having said that, he also believes no land can be regarded as an authentic Dar Al-Islam unless it fulfils two fundamental criteria: rule by a Muslim and rule on the principles of the *shari'a*. Without fulfilling these criteria, the land can be regarded only as a nominal Dar Al-Islam.

Perhaps the most interesting facets of Ismail Lutfi's arguments are those made with respect to the criteria for differentiating between various Dar Al-Harbs. Here, a key point of departure separating one Dar Al-Harb from another is its freedom to wage war with another Dar Al-Harb and the absence of a pact against a common external enemy. When a Dar Al-Harb enters into a defence pact with another Dar Al-Harb against one common enemy, in particular Muslims, both are regarded as belonging to one undifferentiated category.[54]

Differentiating Populations

To determine the appropriate application of Islamic law to individuals, Lutfi suggests that the status of individuals accords with the status of the territory they reside in (Dar Al-Islam or Dar Al-Harb). He establishes the following categories: (1) Non-Muslim citizens of Dar Al-Harb living in Dar Al-Harb, (2) Non-Muslim citizens of Dar Al-Harb in Dar Al-Islam, (3) Non-Muslim citizens of a Dar Al-Harb in a foreign Dar Al-Harb, (4) Muslim citizens of Dar Al-Islam living in Dar Al-Islam, (5) Muslim citizens of Dar Al-Islam in Dar Al-Harb, (6) Non-Muslim citizens of Dar Al-Islam living in Dar Al-Islam, and (7) Non-Muslim citizens of Dar Al-Islam in Dar Al-Harb. Beyond individuals' association with the land, which determines the laws to which they are held, Lutfi also argues that Islamic personal and transaction law could differ when individuals enter into contract with others in each particular context.[55]

Here, Lutfi reinforces the majority opinion of classical Muslim scholars and argues that it is not permissible in Islam to have multiple Dar Al-Islam, nor is it permissible to appoint two Muslim rulers in the same period. In this regard, he explains the current global proliferation of Muslim "lands" and "rulers" by arguing that the nation-state is "excusable" based on the principle of *dharurat* (emergencies), a consensus found in Islamic jurisprudence that temporarily permits the prohibited. Having established this, Lutfi contends that Muslims are obliged to rectify the situation using "all means available", as Islamic jurisprudence dictates that the rule of *dharurat* may only be applied for a minimum duration and must ultimately be overcome. Lutfi further opines that Muslims "should not feel pleased" with such a situation (of the perpetual application of *dharurat*).[56] Needless to say, such a reading goes against the conventional understanding of international relations, and could be interpreted to support a transnational caliphate of sorts, though Lutfi does not mention this explicitly, nor does he elaborate further on this point.

Since there are two types of Dar Al-Harb — one "authentic" and another "nominal" — Muslims living in Dar Al-Harb are confronted with two different sets of guidelines for behaviour. Lutfi argues that Muslims living in an authentic Dar Al-Harb are obliged to migrate (*hijrah*) to a Dar Al-Islam if they are able to do so on the premise that they are likely to face religious persecution and be denied the freedom to observe major religious obligations.[57] As for Muslims living in a nominal Dar Al-Harb, Lutfi contemplates two separate contexts. The first is where a Dar Al-Islam is overtaken by non-Muslims through invasion or a *coup d'état*. In such a situation, Lutfi argues that Muslims living in the land are obliged to perform *jihad* in order to reclaim power so that the rule of Islam can be re-established. If the efforts of these local Muslims are not sufficient to re-establish the rule of Islam, then Muslims living in neighbouring lands are obliged to support their co-religionists. The nature and conduct of this *jihad*, however, depends on a consensus, for the responsibility to decide on the issue lies collectively with Muslims who are directly confronted with the situation, and decision-making is to be undertaken through collective *ijtihad*. The second scenario is where Muslims live in a Dar Al-Harb and enjoy freedom to practise some of their religious obligations. If a Muslim is not able to perform his major obligations or is forced to live in fear for his and his family's welfare if he does, he is instructed to leave the country and should only stay if he is unable to migrate with the family. In other words, under such circumstances migration is obligatory unless conditions are extreme. If, however, Muslims enjoy the freedom to perform their major religious obligations, migration is no longer obligatory.[58]

The final part of Lutfi's discussion on the nature and character of Islamic lands and territories presents a typology of populations under the general banners of Muslims and non-Muslims. For Muslims, Lutfi enumerates three categories, namely (1) citizens of Dar Al-Islam living in a Dar Al-Islam, (2) Muslims living or residing in a Dar Al-Harb either as settlers (citizens) or sojourners, and (3) citizens of Dar Al-Harb (on the above premise) who have not migrated to a Dar Al-Islam.[59] For non-Muslims, he categorizes them broadly along two lines, (a) *Ahl Harb* or people at war, and (b) *Ahl 'Ahd* or people of the covenant of peace. *Ahl 'Ahd* are further qualified as either *zimmi* or non-Muslims who agree to be citizens of a Dar Al-Islam;[60] *Musta'min* or a person who enters into a contract of Al-Aman which binds rival parties to cease hostilities;[61] *Muwadi* or a non-Muslim who has a peace or non-aggression agreement or is a citizen of a country that has such an agreement with Dar Al-Islam;[62] *Muhayid* or a neutral non-Muslim or a non-Muslim who does not wage war against Muslims;[63] and finally, *Harbi* or a non-Muslim citizen of a Dar Al-Harb that is not neutral and that does not enjoy a peace agreement with Dar Al-Islam.[64]

Assessing Ismail Lutfi's views on the issues of identity, citizenship, and pluralism from this text is not an easy task given that his interest lies primarily in the jurisprudential classification of lands and peoples. Be that as it may, it is still possible to distil important insights that speak to these issues. While Lutfi's view accords with classical Islamic thought on the delineation of territorial boundaries along faith lines, he does not subscribe to the idea of perpetual war between Muslims and non-Muslims which is propounded in certain Salafi circles (particularly Salafi Jihadists), nor does he believe in the strict Manichean division of the world into Dar Al-Islam or Dar Al-Harb. There are two indications of this. First, he demonstrates an inclination towards the idea that a Dar Al-Kufr (Land of Disbelief) and Dar Al-Harb may be a land where non-Islamic systems prevail, but that alone does not necessarily translate to hostility towards Muslims. Second, the idea he propounds of a Muhayid state, a state that has entered into a peace treaty with an Islamic state, indicates a belief that not all non-Muslim countries are perforce hostile to Muslims, even as he suggests that an agreement is still required for a state to be regarded neutral.

Though Lutfi does not state it explicitly, based on his typologies of Muslim lands the southern provinces might be regarded as a nominal Dar Al-Islam by virtue of their Islamic character, freedom of worship for Muslims, and the existence of some aspects of Islamic law and practice, albeit without explicit Muslim political leadership of the kind that an authentic Dar Al-Islam demands. Such a perspective would undoubtedly differ from that of some militants who clearly see the southern border provinces as a Dar Al-Harb that needs to be reclaimed and purified from "*kafir*" Siamese influence.[65] Lutfi is nonetheless ambiguous on the issue of whether Muslims living in the Patani Dar Al-Islam are obliged to reclaim it through *jihad*, though it is possible he thinks so, going by the teaching of classical Islamic scholars toward whom he has demonstrated a proclivity. This begs the question of what form of *jihad* would be deemed appropriate to reclaim Patani. Again, it is not clear whether Lutfi means *jihad* in a narrow sense (*jihad* of the sword) or in a wider form through *dakwah*. Indeed, to better understand his idea of *jihad* in the context of Thailand, we now turn to another of his works, *Islam Penjana Kedamaian Sejagat*, which further develops his understanding of war and *jihad* and which was written to address the resurgence of violence and conflict in Thailand's Malay-Muslim minority.

ISLAM PENJANA KEDAMAIAN SEJAGAT (ISLAM AS THE PATHWAY TO HARMONY)

Published in both Malay and Thai, *Islam Penjana Kedamaian Sejagat* (Islam as the Pathway to Harmony) was essentially motivated by the ongoing violence in southern Thailand and the discourse on Islamist extremism that surrounds it. It was, in Lutfi's own words, meant to "rectify misperceptions about the role of Islam in the conflict".[66] While essentially written to refute claims of religious motivation on the part of militants as well as certain quarters in the central government's security apparatus, the book is noteworthy in terms of how it articulates the position of one of southern Thailand's foremost contemporary scholars of Islam on critical subjects such as conflict, warfare, and, in particular, the relationship between Muslims and non-Muslims.

According to its Introduction, *Islam Penjana Kedamaian Sejagat* is an attempt to correct the misperceptions pertaining to Islam that Lutfi suggests have been created by anti-Islamists such as the Zionists through the mass media and biased writings on the subject. He terms this phenomenon "Islam Phobia", and rejects it by stressing a set of conciliatory Islamic values and principles as derived from the Qur'an and *hadith*. Replete with *surah* (verses) from the Qur'an and *ayat* (phrases) from *hadith*, the book centres its argument on the values of "*Kedamaian*" (harmony) and "*Kesejahteraan*" (peace), and to some extent "*Keadilan*" (justice) as well, in order to substantiate its contention that Islam is a peace-loving and harmonious religion that has never intended to cause harm to other religions or be a threat to humanity.

Lutfi makes the argument that the Islamic values set out above are in fact universal values shared by other religions as well. In other words, the values of peace, harmony, and justice are not exclusive to Islam but are universal values regardless of religion, race, or gender.[67] In addition, Lutfi attempts to explicate what being a "good" Muslim entails. For Lutfi, this is central to the enterprise of Islamic education. He points out that a good Muslim should be one who follows the teachings of the Qur'an and by virtue of that the teachings of *Allah*, treats his fellow Muslims as his brothers and provides them with warmth and love for the sake of *Allah*, unites with his fellow Muslims to assist in social and community work, actively seeks to improve himself by increasing his knowledge (in particular, religious knowledge), and finally, is prepared to make sacrifices for the happiness of his fellow Muslims in the name of *Allah*. Not surprisingly, to Lutfi's mind all these traits are manifested when a Muslim abides by the *shari'a* and makes contributions to the *zakat* (Islamic tax) system.[68] As Lutfi notes, Islam teaches that the ties between humans, whether at the individual, communal, or international level, must emphasize "*tolong-menolong*" (helping one another) and "*berkenal-kenalan*" (getting to know one another through interaction). At the same time, Islam also teaches that such ties should not be those that involve enmity, cruelty, and acts of terror. Lutfi notes that the values of "*tolong-menolong*" and "*berkenal-kenalan*" go beyond mere familiarity with a neighbour's name and status. Rather, these values have a deeper meaning in the sense that it brings individuals and communities closer together in the spirit of "*gotong-royong*" and "*bantu-membantu*" (mutual help and support), and in so doing, fosters an integrated, multiracial, and harmonious society.[69]

Islam and Pluralism

Lutfi points out that while there may be those who reject Islam as a religion and way of life, Islam instructs Muslims always to extend a hand of friendship and work together to make this world a harmonious (*damai*), peaceful (*sejahtera*), and just (*adil*) place to live for all mankind, regardless of religion. As this teaching reflects the universal values of humanity (*kemanusiaan*), he stresses that it should not be understood as unique to Islam and may be professed in other religions as well. In the same vein, close friendship ties and interactions across different ethnic and religious boundaries will accrue benefits to all societies, including Muslims. For instance, they present the opportunity for the sharing of knowledge through public education, science, and technology as well as other fields of knowledge that would reap mutual benefits for both Muslims and non-Muslims. By doing this, the focus on the universality of values will foster cross-cultural understanding and reduce the possibility of conflict and misunderstanding between Muslims and non-Muslims, not just within a nation but also among nation-states. This, according to Lutfi, is crucial to the fostering of a harmonious and peaceful global community.

To substantiate his views on the relationship between Islam and cultural pluralism, Lutfi draws on Islamic history by reminding readers that during the time of Prophet Muhammad there were non-Muslims (in particular, Jews and Christians) living in an Islamic state.[70] These non-Muslims lived peacefully alongside their Muslim counterparts because neither the ruler nor the Muslim citizens compelled non-Muslims to convert to Islam. These were teachings of the Prophet Muhammad to the early Muslims that were codified in the

Qur'an and to Lutfi's mind they remain of timeless relevance to all Muslims in any milieu. Fascinatingly, rather than cite a Muslim scholar, Lutfi quotes Thomas Arnold, an English historian, to stress this point. According to Lutfi's reading, Arnold had argued that at the time of the Prophet there had never been any attempt to compel non-Muslim conversion to Islam, nor were there any attempts to drive other religions from Muslim lands.[71]

In his reflection on what Islam teaches about the relationship between Muslims and non-Muslims, Lutfi reasons that Muslims are enjoined always to perform good deeds and interact with non-Muslims so long as they do not pose a threat to Islam. In essence, Muslims are called to treat non-Muslims with the same goodness and compassion that they would extend to fellow Muslims and members of their own family.[72] On the matter of proselytization, Lutfi establishes categorically that Muslims should not forcefully convert non-Muslims. Instead, Muslims should share the "essence" of Islam by presenting its teachings in a conciliatory and consultative manner and on the basis of rational and logical explanation ("*dengan hujah yang logik*"). Muslims are also encouraged to engage in constructive dialogue and debate with non-Muslims over matters of religion, including the teachings of Islam.[73] Non-Muslims then have the right to decide for themselves if they wish to accept Islam.

To illustrate the nature of Muslim relations with non-Muslims, Lutfi provides hypothetical examples, such as that a son who has accepted Islam while his parents have not is exhorted to continue to show care, respect, and devotion to his parents despite differences in their religious beliefs.[74] In another instance, Lutfi cites the historical record of how Christians in Syam (Syria) expressed greater love to Muslims in their midst than they did to their fellow Christians from Rome.[75] This, he surmises, was attributable to the fact that during the classical period Muslims kept to their promises and delivered on them, possessed a tolerant and patient attitude, and refrained from using violence. He quotes a German scholar, Zanghrid Honikah, who spoke of a priest from Constantinople who wrote to him and intimated that Arab Muslims are renowned for their truth and justice as well as their restraint from the use of aggression and terror, especially towards the Christians in Constantinople.[76]

Islam and Warfare

One of the central issues of concern for Lutfi is conflict and warfare. Lutfi sets out the counter-intuitive argument that war (*syariat qital* or *peperangan*) is in fact a way to promote harmony.[77] Lutfi argues that insofar as *peperangan* (war) is concerned, Islam teaches that it should be used either for upholding the truth and maintaining harmony or defending against acts of terror and aggression.[78] In this way, Islam teaches that *peperangan* is something that is inevitable and will confront any community or society.[79] This is because *peperangan* is necessary for a community or society to maintain peace and foster harmony.

At the same time, Lutfi points to the fact that *peperangan* in Islam does not mean for one to actively and literally go into battle and perform acts of terror and aggression for the purpose of self-interest or gains for a particular religious community. Instead, *peperangan* in Islam simply means to ensure harmony and peace by upholding the truth yet also being prepared to fight if and when necessary — especially if the religion (in this case, Islam) is clearly under threat. He explains, however, that Islam prohibits the killing of human beings (especially women, elderly, children and disabled) who do not pose a threat to Islam and its followers. In order to validate his contention, Lutfi turns to the historical record, where the Prophet Muhammad permitted *peperangan* against non-Muslims only when there were acts of injustice and aggression perpetrated against Muslims that undermined Islamic principles and posed an existential threat to Islam. Lutfi argues that even during *peperangan*, the Qur'an exhorts Muslims to remember the call to be just towards the enemy and to demonstrate empathy (*belas kasihan*), especially if the latter has chosen to accept peace and agrees to co-exist in harmony.[80] To substantiate his position, Lutfi cites the work of Imam Al-Qurthubi, who opined that although non-Muslims may have killed the women and children of a particular religious community deliberately to cause hurt, members of that community must not retaliate in similar fashion.

Lutfi stresses how harmony in fact "conditions" *peperangan* because to him, harmony is the basis of linkages in Islam. According to him, Islam teaches its followers to prioritize harmony over conflict or aggression; he maintains that to do this is simply to replicate the example of the Prophet who did all in his power to prevent aggression and the unnecessary loss of life, because he placed paramount importance on harmony and peace. Even though the Prophet had many enemies, especially in Mecca, who threatened to kill him, he did not resort to violence but instead engaged in dialogue to win over the support of his enemies, including his virulent opponents from the Quraisy clan. In other words, Lutfi avers that the Prophet Muhammad taught peace and urged the demonstration of empathy, patience, tolerance, and graciousness when dealing with enemies rather than resorting to violence for particular aims.[81] To illustrate this, he recounts the conduct of Sultan Salahhuddin Al-Ayubi during the period of the crusades with Christians.[82]

Another point Lutfi makes is that the cause of war often has less to do with religion than with material advancement.[83] In fact, he concedes that Islam is often a victim of the greed for material advancement that induces countries to go to war. He gives the examples of Israel's attack on Palestine as well as the American invasion of Iraq, both of which he views as struggles over material resources though masquerading as religiously sanctioned warfare. He asserts that Zionists, whom he argues are the initial cause of these problems, have taken advantage of the situation to condemn Islam and present it in bad light. However, Lutfi is equally categorical in his condemnation of acts of terror in the name of Islam.[84]

Jihad

A sub-section following the discussion on *peperangan* deals with the question of *jihad*. Lutfi subscribes to the classical Islamic tradition stating that certain conditions must be met before *jihad* can be declared. Following its declaration, the conduct of *jihad* must abide strictly by specific guidelines. He maintains that there are different levels of *jihad* — unless one is grounded in a proper understanding of Islam and what the Qur'an says about the conduct of *jihad*, these will complicate matters for those seeking to execute *jihad*.[85] While terrorism involving mass murder and bloodshed is prohibited in Islam, *jihad* is permissible so as long as its purpose is to rescue Islam and its followers from persecution.[86] Lutfi cautions that killing without reason is prohibited in Islam and those who perform such acts will be condemned in the afterlife. Further, he argues that a Muslim cannot kill another Muslim for no justifiable reason and likewise a Muslim cannot kill a non-Muslim if the latter poses no threat to Islam.[87] In other words, a Muslim is permitted to kill a non-Muslim only if the non-Muslim is an existential threat to him and to Islam. If blood is spilt otherwise, these Muslims will be forbidden from entering Heaven and condemned to Hell instead.

Arguably, the most telling perspectives that can be inferred from *Islam Agama Penjana Kedamaian* pertain to the matter of pluralism. The conciliatory nature of Lutfi's understanding of the relationship between Muslims and non-Muslims is revealed in a number of ways that are striking, given his alleged association to Wahhabism. Lutfi's assessment of how Muslims are required to deal with non-Muslim neighbours is anchored first and foremost on the scriptural injunction that there is no compulsion in Islam, particularly on the question of conversion. Moreover, he suggests it is through the sharing of the "essence of Islam" that Muslims can best impress upon non-Muslims the beauty of their religion. To underscore this point, he suggests that

Muslims should be prepared to engage non-Muslims in constructive debate on matters of religion. In doing this, he articulates what is clearly a progressive view, again surprising given the regular accusations levelled at him of being a hardline, scripturalist Wahhabi. Additionally, Lutfi contends in *Islam Penjana Kedamaian* that the cornerstone of the relationship between Muslims and non-Muslims is not war but peace. In stark contrast to extremist ideologues such as Sayyid Qutb (to many the standard-bearer for militant Islam today), Lutfi's view of relations between Muslims and non-Muslims is that it is hardly the perpetual state of conflict that some extremists make it out to be. Again, this raises doubts about popular media representations of Ismail Lutfi as a "hardline Wahhabi cleric" bent on Islamizing Thailand and undermining the Bangkok regime through the use of force. It spotlights the difficulty of strait-jacketing Islamic scholars according to the conventional typologies of thought.

JIHAD QITAL

Jihad — the Qur'anic injunction for believers to strive with their entire being to carry out the commandments of God as part of their submission to God's will — is one of the most controversial concepts in the lexicon of Islam today. While classical Muslim scholars stress that *jihad* can take on many forms, the concept has taken on a threatening note by virtue of the fact that Muslim militants are mobilizing one aspect of *jihad* — which calls for armed struggle against an oppressive and hostile enemy — to sanction and legitimize their actions. The notion that the conflict in southern Thailand enjoys religious sanction as an armed struggle for justice weighs heavily on prevailing perceptions of Islamic schools. In other words, the question that arises is how *jihad*, and in particular armed *jihad* or *jihad qital*, is understood and taught in Islamic schools against the arid realities of life in the southern provinces today.

Views differ among religious educators on whether the ongoing southern Thai conflict could justifiably be considered a *jihad*. For instance, Ismail Lutfi argues fervidly that to describe the ongoing conflict as a religious struggle betrays "a very general and simplistic understanding of *jihad*".[88] In his writings, Lutfi asserts that only recognized religious authority (*pemimpin agung bagi ummat Islam*) can declare *jihad*, and even then it can only be declared after other avenues of *dakwah* have been exhausted.[89] He further instructs that "Islam forbids the spilling of Muslim blood". This view takes on greater currency in the context of ongoing violence in southern Thailand, which has increasingly witnessed the killing of fellow Muslims (including teachers students of Islamic schools) by militants.[90] Lutfi's view on the prohibition of violence in the name of Islam is shared by members of the *Jemaat Tabligh* movement. Their explanation for this injunction, however, differ somewhat from the reformists. For them, violence is forbidden because southern Thailand has not yet seen the conditions for *jihad qital* arise, and hence the spread of Islam should be done via peaceful means.[91]

The benign views discussed above are fairly prevalent, but more malignant perspectives on *jihad* and the violence in southern Thailand have emerged on the discursive landscape. In fact, some educators have articulated somewhat disconcerting opinions on the subject. An *ustaz* with known links to PULO ranted in the course of an interview that *jihad qital* has long been necessary in southern Thailand because Malay-Muslims are being victimized by the oppressive Thai state.[92] Unlike noted contemporary southern Thai Muslim scholars such as Nidae Waba, Ismail Ali, and Ismail Lutfi, this *ustaz* felt that offensive *jihad* was necessary to ensure the freedom not just of religion but of Malay identity in the southern provinces. Another *ustaz* with links to GMIP averred that the time for *jihad qital* had descended upon the "*tiga wilayah*" (three provinces — the local nomenclature for the Malay-Muslim provinces of Narathiwat, Pattani, and Yala).[93] He was especially critical of Ismail Lutfi's more accommodating interpretation of *jihad* in relation to the situation in southern Thailand. Lutfi's view, he suggested, stemmed from his "Saudi-oriented" perspective which focused on developments in Islamic thought during the religion's formative phase under the Prophet in Mecca ("*zaman nabi di Makkah*"), where the message focused on the peaceful spread of Islam ("*menyebarkan shari'a Islam dengan cara damai*") amid opposition from various sources such as the aristocratic Quraiysh tribes who were sceptical of the new religion. In contrast, this *ustaz* argued that the situation of southern Thai Muslims today is in fact similar to that which confronted the Prophet of the Medinan era ("*zaman nabi di Medina*"), an era which was defined, in his words, by the "assault and violation of Muslim lands by non-Muslims (*orang yang mencerobuhi bumi kita*)" from polytheistic Mecca. Under these conditions, *jihad qital* was not only legitimate but necessary. Another educator, when presented with the hypothetical situation in which his students were known to be active militants against the Thai state, opined that he would not stop them because they would be perpetuating a legitimate struggle that is several centuries old. When asked what he thought of the fact that the Siamese had in various instances rendered aid and assistance to Patani, he reportedly responded: "Do you know how humiliating it is for the Malays to seek assistance from Siam?"[94]

It bears noting, however, that many educators are resigned in their attitude to the ongoing violence. They concede that violence has been part and parcel of the history of the south for the past century and is caused by the long-standing neglect of the Malay-Muslim community by Bangkok administrations, a neglect that is likely to persist. Others, when prodded to explain ongoing violence in religious terms, were quick to establish that in their classrooms they taught that the greater, more important *jihad* is the "*jihad* of self".[95]

JIHAD FI SABILLILLAH PENGERTIAN DAN BIDANG (THE UNDERSTANDING AND CALL FOR STRUGGLE IN THE WAY OF ALLAH)

The undated booklet *Jihad Fi Sabilillah Pengertian dan Bidang* was written by Hassan Nikmatullah. Obtained from a rural-based Islamic school in Pattani province, the booklet is an exegesis on the concept of *jihad*, but, as becomes quickly evident, the author's specific preoccupation is to extol the virtues of offensive *jihad*.

The booklet begins by establishing two examples of the understanding of *jihad fi sabilillah*. To the author, *jihad* can be defined either in terms of the performance of rituals such as prayers, *zikr*, and fasting, or as the call to wage war against infidels (*kafir*). The discussion is punctuated with Qur'anic verses to support his claim.[96] He suggests that Muslims have "failed to comprehend the true meaning of *jihad*" and he blames this failure on the *ulama*.[97] In a riposte that is characteristic of Salafi criticisms of traditional religious leaders, the author suggests that *ulama* tended to subscribe only to those meanings of *jihad* propounded by classical Islamic scholars and that it was this rigid and hardened position on *jihad* that accounted for the community's inability to fully comprehend the concept. Hassan defines *jihad fi sabilillah* as "striving for something with one's strength and for the sake of mankind, and without care for anything except for God's blessings".[98] He later argues that *jihad* conducted in this manner "is the most important positive deed in the eyes of Allah".[99]

Conditions for and Advantages of *Jihad Fi Sabilillah*

Hassan provides three conditions for the conduct of *jihad fi sabilillah*: (1) performing *amal* (action in the name of Islam) to the best of one's abilities, (2) performing *amal* sincerely for Allah, and (3) performing *amal* in accordance to the *sunnah* of the Prophet.[100] He expands on the three conditions identified by making extensive references to the Qur'an as well as to numerous *hadith*.[101] The discussion on the conditions for *jihad fi sabilillah* is followed by an elaboration of its advantages, which Hassan divides into two categories: advantages in the current life and in the afterlife. Hassan explains that the advantage of *jihad* in the current life lies in the fact that its conduct will be guided by God and will return in the form of blessings to the believer.[102] Specifically, a person who performs *jihad* will obtain "war gains (bounty)" and will be widely respected, particularly if they triumph over the *kafir*.[103] Moreover, a person who wages *jihad* will be ensured a place in heaven and enjoy its benefits. Finally, the person who conducts *jihad* will have all his sins forgiven.[104]

From here, Hassan discusses the categories of *jihad*. He classifies *jihad* into four categories, namely, (1) *jihad* at a personal level, (2) *jihad* at a societal level, (3) *jihad* at an economic level, and (4) *jihad* at a political level. Citing a *surah* from the Qur'an that relates how Moses challenged the Pharaoh's claims that he was God, Hassan argues that the best form of *jihad* is one which is conducted to uphold justice for the betterment of one's country.[105] To justify his emphasis on armed *jihad*, the author quotes from the Qur'an (Al-Tahrim 9), where it is written, "Oh prophet of God, wage *jihad* against *kafir* and *munafikin* (hypocrites) and ensure that you deal with them in a tough manner as they are inhabitants of hell and hell is the worst place one can live in".[106] From this verse, he suggests that there are two targets of *jihad* — *jihad* against *kafir* and *jihad* against *munafikin*. Hassan also quotes a *hadith* from Imam Muslim in which the Prophet is believed to have said: "There are no prophets that were sent before me to an *ummah* but to stop from doing deeds prevented by God and to ask of them to perform deeds required by God of them. Those among the people who *jihad* to stop an illegal act using their hands are among the *mukmin* (people blessed by God). Those among the people who *jihad* to stop an illegal act using their tongue are among the *mukmin* (people blessed by God) and those among the people who *jihad* to stop an illegal act using their heart are among the *mukmin* but this is the weakest form of *iman* (faith)".[107] Hassan deduces from this *hadith* that the Prophet was exhorting Muslims to conduct armed *jihad* in order to ensure peace and "extinguish the fire of anarchy" that arises from the injustice of the government. Having affirmed the centrality of "*jihad* of the hand", Hassan proceeds to cite other examples of *jihad* which include doing good to one's parents, supporting widows, loyalty to and taking care of spouses and their property, and personal *jihad* through prayer and fasting.[108] Considering that the attention he gives to them is discernibly less than that paid to armed *jihad*, these examples are clearly of secondary importance in his mind.

The booklet *Jihad Fi Sabilillah Pengertian dan Bidang* has two distinguishable traits. First, it clearly is Salafist in orientation, given the author's direct criticism of the traditionalist *ulama* for "misleading" the

Muslim community. Second, despite the author's attempts to elucidate the various natures of *jihad*, it is clear from the flow of the text that he privileges *jihad qital* or armed *jihad*. The Salafist-Jihadist emphasis in this book contravenes not just the perspectives of more moderate Salafi-reformists like Ismail Lutfi, but also popular Sufi readings of *jihad*, which according to Sufi proponents should "originate from the heart, not the hand".[109] Moreover, while classical Islam provides strict guidelines and codes of conduct for *jihad*, especially *jihad qital*, the author fails to account for this very important dimension in his discussion. For instance, there is no attempt to distinguish between *jihad* as *fard 'kifaya* (referring to the offensive *jihad* which only a few need undertake) and as *fard 'ayn* (referring to the defensive *jihad* which all Muslims are obliged to undertake in their own way). Nor does the author feel any need to highlight one of the most controversial and well-concealed features of the ethics and law regarding *jihad* — that in the Qur'an (22:40) it is intimated that Islam permits Muslims to carry arms to defend those who are oppressed and persecuted regardless of race or religion.[110]

In addition, the author fails to explain the legalistic and regulatory terms of *jihad*, particularly the centrality of the imam in the call to arms, where in classical Islamic thought *jihad qital* can only be undertaken upon the sanction of the imam or *mujtahid*, who serves concurrently as the legitimizing authority as well as the "commander-in-chief". The fact that *jihad qital* cannot be launched without the issuance of prior notice through three warnings, and that there are legitimate and illegitimate targets of armed *jihad* (for example, civilians or those not trained in weapons are not to be targeted) is also overlooked. Nor does the book discuss terms for the termination of *jihad* in accordance to the Prophet's injunction that reads, "fight until oppression ends and God's laws prevail. But if [the enemy] desists, then you must also cease hostilities".[111] Finally, discussion of the societal aspects of *jihad qital* — particularly the fact that parental approval is required for the offensive *jihad* of *fard 'kifaya* or that under certain circumstances non-Muslims can be enlisted for *jihad* (even if they are of the same religion as the enemy) — are skirted.

In other words, the traditional legal and societal strictures that classical Islamic thought set in place to regulate the conduct of *jihad*, particularly *jihad qital*, have been ignored by the author of this booklet.

BERJIHAD DI PATTANI (THE CONDUCT OF A HOLY STRUGGLE IN PATTANI)

The nexus between history, religion, identity, and education climaxed on 28 April 2004, when militants undertook an audacious series of coordinated attacks across Pattani, Yala, and Songkhla that ended in the massacre of thirty-two militants and one civilian at the historical Krisek (Krue Se) mosque. It was after this attack that security officials uncovered a controversial Jawi manuscript entitled *Berjihad di Pattani* (Holy Struggle for Pattani). According to reports, *Berjihad* was found on the bodies of several dead militants in Krisek and is believed to have circulated in a number of Islamic schools in the southern provinces, becoming not only part of their curriculum but of the resistance narrative as well. In other words, the book highlighted the salience of historical memory and offered a systematic if theologically flawed articulation of the religious dimensions of the southern Thai conflict.

Allegedly penned in an obscure town in Kelantan (northern Malaysia), *Berjihad di Pattani* calls categorically for a holy war of liberation for the kingdom of Patani from "colonialists".[112] Liberally peppered with metaphorical references and verses from the Qur'an, *Berjihad* reflects in its polemics the familiar radical Islamist diatribe that conjures a Manichean world struggle between Islam and the *Jahiliyyah*.[113] That aside, what is striking about *Berjihad* is the objectives to which Islamic idioms are directed — mobilization of the population to support and sacrifice for the reinstatement of Patani Darussalam. Alluding to the historical struggle for Patani, the author wrote:

> We should be ashamed of ourselves for sitting idly and doing nothing while the colonialists trampled our brothers and sisters. The wealth that belongs to us have been seized. Our rights and freedom have been curbed, and our religion and culture has been sullied .... Our late parents, brothers, and sisters sacrificed their lives for their land as warriors; they left behind a generation with warrior blood flowing in their veins. Today, let us make a call, so that the warrior blood will flow again and the generation will emerge again.[114]

He calls specifically for martyrdom, which emerges as a central theme in the book, in order to fulfil this objective: "*Wira Shuhada* (martyrs), how glorious we will be if we fall as warriors of our land.... When Martyrs are killed, they are not dead but alive next to God ... (and) will watch and listen to every piece of news to see if their children will follow in their footsteps".[115] Another striking feature of the polemics in *Berjihad* is the writer's attack not only on "colonialists" as *Jahili* (people of ignorance), but also on Muslims. For instance, he suggests that while some Muslims may be performing the Five Pillars of the faith, "their actions or practices are a disguise, for their hearts are filled with hatred and fury against Islam".[116] Later, he assails them as "*Munafikin*" or hypocrites, saying that "Allah not only forbids us from electing the hypocrites as leaders, but Allah also forbids the believers from offering prayers for the dear hypocrites and from standing at their graves to offer prayer".[117] *Berjihad* is equally notable for what is *not* mentioned in its exegesis — the spectre of global *jihadi* struggle that so pre-occupies many Muslim militants and terrorists today is not raised, nor are the anti-Western and anti-Zionist motivations that fixate Islamists and *jihadis* worldwide. In fact, the book does not even allude to Muslim suffering and persecution elsewhere in the *ummah*. Even in its highly polemical and ideological form, the points of reference in *Berjihad* are specific, narrow, exclusive, and local.

There are several points worth noting in this attempt to mobilize religion for the justification of violence in southern Thailand. First, and perhaps most important for current purposes, is that the numerous *surah* citations fail to disguise the political nature of the document. The author of *Berjihad* makes it very clear that his objective is the liberation of Patani and the creation of a separate state. Even the question of the Islamic character of this new state and the implementation of the *shari'a*, for which all card-carrying Islamists labour ceaselessly (albeit often with their own interpretations), receives only passing mention and appears secondary to this overarching objective. Unlike the highly ideological Sayyid Qutb, the author is not interested in delving into the titanic struggle between Dar Al-Islam and Dar Al-Harb, nor is he overly concerned about the alleged global threat posed by the *Jahili* to Islam, even if this is alluded to at a few token junctures without any further elaboration. The sole concern of *Berjihad* is, in its own words, the "liberation of our beloved country" from "the disbelievers' occupation". This fundamentally contradicts the account provided in a Time Magazine report that mistakenly claimed "paucity of references to the liberation of the south" in *Berjihad* stating, "it looks like they don't care for autonomy".[118] In fact, much effort is directed at rekindling memories of the Malay-Muslim "freedom fighters" and "*jihad* warriors" of a previous generation who fought and died valiantly for the same political cause. The final chapter tellingly provides a systematic exposition of the executive and legislative elements of the Patani state that would be established after the ejection of the "colonialists". Of particular interest is the fact that the "rightful" leader of the new state of Patani is envisaged to be "a royalty related to the Sultan of Kelantan".[119] This speaks not only to the historical ties that Malay-Muslims share across the Thai-Malaysian border, but also to the *ancien régime*, whose reinstatement appears to be the objective of the *Berjihad* separatists. In this way, the book contravenes one of the fundamental themes of Islam — that the faith supplants tribal identities and ties.

Berjihad is also notable for its attempts to amplify latent antagonisms within the Muslim community in Thailand. The fact that the author engages indirectly in *takfir* (the highly politicized exercise of labelling fellow Muslims as infidels often associated with radical Salafis and Wahhabis) and makes blatant calls for the martyrdom fighters to attack Muslim "hypocrites" betrays an attempt to capitalize on existing fissures within the Thai Muslim community. The document reserves its most virulent attacks for members of the Muslim elite who have been co-opted into the Thai state. At one point, the author disparages the practice of veneration often associated with Shi'a Islam, though not exclusive to it. Part of his overall condemnation of Thai Muslims in positions of authority conceivably includes a veiled attack on the Chularajmontri as well.[120]

On the other hand, the demonstrations of orthodoxy associated with the condemnation of Shi'a practices paper over the influence of Sufi and animistic beliefs and practices blended into *Berjihad* and the events of April 28. Many of the religious rites associated with the April 28 attacks bore the imprint of militant Sufism seen previously in Chechnya, Sudan, Morocco, and Algeria. Numerous reports spoke of how the militants had engaged in practices such as the use of prayer beads, holy water, and "consecrated sand".[121] This connection with mysticism was also confirmed when Abdulwahab Datu, headmaster of Tarpia Tulwatan Mullaniti Islamic School in Yala, informed security officials during interrogation that he had been acquainted with the author of *Berjihad* (Poh Su Ismail) but had subsequently distanced himself because he questioned the latter's belief in and employment of supernatural powers.[122] References to Sufi beliefs are also contained in the *Berjihad* document itself, particularly in relation to physical invincibility.[123] Given the esoteric nature of this brand of Sufism, it was not surprising to discover that the militants in the attacks were apparently covertly recruited and indoctrinated in liberation ideology — through small study groups or cells based in religious schools.[124]

Notes

1   Iik A. Mansurnoor, "Intellectual Networking among Muslim Scholars in Southeast Asia with a Special Reference to Patani Works on Society, Coexistence and External Relations" (paper presented at the First Inter-Dialogue Conference on Southern Thailand, Pattani, 13–15 June 2002), p. 5.

2   Martin van Bruinessen, "Kitab Kuning: Books in Arabic Script Used in the Pesantren Milieu", *Bijdragen tot de Taal-, Land- en Volkenkunde* 146 (1990): 226–69; Saroja Dorairajoo, "From Mecca to Yala: Negotiating Islam in Present-Day Southern Thailand" (paper presented at the symposium Islam in Southeast Asia and China: Regional Faithlines and Faultlines in the Global Ummah, City University of Hong Kong, 28 Nov–1 Dec 2002), pp. 11–13.

3   See Virginia Matheson and M.B. Hooker, "Jawi Literature in Patani: The Maintenance of an Islamic Tradition", *JMBRAS* 61, no. 1 (1988): 14–15; "Al-Ghazaly Modern Syekh Nawawi Al-Bantani", <www.sufinews.com> (accessed 8 April 2004). See also Mohd. Noor bin Ngah, *Kitab Jawi: Islamic Thought of the Malay-Muslim Scholars* (Singapore: ISEAS, 1983).

4   See Peter Riddell, *Islam in the Malay-Indonesian World: Transmission and Responses* (Hawaii: University of Hawaii Press, 2001), pp. 199–200. See also Hasan Madmarn, "Traditional Muslim Institutions in Southern Thailand: A Critical Study of Islamic Education and Arabic Influence in the Pondok and Madrasah Systems of Patani" (Ph.D. dissertation, University of Utah, 1990).

5   Alexander Horstmann, *Class, Culture and Space: The Construction and Shaping of Communal Space in South Thailand* (Tokyo: Research Institute for the Languages and Cultures of Asia and Africa, 2002), p. 74.

6   According to scholars at the College of Islamic Studies, Prince of Songkhla University, most *ustaz* in southern Thailand are specialists/graduates in *shari'a* and *usul-uddin*. Very few are specialists in *fiqh*. While the popularity of *pondok* and Islamic private schools in the current milieu depends much on expertise in specific aspects of Islamic curriculum among their teachers, on the basis of teacher qualifications it appears that *shari'a* is by far the most popular topic and one that can be considered a forte of the Islamic education system in Thailand insofar as the Malay-Muslim provinces are concerned. This was confirmed in random interviews with some thirty Islamic private school teachers between January and April 2005.

7   Interview at Sad Samaki School, Pattani, 16 January 2006.

8   Interview with Ismail Lutfi, Pattani, 14 January 2006. This view was reinforced in the course of an interview with a reformist *ustaz*, who opined that there was "no need" to privilege a particular Mazhab. Telephone interview, 16 January 2006.

9   This includes the reformist tradition associated with Muhammad Ibn Abd Al-Wahab. Natana Delong-Bas reminds us that Wahhab was in fact schooled in the classical schools of jurisprudence and as such was able to declare his continuity with the Islamic intellectual tradition, thereby "exonerating him from the charges of his critics that he was engaged in innovation (*bid'a*)." See Natana J. Delong-Bas, *Wahhabi Islam: From Revival and Reform to Global Jihad* (London and New York: I.B. Tauris, 2004), p. 282. It is important to note, however, that while the reformists were proponents of *ijtihad*, in practice it was never something that was permitted for all Muslims. Indeed, the reformist-Wahhabi position remains that it is the religious scholar who is deemed qualified to exercise *ijtihad*.

10 Muhammad Nur bin Muhammad bin Ismail Ismail Al-Fatani, *Kifayah Al-Muhtadi* [Provision for a Person Who Receives Guidance] (Pattani: Muhammad An-Nahdi and Sons Publication House, 1932), p. 1.

11 The Muktazilites adopted an allegorical understanding and refused to accept the literal meaning of the phrase because they saw it as tantamount to attributing

human traits to God. This position is represented by the great Islamic philosophers such as Ibn Sina or Avicenna (980–1037) and Ibn Rushd or Averroes (1126–1198), who were of the view that while God was fundamentally indefinable, he nevertheless existed within the framework of human reason, and hence all theological arguments must stand the scrutiny of principles of rational thought and philosophy. On the other hand, the Salafi position represented by the Asharite school maintains that while human reason is important, it must be subordinated to the Qur'an and *sunnah* of the Prophet. They counter the Muktazilite emphasis on rationality by arguing that reliance on rational speculation would negate the need for prophets and revelations, and this would lead to the dominance of the will of man over the will of God. To them, human reason and rationality was ambiguous and changing, whereas holy scripture was stable and unchanging.

[12] Muhammad Nur, *Kifayah Al-Muhtadi*, p. 11.

[13] Ibid., pp. 95–96.

[14] See "Al-Qunut in salatul fajr" <http://www.usc.edu/dept/MSA/law/fiqhussunnah/fus2_13.html> (Accessed 12 September 2007). This opinion is also shared by the Hanafi and Hanbali schools of jurisprudence.

[15] See Ismail Lutfi Japakiya, *Hayat Tayyibah: Dari Kalimat Tayyibah Hingga Masakin Tayyibah* [The Good Life: From A Good Word to A Good Abode] (Pattani: Majlis Al-Ilm Fattani, 2001), pp. 38–39.

[16] Syeikh Samad al-Talimbani, *Hidayatul Salatin* [Guidance for Sultans] (Pattani, n.d.) , p. 40.

[17] Ibid., p. 49.

[18] Raymond Scupin, ed., *Aspects of Development: Islamic Education in Thailand and Malaysia* (Bangi: Institut Bahasa Kesusasteraan dan Kebudayaan Melayu, Universiti Kebangsaan Malaysia, 1990), p. 8.

[19] Michel Gilquin, *The Muslims of Thailand*. Translated by Michael Smithies (Chiang Mai: Silkworm Books, 2005), p. 57.

[20] Scupin, ed., *Aspects of Development*, p. 8.

[21] Ismail Lutfi Fatani, *Ikhtilaf Ad-Darain wa Atsaruhu fi Ahkam Al-Munakahat wa Al-Muamalat* [The Effect of Two Dars (Dar Al-Islam and Dar Al-Harb) on Islamic Personal and Transaction Laws], pp. 72–73.

[22] Interview at Chongraksat Witthaya, Pattani, 14 February 2006.

[23] Ibid.

[24] During the course of fieldwork interviews in January 2006 religious teachers from at least three Islamic private schools expressed this opinion. Given the controversial nature of such perspectives and their possible implications, I have decided to withhold the names of these schools.

[25] Hasan Madmarn, *Pondok and Madrasah*. Bangi: Penerbit Universiti Kebangsaan Malaysia, 1999, p. 124.

[26] Ibid., p. 84.

[27] "Teaching Thai: Innovative approach blends in Malay", *The Nation*, 14 August 2005.

28   Hasan Madmarn, *Pondok and Madrasah*, p. 88.

29   Ibrahim Shukri, *Sejarah Kerajaan Melayu Patani* [History of the Malay Kingdom of Patani], translated by Conner Bailey and John Miksic (Athens, OH: Centre for International Studies, Ohio University, 1985); Nik Anuar Nik Mahmud, *Sejarah Perjuangan Melayu Patani, 1785–1954* [History of the Struggle of the Patani Malays, 1785–1954] (Bangi: Penerbit Universiti Kebangsaan Malaysia, 1999).

30   A more contemptuous attitude towards Siam can be found in the *Hikayat Kelantan* (Kelantan Annals), where Kelantan Rajas apparently dismissed Siamese as "uncivilized infidels". See Mohd Taib Osman, "Hikayat Seri Kelantan" [The History of Seri Kelantan] (M.A. dissertation, University of Malaya, 1961).

31   Shukri, *Sejarah Kerajaan* [History of the Government], p. 77.

32   Ibid., p. 75.

33   See Abdullah Zaidi bin Hassan, "*Syaikh Ahmad Bin Muhammad Zain Al-Fatani — Pemikir Bangsa*" [Syaikh Ahmad Bin Muhammad Zain Al-Fatani — The Nation's Thinker] <http://www.geocities.com/traditionalislam/syaikh_ahmad_alFatani.htm> (accessed 15 August 2006). See also Wan Mohd Shaghir Abdullah, *Syaikh Ahmad al-Fatani* (Kuala Lumpur: Khazanah Fathaniah, n.d.).

34   Interview with a Yala-based Muslim educator, Bangkok, 12 July 2005.

35   See Andrew Cornish, *Whose Place is This? Malay Rubber Producers and Thai Government Officials in Yala* (Bangkok: White Lotus Press, 1997).

36   Quoted in Teddy Prasetyo, "Thailand: Buddhism-Islam dialogue aimed at ending violence and promoting greater religious understanding", *Current Dialogue (World Council of Churches)* 46 (December 2005) <www.wcc-coe.org/wcc/what/interreligious/cd46-12.html> (accessed 26 June 2007).

37   Email interview with an *ustazah*, 10 July 2006.

38   Interview at Tabia Witthaya, Yala, 2 August 2006.

39   Email interview with an *ustazah*, 10 July 2006.

40   Ismail Lutfi Fatani, *Ikhtilaf Ad-Darain wa Atsaruhu fi Ahkam Al-Munakahat wa Al-Muamalat* [The Effect of Two Dars (Dar Al-Islam and Dar Al-Harb) on Islamic Personal and Transaction Laws] Second Edition (Dar As-Salam, Cairo, 1998), pp. 86–87.

41   Ibid., p. 57.

42   Ibid., pp. 33–35; 72–74.

43   Ibid., p. 57.

44   Ibid., pp. 53–57.

45   *Zimmi* enjoy rights of protection for their lives and property and freedom to practise their religion while under Muslim rule. In return, they carry the following responsibilities: payment of *jizyah* in lieu of military service, upholding Islamic law in contracts, transactions, and torts, avoidance of blasphemous acts towards Islam and Muslims, and prohibition from committing any act in public that is permissible to them but forbidden in Islam, i.e. consumption of alcohol.

46   Ibid., pp. 68–70.

47   Ibid., pp. 70–72.

48   Ibid., pp. 66–68.
49   Ibid., p. 72.
50   Ibid., pp. 72–73.
51   Ibid., pp. 73–74.
52   Ibid., pp. 75–76.
53   Ibid., p. 77.
54   Ibid., pp. 81–84.
55   Ibid., pp. 84–87.
56   Ibid., p. 93.
57   Ibid., pp. 96–100.
58   Ibid., pp. 104–7.
59   Ibid., pp. 111–12.
60   Ibid., pp. 112–25.
61   Lutfi further elaborates that such a contract may be permanent or temporary. A permanent contract of Al-Aman by a non-Muslim with a Dar Al-Islam can only be made if he agrees to be a *zimmi*. A temporary contract is made when a person enters a country (i.e., a Muslim or *zimmi* enters a Dar Al-Harb or a non-Muslim enters a Dar Al-Islam) with proper permit as a official, trader, or visitor on other purposes. In today's context, such a permit may only be issued by a government although an individual could be the guarantor. A *mustamin* is protected from any aggression towards his life or property. The contract of Al-Aman binds all Muslims. See ibid., pp. 127–30.
62   Such agreement is permissible in Islam but not obligatory. The agreement must accord with the interest of Muslims. Although the agreement cannot be a permanent one, there is no restriction to the length of the period. The length is determined based on need and interest(s). Also, the agreement can only be made by a Muslim ruler or his representative on behalf of Muslims. Like *mustamin*, *muwadi* is similarly protected. See ibid., pp. 131–35.
63   Ibid., pp. 137–39.
64   If found in Dar Al-Islam without proper permit of entry, a *harbi* can be taken prisoner or killed and his property may be confiscated. However, the government has the power to pardon him.
65   See Human Rights Watch, "No One is Safe: Insurgent Attacks on Civilians in Thailand's Southern Border Provinces", *Human Rights Watch* 19, no. 13(C) (August 2007): 6.
66   Interview with Ismail Lutfi, Pattani, 14 January 2006.
67   Ismail Lutfi Japakiya, *Islam Agama Penjana Kedamaian Sejagat* [Islam as the Pathway to Harmony] (Alor Star: Pustaka Darussalam, 2005), p. 2.
68   Ibid., p. 22.
69   Ibid., pp. 46–47.
70   Ibid., p. 49.
71   Ibid., p. 50.
72   Ibid., pp. 69–76.

73 Ibid., p. 70.
74 Ibid., pp. 71–72.
75 Ibid., p. 74.
76 Ibid., pp. 74–75.
77 Ibid., pp. 50–53.
78 Ibid., p. 51.
79 Ibid., p. 52.
80 Ibid., p. 65.
81 Ibid., p. 66.
82 According to Lutfi, although Muslims were being massacred by Christians, Salahuddin opted for a kinder, gentler touch and demonstrated patience and tolerance towards the Christians. Even as Salahuddin neared victory, he would pardon the perpetrators in full knowledge that these enemies would return to fight him once they had regained their strength.
83 Ismail Lutfi, *Islam Agama Penjana Kedamaian Sejagat*, pp. 66–67.
84 Ibid., p. 68.
85 Ibid., pp. 76–77.
86 Ibid., p. 77.
87 Ibid., pp. 79–83.
88 Interview with Ismail Lutfi, Pattani, 14 January 2006.
89 Ismail Lutfi, *Islam Penjana Kedamaian Sejagat*, p. 76.
90 Ibid., p. 81.
91 Interview at Markaz Dakwah Yala, Yala, 14 January 2006. This *ustaz*, however, was not specific as to what he meant by the "conditions" for *jihad qital*.
92 *Ustaz* interview, Pattani, 8 May 2006.
93 *Ustaz* interview, Pattani, 10 May 2006.
94 This anecdote was shared by Don Pathan during a seminar at the Rajaratnam School of International Studies, Singapore, 9 July 2007.
95 Owing to the sensitivity of this topic, not many *ustaz* were prepared to comment. Only those from Azizstan and Bamrung Islam were prepared to share their perspective on *jihad*.
96 Hassan Hikmatullah, *Jihad Fi Sabilillah Pengertian dan Bidang* [The Understanding and Call for Struggle in the Way of Allah], n.d., p. 4.
97 Ibid., p. 5.
98 Ibid., p. 9.
99 Ibid., p. 38.
100 Ibid., p. 10.
101 Ibid., pp. 11–32.
102 Ibid., pp. 34–35.
103 Ibid., p. 36.
104 Ibid., p. 39.
105 Ibid., p. 44.
106 Ibid., p. 45.

107 Ibid., p. 46.
108 Ibid., pp. 47–53.
109 *Ustaz* interview, Pattani, 13 January 2006.
110 See Muhammad Haniff Hassan and Mohamed bin Ali, *Questions and Answers on Jihad* (Singapore: The Islamic Religious Council of Singapore (MUIS), 2007), p. 6.
111 Al-Quran 2:193.
112 The author of *Berjihad di Pattani* is believed to be a Kelantan native who has gone by the aliases of Poh Su, Poh Su Ismail, and Ismail Jaafar.
113 *Berjihad Di Pattani*, author's personal copy, 10 August 2002, p. 2.
114 Ibid., p. 5.
115 Ibid. The author cites *Al-I-Imran* 3:169 to substantiate this call, and *Hadith Shaheeh Muslim*, book 1, p. 65, Hadith 113 to justify the use of violence.
116 Ibid., p. 8.
117 Ibid., p. 9.
118 See "Southern Front", *Time*, 11 October 2004. Needless to say, the report's claims do not appear to be accurate, according to my copy of *Berjihad di Pattani*.
119 *Berjihad*, p. 24.
120 The author writes to the following effect: "Allah not only forbids us from electing the hypocrites as leaders, but Allah forbids the believers from offering prayers for the dead hypocrites and from standing at their graves to offer prayer." Ibid., p. 9.
121 Report of the Independent Fact-Finding Commission on the Krue Se Incident, released on 24 April 2005.
122 "Imam admits to contact with separatists", *The Nation*, 1 September 2004.
123 For instance, at one point the author writes: "We Muslims, who believe in Allah and the Prophet, never rely on modern weapons. It is an obligation for us to hope for Allah's help. For He is the only One who has weapons that are most powerful and have the greatest capabilities"; and elsewhere, "If Allah is willing, a rain of bullets could not harm us". See *Berjihad*, p. 7 and p. 17.
124 This was verified during the interrogations of some suspected of involvement with the 28 April militants. See "Imam admits to contact with separatists", *The Nation*, 1 September 2004. This was also confirmed in my interview with military intelligence officials in Bangkok on July 13, 2005, where they opined that the 28 April event "was not linked to the central leadership of the insurgency".

5

NETWORKS AND CROSSCURRENTS

The previous chapters have demonstrated how Islamic education has become the frontline in the battle for influence and adherence between traditionalist and reformist Muslim scholars and community leaders in southern Thailand. By way of the *Kaum Tua–Kaum Muda* intellectual and theological contestation of the past, the book has discussed the intellectual underpinnings of the newly emergent reformist movement, which has taken a decidedly Salafist doctrinal and epistemological bent. Not only do traditionalists have to face the increasingly formidable challenge presented by the reformists, including proponents of literalist constructions of Islam, but they also have to contend with other representations of the faith that have emerged on southern Thailand's socio-religious landscape over the past few years, These are not only gaining popularity, but also jostling for legitimacy, authenticity, and influence. Two in particular warrant mention — the *Jemaat Tabligh* and Shi'a Islam.

Though the *Jemaat Tabligh* and Shi'a Islam had established a presence in the southern provinces by the mid-twentieth century, their activism accelerated considerably between 1980 and 1996 as a result of two factors. First, the early 1980s witnessed the intensification of a global Islamic awakening that rode the waves of the Iranian Revolution and the Mujahideen struggle against Soviet imperialism in Afghanistan in 1979. The Revolution represented the triumph of Islam over a superpower-backed authoritarian regime and the creation of a modern Islamic polity, signalling the emergence of an authentic Islamic ideology that could challenge the hegemony and dominance of Western conceptualizations of statehood. Needless to say, southern Thailand was not immune as the psychological impact of the Revolution rippled across the Muslim world. Describing the impact of the Revolution on Muslims in southern Thailand, Surin Pitsuwan remarked:

> I think the context of the situation certainly has led people to express their grievances in Islamic terms, in religious terms. It is not an abuse in Islam. It is not an abuse of Islamic teachings. They are trying to express the situation in Islamic terms in their Islamic worldview and it is very powerful.[1]

Together with the Mujahideen resistance against the Soviet invasion of Afghanistan which rallied Muslims from across the world to the cause of *jihad*, the Iranian Revolution was a symbol of the empowerment of the *ummah*. Second, this period also coincided with greater political openness in Thailand as a result of democratization. In tandem with the surge in Islamic consciousness and activism, this process of democratization provided the conditions for new Islamic groups and movements to assert a noticeable presence and gain a foothold in the kingdom.

THE *JEMAAT TABLIGH* MOVEMENT

The *Jemaat Tabligh* is an increasingly assertive socio-religious force in the Thai Muslim community that is rooted in broader reformist tradition. An Islamic grassroots *dakwah* (missionary) movement focused on the "purification" of the Islamic community, the *Jemaat Tabligh* originated from the South Asian continent as part of an Islamic reform movement of the mid-nineteenth century emphasizing religiosity, observance, and personal devotion. The focus of *Tabligh* activism is the replication of the Prophetic lifestyle as dictated in the *hadith*. This expression of religiosity, the *Tabligh* movement further maintains, is open to lay preachers and worshippers and not solely confined to a coterie of religious scholars. By this token, the most vivid expression of *Tabligh* activism has been the missionary travels of Muslim commoners and lay preachers alike.

While the activities of *Jemaat Tabligh* are highly mobile, decentralized, and transnational in nature, in southern Thailand most of its activities are centred at the Markaz Dakwah Yala in the outskirts of Yala town and to a lesser extent in Bangkok, where *shura* councils consisting of groups of elders meet to vet the readiness of followers to conduct their *dakwah*, which is usually either three days a month or forty days a year. *Tabligh* members come from varied backgrounds, include professionals such as engineers, doctors, teachers, lawyers, and university students, as well as farmers and businessmen.[2]

The genesis of the *Tabligh* movement in southern Thailand can be traced to the 1960s, when *Jemaat* (missionary groups) from Kota Bahru (Malaysia), led by the son-in-law of *Jemaat Tabligh* founder Muhammad Ilyas, visited Yala and established the first *Tabligh* centre there. It was in the 1980s, though, that the popularity of *Jemaat Tabligh* really expanded. The first Markaz Dakwah Jemaat in Thailand, also known as Masjid Jami', was established in 1983 by Ustaz Abdurrahman Phatlung in Sungei Golok, Narathiwat, in close proximity to Rantau Panjang in the northern Malaysian state of Kelantan, which also hosts a significant *Jemaat Tabligh* presence. In 1993, the Markaz Dakwah Jemaat relocated to its current premises in Yala which cover 1.5 acres. The building was constructed at a cost of 110 million baht (approximately US$3 million) which, according to members of the community, was collected from *zakat* among followers and *waqf* from commercial and residential properties located in the vicinity. Occasional contributions have also been made by foreign pilgrims who visit the Markaz Dakwah Yala to undertake their own *dakwah*.

The presence of several notable religious teachers among the ranks of the *Jemaat Tabligh* lent a much-needed credibility to the hitherto unfamiliar Islamic movement which locals observed with a mix of interest and caution. Among the more prominent of these leaders were Ustaz Mahmud bin Hayee Ismail, trained in Islamic studies first at Pondok Paderu in Yala and then in *dakwah* at universities in Jordan and Pakistan. Mahmud established Madrasah Tahfiz Alkuran, the first religious school in southern Thailand known to be associated with the *Jemaat Tabligh*, in Yala province approximately fifty years ago. Aside from local *dakwah* activities, Mahmud has given southern Thailand's *Jemaat Tabligh* movement the status of an international brand with his *Tabligh* work in Asia, Europe, and Africa. According to educators at Madrasah Tahfiz Alkuran, the school was established for the purpose of "returning Muslims to the Qur'an so as to attain true spiritual peace in their lives similar to that which the followers of the holy Prophet enjoyed".[3] Another prominent religious teacher associated with the *Jemaat Tabligh* is Ustaz Zakaria Al-Fathoni. Based in Yala, Ustaz Zakaria is a popular *Tabligh* speaker widely travelled in the Southeast Asian region. He is the head of *Jemaat Mastura*, the female arm of the *Jemaat Tabligh*.[4]

There are around sixty schools in Thailand that have either been directly established by *Jemaat Tabligh* or are closely affiliated with it. Known by the generic name of Madrasah Tahfiz Alkuran after the original school in Yaha, Yala, most of these schools are located around Bangkok (Minburi), Nakhon Si Thammarat, Tak (Mae-sod), Yala (Klorek and Bachok), and Narathiwat (Sungei Golok, Dusun Nyor, and Chanet).[5] The original Madrasah Tahfiz

Alkuran is a three-building institution currently headed by Al-Hafiz Abdullah Yamaloh. Unlike mainstream Islamic private schools, *Tabligh* schools are wholly private institutions as they are not registered with the government. Many are in fact recipients of support from South African *Tabligh* organizations and members. The students who graduate from these local *Tabligh* schools often proceed to Pakistan to further their Islamic education in schools linked to the *Jemaat Tabligh*.[6] Between the Markaz Dakwah Yala, whose religious classes are supervised by Ustaz Abdurrahman Phatlung, and Madrasah Tahfiz Alkuran, which remains the largest *Tabligh*-linked religious school in southern Thailand, *Jemaat Tabligh* schools have approximately 5,000 students in total.[7] Most of these students either have or will proceed to *Tabligh* institutions in South Africa, Yemen, Sudan, Jordan, Pakistan, Bangladesh, and India.[8]

Despite the fact that they run several *madrasah* throughout the country, as elsewhere in Southeast Asia, the *Jemaat Tabligh* does not advocate an institutionalized track of formal education, at least not in the manner of mainstream Islamic schools. Preaching and teaching in the various *Tabligh* centres, as well as in the course of *dakwah* activities, generally focus on the key *Tabligh* text, *Tablighi Nisaab*, written by Maulana Zakariyyah Khandelwi. This text is the cornerstone of the *Tabligh* Islamic studies curriculum, along with the *Fazail A'maal*, a collection of *hadith* written in Urdu. Lessons on *tahfiz al-Quran* are also conducted for younger members of the *Jemaat Tabligh* community. Beyond that, occasional religious lectures and lessons are conducted at the *Tabligh* centre, including some that focus on polemics and debating skills for the purpose of countering the evangelism of other religious groups, particularly Christian, and to a lesser extent Hindu, missionaries.[9] Newly initiated *Tabligh* members are taught Urdu, the language of the global *Jemaat Tabligh* movement, in preparation for transborder *dakwah Tabligh* activity.[10] Apart from *Tabligh*-linked schools, it should be noted that many *Tabligh* members are also teachers and students in mainstream Islamic private schools. The apparent separation between *Tabligh* education and conventional Islamic education is less clear than at first glance.[11]

While *Jemaat Tabligh* groups often come under intense scrutiny elsewhere, in Thailand the movement has mostly been left alone by the Thai government. Indeed, the government has endorsed and supported the movement. This is evident from actions such as Bangkok's support for an inaugural *Tabligh* convention in 1982 at an army camp in Kai Sirintong, Pattani. From the Thai government's perspective, supporting the *Jemaat Tabligh* has yielded welcome dividends: large numbers of Malay-Muslim separatists and insurgents have evidently abandoned their struggle and surrendered their arms after taking up membership in the *Jemaat*.[12] The influence of the *Jemaat Tabligh* in

Thailand peaked during the period 1986–96, when it was led by the charismatic Emir Yusoff Khan Pakara, a native of Tak province. Since his passing, the movement has become somewhat decentralized, with several centres of *Jemaat Tabligh* activity throughout the south and in Bangkok, mostly operating independently of each other. The *Jemaat Tabligh* in Thailand continues to enjoy strong ties with Pakistan, Bangladesh, and increasingly as noted earlier, South Africa. The current *Tabligh* centre, the 1.5-acre Markaz Dakwah Yala, is arguably the largest *Tabligh* centre in the Asia-Pacific region and has been endowed with a special sanctity in the eyes of local Muslims. A lecturer at the Yala Islamic University enthused: "I love to pray at the Markaz because it is almost like praying in Mecca".[13] Needless to say, the popularity of the Markaz is not confined to locals: co-religionists from Cambodia, Indonesia, Malaysia, Singapore, and the Philippines are also drawn to the Yala centre and regularly visit the mosque to undertake their own *dakwah*.

As a *dakwah* movement, the *Jemaat Tabligh* differs from others in that it concentrates its efforts in rural communities.[14] Since the mid-1980s, *Jemaat Tabligh* adherents, including foreign *Jemaat*, have been travelling regularly to Muslim villages in the southern provinces as part of their *dakwah*, preaching their own version of a pure Islam along the way.[15] *Tabligh* members liken this to the Prophet's own missionary efforts as a travelling teacher and preacher, which they attempt to emulate in their endeavour to spread Islam's message throughout the region. These *Jemaat Tabligh* members are known to visit most, if not all, of the villages in the southern provinces at least once a week, and to cover every house in each village. The *Tabligh* movement in southern Thailand is led by locals who are usually educated in Pakistan. They support the groups of *Tabligh* travelling preachers who undertake door-to-door preaching. They also organize study circles at local mosques called *Masjidwar Jemaat*. An estimated thirty of the sixty *tahfiz* schools associated with the movement are located in the southern provinces. In most instances, enrolment figures in these schools are small. Nevertheless, true to the transnational nature of the movement, as well as the legacy and reputation of Ustaz Mahmud, the activism of Thailand's *Jemaat Tabligh* movement extends beyond Thai borders. For example, several prominent Thai *Tabligh* members are religious teachers and *imam* (including Imam Salat Tarawih or leaders of the Ramadhan prayers) in Malaysia and Brunei Darussalam.

Jemaat Tabligh members are known for their ascetic lifestyle. Replicating the Prophet's *hijrah* (migration from Mecca to Medina), the *Jemaat Tabligh* is in essence a "revolving door" movement, where *Tabligh* members are recruited "on-the-move" and often leave their homes and villages for periods ranging from three days to four months in order to undertake *dakwah*. Some *ustaz* even leave their schools, sometimes indefinitely, for the purpose of undertaking their *dakwah*. This austere approach to prosyletization, however, has been criticized by traditionalist and reformist scholars alike. In other words, the emergence of the *Jemaat Tabligh* has introduced another layer of complexity to the tensions within the Muslim community in Thailand, particularly in the south.

In the local community, there is considerable disagreement about the *Jemaat Tabligh* as a new interpretation of the faith and expression of religiosity. Some feel it is the epitome of piety while others assail it as misguided, and for misguiding Muslims. Reasons cited for opposing the *Tabligh* movement range from the practical to the epistemological, theological, and doctrinal. On a mundane level, the *thawb* (white robes) and *taqiya* (turbans) worn by *Jemaat Tabligh* members to imitate the dress of the Prophet as well as to ward off the devil, are foreign to the southern Thai provinces. More substantive differences lie beneath the surface, particularly between the *Jemaat Tabligh* and some Salafi reformists. In the main, the latter have raised doubts as to the doctrinal authenticity and purity of the *Jemaat Tabligh* and criticized its apparent use of Sufi techniques to instruct new recruits on meditation and self-control.[16] The opposition of Salafi reformists may be explained at least in part by the fact that the *Jemaat Tabligh* is frowned upon in Saudi Arabia, a major source of reformist thinking. Religious scholars have further argued that an approach to *dakwah* which results in what they consider to be the abandonment of family and, in the case of religious teachers who take leave from their schools, neglect of educational responsibilities, is not representative of the Prophet and the Salaf. Indeed, an *ustaz* interviewed remarked tersely that some *Tabligh* members were setting a bad example, for "while they ventured to other villages to preach, their wives back home do not pray nor wear the headscarf, and the children are left without a disciplinarian".[17] He noted that participation in *Tabligh* activities also meant that women had to support the household in their husband's absence, and this had a negative effect on child discipline at home.[18] Another traditionalist teacher accused the "*dakwah* people" (which *Tabligh* members are sometimes referred to colloquially) of being closed-minded: "When I asked them about what their wife and children are going to eat, they said God's work is above everything else. All they say is *Allah* this, *Allah* that. *Dakwah* is about form and not much substance".[19]

Intellectually, some Salafi reformist scholars dismiss the *Tabligh* movement altogether, disparaging its members as Muslims who are "misdirected". *Jemaat Tabligh* members have been criticized for their purportedly weak knowledge of Islam. For instance, *Tabligh* instructors are often taken to task for their alleged use of "lesser" *hadith* such as those contained in the *Fazail A'maal*.[20] Similarly, the *Jemaat Tabligh* has been treated with considerable caution by certain segments of the orthodox Malay-Muslim Shafi'i-Sunni community because of the pressure it exerts on these communities to turn away from their age-old cultural traditions. Hence, while some Salafi reformists view the *Jemaat Tabligh* as "too Sufi" in orientation, traditionalists are of the converse opinion that it is "not Sufi enough". As in the case of Salafi reformist influence, in the eyes of traditionalists and orthodox Muslims the *Jemaat Tabligh* threatens to undermine traditional Thai Islam and polarize Muslim society. In fact, anthropologists have documented that the tension between the *Jemaat Tabligh* and traditional/orthodox Muslims is expressed, for example, in encounters where younger, more charismatic *Jemaat Tabligh* leaders overtly contest the stature and authority of senior teachers and *imam* in the *pondok*, Islamic private schools, and local mosques.[21] The profile of *Jemaat Tabligh* leaders in Thailand also differs from those of the orthodox Malay-Muslim community in terms of their education: the former are usually educated in Pakistan and the latter in Saudi Arabia, Egypt, and Indonesia. It is unclear, however, if this contributes further to the gulf between the movement and its more orthodox and traditionalist counterparts.

Notwithstanding its detractors, the *Jemaat Tabligh* clearly has its fair share of local sympathizers and supporters. Some traditional Muslims take a more accepting view and suggest that *Tabligh* activism, among other things, offers an avenue for poor Muslims to practise or renew their Islamic faith. Some traditionalist *ustaz* interviewed saw no problems with *Jemaat Tabligh*, while others believe that the increasing influence of the *Tabligh* movement in Thailand is not necessarily a bad thing. While it is difficult to ascertain exact figures, two important observations may be made. First, the *Jemaat Tabligh* is indeed expanding its activities.[22] *Jemaat Tabligh* members have been canvassing southern Thai Muslim communities vigorously over the past few years, and the likelihood that every village in the three Malay-Muslim provinces of Yala, Pattani, and Narathiwat has *Tabligh* members in their midst is very high.[23] Second, like the reformists, the *Jemaat Tabligh* is viewed in certain quarters of the traditional religious establishment as another challenge to its authority and legitimacy, and therein lies sources of friction for the Malay-Muslim community.

SHI'A ISLAM

Thailand's Shi'a community is believed to number around 100,000, consisting mostly of members of the Pakistani, Indian, and Persian diasporas in Bangkok.

Most of these Muslims descended from middle-class, educated families of traders, artisans, and scholars. Of the 180 mosques in Bangkok, four are Shi'a. Additionally, the Shi'a community runs five or six religious schools in Bangkok and one in Nakhon Si Thammarat. The most popular among these schools is the Imam Khomeini School in Dhonburi. These Shi'a schools are privately funded and operate on a half-day basis (evenings and weekends) with small class sizes. The curriculum revolves around the study of the Qur'an as well as Mazhab Jafari, the most popular Shi'a school of jurisprudential thought in Thailand.

The Shi'a community in Thailand is led by Ayatollah Syed Suleiman, a graduate of Islamiah University (Qum) who maintains close ties with the Iranian government and who has facilitated the training of around 100 Thai Shi'a scholars in Iran since the Iranian Revolution. The education of these Thai Shi'a students was undertaken with the support of Iranian government scholarships. Though the Shi'a community remains small in number, it makes up for this with its impressive activism that has resulted in extensive exposure in the national media. For instance, in the last two years the Shi'a community has broadcast messages over Ramadhan. It has a vigorous publication programme that reproduces Shi'a religious material and includes the translation of Iranian Islamic scholarship into Thai. In southern Thailand, the Shi'a community is active in Muang, Yala, and Yarang, Pattani. Shi'a activism in these regions is primarily organized and led by two individuals — Anwar and Ishak Budi. Both were recipients of scholarships from Iran and formerly taught as *ustaz* in religious schools in Pattani. Currently, they are businessmen who actively promote Shi'a Islam in the south by distributing Shi'a publications in this predominantly Sunni area.

Because the Shi'a community is very small in the south, it is not seen as a major threat to traditional Islam compared to the reformist movement. Having said that, Shi'ism in Thailand has at times been vocally critical of the Malay-Muslim Sunni parochialism that has fed the violence in the south. This points to some of the tensions between the two communities.[24] In Bangkok, traditional Muslim parents have expressed concern about the expanding presence of the Shi'a community. For example, when parents found out in 2002 that Santichon Islamic School in Bangkok had hired an Iraqi Shi'a to teach English, many threatened to withdraw their students unless the teacher was repatriated.[25]

EDUCATIONAL NETWORKS

The considerable reputation that Islamic education in Thailand established in the nineteenth century translated into an increasing popularity of Patani's *pondok* schools and a rising demand for Thai Muslim scholars, as Muslim students flocked to southern Thailand from all over Southeast Asia. Patani's vaunted reputation as a centre for Islamic learning was further augmented through the *dakwah* activism of Thai *alim* who visited Indonesia, Malaysia, and Cambodia and were welcomed as learned *musafir* (travellers) in various villages.[26] Patani had an especially significant role to play in the expansion of Islamic knowledge in the Malay Peninsula. Robert Winzeler has noted that "important religious leaders in Kelantan trace their families back to Patani and it is thus not unlikely that the traditional schools derive at some point from this area as well".[27] In fact, the influential role played by Patani religious scholars in the development of Islamic thought in the Malay Peninsula may be seen in the fact that renowned Malay scholars such as Tok Kenali and Haji Nik Mahmud Muhammad Ismail were taught by a Patani teacher, Sheikh Ahmad bin Muhammad Zayn bin Mustafa bin Muhammad al-Fatani (Sheikh Ahmad Al-Fatani), who taught out of Mecca in the early twentieth century.[28]

This reputation as a centre of Islamic learning has waned considerably over time as a result of decades of tension between the central Bangkok government and the Malay-Muslim south. Not surprisingly, these tensions have negatively affected foreign student enrolment in Islamic schools in the southern provinces. As suggested earlier, the assimilationist policies directed at Islamic schools eroded the quality of Islamic education in Thailand. While foreign students can still be found in the Islamic private schools and *pondok* throughout southern Thailand today, their numbers pale in comparison to the pre-war era. Moreover, while in previous epochs students from the Muslim heartlands of the Indonesian archipelago and the Malay Peninsula converged on Patani in search of renowned *tok guru* and *ulama*, the foreign student population today consists mostly of Muslims from Cambodia and Myanmar, though a handful of Malaysian, Indonesians, and Singaporeans are currently studying in the traditional *pondok* as well. In the same vein, tertiary education institutions in the southern provinces have enjoyed only limited success in their attempts to attract foreign students, although the Yala Islamic University has experienced a small but steady stream in its short lifespan, with about 100 foreigners currently enrolled in the departments of *shari'a* and *usul-addin* at the faculty of Islamic studies.[29] Likewise, the number of foreign teachers actively teaching in the southern provinces is but a fraction of the total number of religious educators. For instance, of the 150 instructors currently employed at Yala Islamic University, eight are of foreign nationality, from Malaysia, Indonesia, Algeria, Sudan, Iraq, and Saudi Arabia. In other words, Islamic education has become an essentially local enterprise in southern Thailand.

The decline in the number of foreigners studying in southern Thailand corresponds to a rise in the number of Thai Malay-Muslims who pursue their education overseas. Indeed, the number of foreign-trained local educators teaching in the south appears to have increased as a result of the outflow of southern Thai Muslims to the major centres of Islamic learning throughout the world. Most of the faculty at the College of Islamic Studies, Prince of Songkhla University, and Yala Islamic University received their advanced training from foreign institutions. Many of these educators are graduates of prestigious Egyptian and Saudi universities, though there is an increasing number returning from Malaysia and Indonesia as well. While the number of Islamic private school teachers educated overseas is difficult to determine, anecdotal evidence suggests that their numbers are large.

The preponderance of foreign-trained educators has not translated into the establishment of significant formal educational networks. Indeed, links with foreign institutions are for the most part limited to individual students receiving scholarships from foreign sponsors to further their religious education at these institutions. That is not to say, of course, that there have been no attempts to institutionalize networks in some form or other. For instance, Thamma Witthaya Islamic private school in Yala regularly sends its students to Al-Azhar University as well as schools and universities in Indonesia.[30] In the latter case, this collaboration in student exchange is premised on a Memorandum of Understanding in which Indonesian universities commit to hosting on an annual basis a select number of Thamma Witthaya graduates. Likewise, informal alumni associations have been formed by graduates of universities in Egypt, Saudi Arabia, and Pakistan.

Local education networks are built around student organizations and school associations. The most prominent student organization for Muslim students is the Thai Muslim Students Association (TMSA). Established in 1965 by Wan Muhammad Nor Matha, now a prominent Malay-Muslim figure, the TMSA modelled itself along the lines of an activist non-governmental organization that took up the cause of Muslim tertiary education. Like most Muslim student organizations established during the turbulent era of the 1960s and 1970s, the TMSA evinced reformist inclinations in its embrace of the Islamic resurgence. According to one of its founding members, the TMSA "was created to facilitate collaboration between all Muslim societies in Thailand in tertiary education institutions (national and private universities), and functioned as a civil society movement".[31] In 1967 graduates from TMSA moved to form the YMAT (Young Muslim Association of Thailand), which established strong ties with *Angkatan Belia Islam Malaysia* (Islamic Youth Movement of Malaysia), a vocal and active civil society pressure group then headed by the charismatic Anwar Ibrahim and that operated in the highly politicized arena of Malaysia's tertiary education system. ABIM-style political activism, however, did not appeal to all members of the YMAT and this became a matter of great debate among its founding leadership. The tensions that arose within the organization as a consequence of its alignment with ABIM undermined the organization's ability to represent the interests of Muslim students in Thailand with one coherent voice. Beyond that, the zealous reformist ideals demonstrated by YMAT led to occasional altercations with traditional Muslim community leaders over matters like improvements to the structure and curriculum of the *pondok*.[32]

LOCAL EDUCATIONAL FOUNDATIONS

Islamic schools in southern Thailand function as independent bodies that are run either by their own management committees or by foundations. Though schools are often aligned in terms of ideology, most Islamic schools are in fact autonomous on matters of administration. There have, however, been various attempts to foster closer cooperation and dialogue among Islamic schools so as to present a more unified and coherent voice in the face of pressures from the Thai state for educational reform. These attempts reached a watershed on 9 May 2004. In the wake of a resurgence of violence in the southern provinces that once again drew the attention of the Thai government to Islamic schools, the Central Islamic Committee of Thailand, formed in 1997 as the sole statutory organization in the country in charge of Islamic religious affairs, brought the Islamic schools under two umbrella organizations — the Pondok Association (*Persatuan Pondok*) and Islamic Private School Association (*Persatuan Sekolah Agama Rakyat*). While these two associations were charged with the objective of improving the administration and curriculum of Islamic religious institutions, it was clear that their formation was also motivated by political exigency — it was a move by the local Malay-Muslim leadership to formulate a coherent policy on matters pertaining to Islamic education and to articulate a unified position in this regard.

Aside from the overarching umbrella of these two associations, a number of Islamic private schools also came within the administrative ambit of Islamic foundations (*Yayasan* in Malay and *Mulniti* in Thai) and mosques. These foundations are often established either by an influential and/or wealthy individual (who may or may not be the principal) or by a group of individuals that oversees the running and funding of a school. The figures for the number of schools under foundations and mosques in the southern provinces are listed in Table 5.1. A full list of the names of schools and the foundations they are affiliated with can be found in Appendix I.

TABLE 5.1
Islamic Private Schools under Jurisdiction of Mosques and/or
Islamic Foundations

Yala	Narathiwat	Pattani	Satun	Songkhla
16	13	12	4	13

TRANSNATIONAL NETWORKS

Models of religious education across the Muslim world have evolved against the backdrop of various cultural milieus, nation-building experiences, and social, political, and economic circumstances. In some respects, the challenges faced by each system are unique to its specific context. On the other hand, the universal nature of Islamic faith demands that any study of Islamic education also consider transnational networks across the *ummah*. There have been several hearths of Islamic thought and influence upon which the *ummah* has converged in search of knowledge. Mamoun Fandy suggests three:

> Because of Egypt's large population and its power as a cultural centre, the Egyptian educational system affected the whole Arab world. The Saudi Arabian approach to education — especially Islamic education — influences the rest of the Muslim world because of the country's wealth and its special status as the birthplace of Islam and home to the two holy mosques. Pakistan, where the 'madrassa system' evolved, is the Islamic centre of South Asia, and a frontier where Islam meets Asian religions. [33]

A major study on the origins of reformist Islamic thought in Southeast Asia by Azyumardi Azra, the prominent Indonesian Islamic scholar, observes:

> The transmission of Islamic renewalism and reformism in the scholarly networks involved very complex processes. There were highly intricate crisscrossings of scholars within the networks, by way of both their studies of Islamic sciences, particularly *hadith*, and their adherence of Islamic mystical brotherhood (*tariqahs*). An examination of this crisscrossing of the networks, and of works produced by scholars in the networks, throws much light on how Islamic renewalism and reformism were transmitted from centres of the networks to many parts of the world.[34]

These networks, it should be added, are seldom institutionalized, though they are gradually taking on a more formal shape through scholarships and the establishment of official and unofficial alumni associations.

As noted earlier, foreign influences have played an increasingly prominent role in defining the parameters of Islamic knowledge within the Malay-Muslim community, by virtue of the fact that Malay-Muslim students are venturing abroad to further their religious education. In particular, pull factors such as the global Islamic resurgence of the late 1960s and early 1970s as well as the rise of petro-Islam coincided with push factors in the form of the intense government scrutiny of local Islamic schools as well as the dearth of tertiary education opportunities at home. The extent of this exodus provoked Surin Pitsuwan to observe that as a consequence of this outflow, "for the first time, the community was faced with a shortage of qualified religious intellectuals".[35] There is of course a slight exaggeration given that many of these students would return to contribute to the local intellectual environment. Nonetheless, the departure of Malay-Muslims is also a matter of concern for security agencies, since many among the Malay-Muslim diaspora were "recruited" by separatist groups such as PULO that had liaison officials stationed in Libya and Saudi Arabia for the precise purpose of enlisting new arrivals to the cause of Patani independence.[36]

Given the tendency of local Muslim parents to prize Islamic over secular education, it follows that an overseas education in North Africa (Egypt) and the Middle East (Saudi Arabia) is rated highly within the community. Because of this, the influence that foreign ideas enjoy in the outlook of Muslims in Thailand in general, and southern Thailand in particular, cannot be over-emphasized. Religious teachers trained in the major centres of Islamic learning command greater recognition and respect in local communities. Likewise, schools with foreign-trained *tok guru* and *ustaz* are often more popular than those with locally-trained religious teachers.[37] In both instances, the prevailing perception is that a foreign education from the Middle East, the heartland of Islam, is more highly valued as it allows more exposure to Arabic, the authentic language of the Qur'an, and, concomitantly, access to a deeper level of religious understanding and discourse that would by and large not be available in Thailand.

There is also a view gaining currency among Malay-Muslim parents, students, and even educators that Islamic education in southern Thailand is no longer of the same quality as it was during the height of Patani's fame.[38] Indeed, one *ustaz* interviewed opined that Thai Muslims are going abroad to study Islam because "times have changed and many prefer to go abroad because that is where the true religion of Islam can be found".[39] Another lamented that "things have changed and it is different from times before. Patani today is not the same as Patani of yesterday".[40] While this tells of the erosion of Patani's legacy of authority in Islamic knowledge, there are still many who romanticize the Patani tradition. One parent interviewed, for instance, opined that compared to foreign-trained religious teachers, local *tok guru* "possess more humility and honesty (*sifat tawadha [rendah diri] dan iklas lagi berkat)*".[41]

The prevailing preference for foreign training is reflected in the statistics. In a random survey of twenty-five *pondok* and Islamic private schools in the three Malay-Muslim provinces, 127 of 297 teachers received their training from abroad.[42] Most graduated with degrees in *usul-addin*, while smaller numbers majored in *shari'a*, *dakwah*, and the Arabic language.

The figures for the number of Malay-Muslim students from southern Thailand studying abroad fluctuate depending on the source. For instance, defence ministry sources estimate that up to 10,000 Thai Muslims (mostly from the southern provinces) are studying abroad in Islamic institutions. Officals from the education ministry, however, place the figure at 6,000.[43] Figures provided by the Islamic Private School Association are even more conservative — the secretary estimates that there are only about 2,000.[44] From the following assessment, however, it is likely that the figure lies between 4,000 and 6,000.

Saudi Arabia

Wan Kadir Che Man had previously estimated that throughout the 1960s and 1970s up to 30,000 Malay-Muslims from Thailand were residing in Saudi Arabia.[45] Some sources state that over the past fifteen years, 2,500 Thai Muslims have graduated from universities in Saudi Arabia.[46] According to the Thai Embassy in Saudi Arabia, about twenty Malay-Muslim students make their way to Saudi Arabia for tertiary education every year, funded by the Saudi government.[47] This surprisingly low figure is undoubtedly a consequence of the government scrutiny and moratorium discussed earlier.[48] Nevertheless, Saudi alumni suggest that a larger number of Malay-Muslim students has actually managed to obtain funding for education from private Saudi sources through networks within the Saudi Arabia Alumni Association, which has a membership of about 200.[49]

In Saudi Arabia, Malay-Muslim students are mostly spread across six institutions — Medina University in Medina, Al-Riyadh University, Islamic University of Imam Muhammad bin Saud and Al-Mahad Al-Ali Al-Kudo in Riyadh, and Mecca's Umm Al-Qura University and Al-Mahad Al-Soutiyah. The highest student concentrations are currently found at Al-Riyadh University (32), Medina University (27), and Umm Al-Qura (12).[50] Disciplines commonly pursued are *hadith*, *tafsir*, *fiqh*, *dakwah*, *aqidah*, and philosophy.

Prominent Islamic scholars who have graduated from Saudi-based tertiary Islamic education institutions include:

1. Dr. Ismail Lutfi Japakiya, Rector of Yala Islamic University and Member of Parliament (Ph.D. in *Shari'a* from Islamic University of Imam Muhammad bin Saud);
2. Prof. Dr. Ismael Ali, Director of Islamic Studies College, Prince of Songkhla University and Member of Parliament (Ph.D. in *Shari'a* from Medina University);
3. Dr. Abdulhalim Saisee, Lecturer, Yala Islamic University (Ph.D. in *Aqidah* from Umm Al-Qura University);
4. Dr. Jihad Bunga-tanyong (recently deceased), Principal, Islahiyah Islamic Private School, Muang, Yala (Ph.D. in *Aqidah* from Umm Al-Qura University);
5. Dr. Abdulgani Saleming, Lecturer, Islamic Studies College, Prince of Songkhla University (Ph.D. in *Shari'a* from Medina University);
6. Hasan Koto, Lecturer, Yala Islamic University (M.A. in *Aqidah* from Umm Al-Qura University);
7. Amin Andalis, (M.A. in Arabic Studies from Medina University);
8. Abdulgani Dami, Principal, Ratprachanukroh Islamic Private School, Thung Yang Daeng, Pattani (M.A. in *Shari'a* from Umm Al-Qura University);
9. Ahmad Mustafa Bango-sina, Principal, Suksawad Wittaya Islamic Private School, Yaha, Yala (M.A. in *Tafsir al-Qur'an* from Islamic University of Imam Muhammad bin Saud).

Estimates obtained from the Islamic Private School Association are that up to 93 per cent of graduates from Saudi institutions are serving as religious teachers and scholars in the three southern provinces.[51] It is further estimated that up to 85 per cent of these students had been supported by scholarships from their host institution. Saudi missionaries have also been known to make regular trips to southern Thailand to assess and oversee Islamic studies instruction in the area.[52] Aside from pursuing tertiary education in Islamic studies, Thai students in Saudi Arabia also play an important role as guides for the approximately 10,000 Thai Muslims who make the *hajj* pilgrimage to Mecca every year, during which time each student is responsible for about 200 pilgrims.[53] Beyond studying at the established universities, a number of Thai Malay-Muslim students continue to attend the traditional Malay *halaqah* at the Masjid al-Haram, where several prominent Islamic scholars from the southern provinces, including

Ismail Sepanjang, a famous *tok guru* from Pattani, continue the tradition of Patani Islamic scholarship in Mecca.[54]

Students who study in Saudi Arabia mostly enjoy financial support from the kingdom. Others obtain financial assistance from a number of Muslim charities, religious organizations, and Saudi private business interests. As mentioned earlier, funding from the Saudi Arabian government for scholarships has effectively been curtailed at the insistence of the Thai government for political and security reasons — namely, concern for the spread of Wahhabi ideas.[55] This has adversely affected the enrolment of Thai students in Saudi Arabian institutions. It might be argued that the kingdom is no longer as popular a destination for tertiary Islamic education as before, because of the government's position as well as the desire among students not to be viewed with suspicion.

The Thai government's apprehension about Saudi involvement in local Islamic education was revealed in the course of planning for a faculty of Islamic Studies at Princess of Narathiwatrajnakarin University in Narathiwat, when after intensive discussions it was Al-Azhar University and not Medina University that was requested to serve as the consultant institution in curriculum planning.[56] That is not to say, though, that collaboration with Saudi universities do not exist. The College of Islamic Studies at Prince of Songkhla University maintains a longstanding collaboration with Medina University. This takes the form of an annual scholarship programme that includes a one-month intensive preparatory course in the Arabic language for students. The top performers in this one-month course are given scholarships to Saudi Arabia. Some local education officials and traditional educators are concerned that Saudi-funded Islamic private schools in southern Thailand may be serving as conduits for the Wahhabi brand of Salafism that is openly critical of the traditionalist position on *fiqh*, *tassawuf*, and Sufism.[57] After all, followers of Ibn Abd Al-Wahhab were not only fierce critics of traditional Islamic practices in the Arab Peninsula, but also on occasion used force to eradicate these practices. In any case, a significant number of Salafi reformists were trained in Saudi Arabia.

Currently, there are substantial numbers of Saudi-trained scholars in more than twenty Islamic private schools in the three southern provinces. Some of these schools may be Salafi-Wahhabi in ideological orientation, judging by some of their literature.[58] A list of schools with a substantial number of Saudi-trained teachers is provided in Appendix II. According to local community leaders, most of the students who move on to tertiary institutions in Saudi Arabia likely studied at the Islamic private schools that have Saudi-trained teachers on staff.

Egypt

Egypt is a major destination for Thai Muslim students. Egyptian universities have long enjoyed a reputation not only as major centres of Islamic learning, but also as affordable tertiary education destinations. The latter owes largely to the fact that schools such as Al-Azhar are *waqf* property, implying that profit is not a major consideration in its activities and that community funds are readily available to support Islamic education. This has in turn translated to numerous scholarships and financial aid opportunities for foreign Muslim students pursuing Islamic studies.[59] Even for self-funded students, education in Egypt is arguably less expensive when compared to other destinations in the Middle East.

Citing records from the Thai Students' Association in Cairo, Hasan Madmarn estimated that there were approximately 750 Thais studying in Egypt in 1987, of which 300 had been given scholarships.[60] Within a decade, the number had increased more than two-fold to 1,700.[61] According to Surin Pitsuwan, there were as many as 3,000 Thai Muslims studying in Egypt in 2006.[62] Hasan Madmarn further suggests that an average of 200 students per year make their way to Egypt for tertiary Islamic education. The most popular tertiary education institutions in Egypt among Thai Muslims are Al-Azhar University (Cairo), Al-Qahirah University (Cairo University), Zamalik University (Zamalik), and the American University of Cairo, where currently two Malay-Muslims are studying. Malay-Muslims have also enrolled at the Al-mahad Al-Azhariyah in Al-Azhar University which provides pre-university placement education. Students from the three southern Thai provinces who study at universities in Egypt mostly take up the fields of *usul-uddin*, *dakwah*, *shari'a*, *falsafah Islamiyah*, Arabic language, and English language. While many Malay-Muslims are admitted to tertiary education institutions in Egypt after completing their secondary education in the Islamic private school system, some in fact undertake their secondary education (*mutawassit* and *thanawi* levels) in Egypt itself before moving on to prestigious tertiary institutions there.[63] This is a notable departure from the norm in most other Muslim countries, where Malay-Muslims by and large enter the system only at the stage of tertiary education. Most of these students are funded either by their respective host institutions (this system of providing free public education has existed since the Nasser administration) or by Islamic charities. A small number of Malay-Muslims do, however, also obtain Thai government scholarships administered through the Islamic Central Committee.

Thus far only two Muslim intellectuals from southern Thailand obtained their doctorates from Egyptian universities. They are Dr. Abdul-Rasyed Yala, an *ustaz* and administrator of Thamma Wittaya Mullanithi School, Yala

District, who has a Ph.D. in Arabic from Al-Azhar, Cairo, and Dr. Mariyam Alfatoni, who also graduated from Al-Azhar with a Ph.D. in Arabic. Other prominent alumni include Abdulaziz Yanya, founding chairman of the *Persatuan Pondok* (Pondok Association) and secretary of the *Persatuan Sekolah Agama Rakyat* (Islamic Private School Association), who completed his M.A. degree in Arabic at Al-Azhar University, Cairo.

According to estimates obtained from the Islamic Private School Association, up to 95 per cent of graduates from Egyptian institutions of higher learning have returned to take up positions as religious educators in southern Thailand. A list of schools with substantial numbers of Egyptian alumni are listed in Appendix III.

Sudan

According to Thai alumni, there are approximately 400 Thai Malay-Muslim students currently studying in Islamic tertiary institutions in Sudan.[64] In addition, an estimated sixty register to study in Sudanese institutions each year.[65] These students are mostly found in Ommu Darman Al-Islamiyah University (OIU) and Ommu Darman Al-Ahliyah University in Ommu Darman, as well as International University of Africa (IUA), University of Khartoum, Alkuran Al-Karim University, and Al-Nilien University in Khartoum. Of the Malay-Muslim students studying in these institutions, the vast majority are enrolled in degree programmes in Islamic studies and *shari'a*, with a smaller number majoring in Arabic and *dakwah*. A small minority from Ommu Darman Al-Islamiyah University, which has the highest concentration of Malay-Muslim undergraduate students in the country, also graduate with academic degrees in fields such as medicine, engineering, education, communications, and economics.[66] Students enrolled in Al-Nilien and the University of Khartoum, on the other hand, are graduate students reading for masters and doctorate degrees in Islamic studies. Except for Ommu Darman Al-Ahliyah University where the medium of instruction is English, Islamic studies departments in Sudanese tertiary education institutions employ Arabic as their teaching language. While graduate students are funded by their respective host universities, undergraduates mostly receive support from Islamic charities and private donations (both locally and across the Arab world).

Almost all the students in Sudan come from southern Thailand's Islamic private school system. This includes both Salafi-reformist as well as traditionalist schools, though the vast majority of Malay-Muslim students educated in Sudan are traditionalist (both Sufi and Shafi'i) in their doctrinal persuasion.[67] It has been suggested that most of the students with a Salafi-reformist bent were already oriented towards this theological direction prior to their departure for Sudan, as a consequence of their training in reformist Islamic private schools in southern Thailand.[68] In other words, Sudan does not appear to be a major source of Salafi-reformist influence on Thailand's Malay-Muslim student diaspora. To the extent that there are a small number of students educated in Sudan who are inclined towards Salafi reformism and possibly Wahhabism as well, it has been suggested that they would likely have crossed over to Sudan from Islamic schools in Saudi Arabia.[69] In the case of reformist schools from southern Thailand, most of the students come from Islahiyah (Tambon Budi, Muang, Yala), Suksawad Wittaya (Tambon Bangosine, Yaha, Yala), and Sukan Sasana Wittaya (Tambon Bangpo, Muang, Narathiwat). For traditionalist schools, the strongest connections are with Islam Sasana Wittaya (Tambon Sakam, Mayo, Pattani) and Dara Wittaya (Tambon Tanyongmas, Rangeh, Narathiwat).[70] As suggested earlier, a small minority enter the tertiary education system following graduation from *thanawiyah* (secondary) schools in Saudi Arabia and Sudan.[71]

Prominent Sudan-trained Islamic studies scholars in southern Thailand include:

1. Dr. Ahmed Telagasembilan, Ustaz, Yarang (M.A. in Arabic from Al-Duwaliyah Al-Arabiayah, Khartoum, and Ph.D. in Shari'a from International University of Africa, Khartoum).
2. Dr. Azmi Yingo, Lecturer, Terengganu, Malaysia (B.A. in Shari'a from Morocco, M.A. in Shari'a Universiti Utara Malaysia, Kedah, Malaysia and Ph.D. in Shari'a from University of Khartoum, Khartoum).
3. Dr. Ahmed Fouzi Salemae, Lecturer, Yala Islamic University (B.A. in Dakwah from International University of Africa, Khartoum, M.A. in Islamic History from Al-Nilien University, Khartoum, and Ph.D. in Islamic History from University of Khartoum, Khartoum).
4. Dr. Weeyusof Sidik, Ustaz, Samaddee Wittaya Islamic School, Saiburi, Pattani (B.A. in Geology from International University of Africa, Khartoum, M.A. in African Studies from International University of Africa, Khartoum, and Ph.D. in Engineering from University of Khartoum, Khartoum).
5. Dr. Sohibulbahree Thon (B.A. in Arabic from Algeria, M.A. and Ph.D. in Arabic from International University of Africa, Khartoum, and University of Khartoum, Khartoum).
6. Ahmed Saddik, Director of Dakwah Foundation, Pattani (B.A. and M.A.

in Economics from Ommu Darman Al-Islamiyah University, Ommu
Darman).

7. Ibrahim Janah, Director of Arabic Language Center, Yala Islamic College
   (B.A. and M.A. in Arabic from International University of Africa and
   Al-Duwaliyah Al-Arabiayah University).

8. Abdulkoder Phomeng, Ph.D. (Shari'a) student, (Ommu Darman
   Al-Islamiyah University, Ommu Darman).

9. Othman Talokmekna, Ph.D. (Arabic) student at Islamic International
   University, Kuala Lumpur, Malaysia (B.A. in Education from Ommu
   Darman Al-Islamiyah University, Ommu Darman, and M.A. in Arabic
   from Al-Duwaliyah Al-Arabiayah University).

10. Aisyah Visetrutt (Ms.), Lecturer in Arabic, Prince of Songkhla University,
    Pattani (B.A. and M.A. in Arabic from International University of Africa,
    Khartoum and Al-Duwaliyah Al-Arabiayah University).

11. Abdul-Rahman Bukitsamae, Ustaz, Darussalam Islamic School, Rangeh
    district, Narathiwat (B.A. in Islamic Studies and Dakwah from Ommu
    Darman Al-Islamiyah University, Ommu Darman).

Jordan

It is estimated by alumni sources that approximately ten to fifteen Malay-
Muslims attend tertiary Islamic education institutions in Jordan annually.[72]
The institutions of choice include Yarmuk University and Yarasy University
in Irbid, Mu'tah University in Krak, University of Jordan in Amman,
Al Al-Bayt University in Mafraq, and Balqok University in Salt. Up to 70 per
cent of the Malay-Muslim students attend Yarmuk, where the vast number
pursue a degree in *shari'a*.[73] Like many Malay-Muslim overseas students,
most return to teach in Islamic private schools throughout the southern
provinces. Samarnmit Witthaya School in Yingo, Narathiwat, houses an
unofficial Jordanian alumni association consisting of six graduates, including
the headmaster of the school, Ustaz Mahamalutfi Hayeesamae, a graduate in
fiqh from University of Jordan. Likewise, many Malay-Muslim students in
Jordan are themselves graduates of Samarnmit, though a small number
originate from public high schools as well. A number of graduates have
assumed administrative positions in provincial and regional religious
bureaucracies.[74]

Students enrolled in Jordanian universities are given scholarships as well
as a stipend of 200 dinar (approximately 14,000 baht) a month. Both sources
of financial aid are provided by the Jordanian education ministry.[75]

South Asia

Thailand's Muslim community has traditionally favoured the Middle East as the destination of choice for tertiary Islamic studies. In recent times, however, interest in South Asia, Pakistan in particular, has increased noticeably. The burgeoning popularity of South Asia has partly been a function of the expansion of *Jemaat Tabligh* activism in the country and the links the movement maintains with *Tabligh* centres in South Asia. According to statistics obtained from Pattani Darussalam Alumni Organisation — Pakistan (*Organisasi Pelajar Lama Pattani Darussalam Pakistan*), there are a total of 1,700 Thai students currently studying in Pakistan.[76] The figures for India and Bangladesh are significantly smaller. Among the various Islamic studies institutions hosting Thai Muslims are Aligarh Muslim University, Nadwah Islamiah, Bangalore University, Burdwan University, Delhi University, and Darul Uloom in India, University of Islamic Studies, Pislabad University, Wifakul Madaris University, International Islamic University in Pakistan, and Islamic University and Dhaka University in Bangladesh.[77] While most returning students continue to subscribe to traditionalist Islam premised on Shafi'i jurisprudence, a handful have also brought back the reformist ideas of the Deobandi tradition. The footprint of Deobandi Islamic thought is however, markedly smaller than that the Salafi reformism propagated by Middle Eastern graduates.

Malaysia

There are currently an estimated 500 Thai Muslims studying in Islamic institutions across Malaysia, including secondary schools and private Islamic schools.[78] Among the fifty or so students who enrol in Islamic schools in Malaysia every year, the vast majority comes from the local Islamic private school system.[79] Significantly, this number does not include those students who reside along the Thai-Malaysian border in towns such as Tak Bai and Sungei Golok. Many of these students possess Malaysian identity registration cards and are registered in Islamic schools in Kelantan as Malaysian citizens. Of the figure mentioned above, it is estimated that up to eighty percent pursue courses in Islamic studies. An equal number is estimated to enter the field of education upon their graduation, either as lecturers in universities in the southern provinces (particularly those with graduate degrees) or as *ustaz* in various Islamic private schools in the region. Some also work in provincial Islamic committees and in mosques as *imam*.

In terms of tertiary education institutions, the students in Malaysia primarily study at the International Islamic University in Kuala Lumpur,

Universiti Kebangsaan Malaysia (National University of Malaysia in Bangi), and Universiti Malaya (Malaya University in Kuala Lumpur). A smaller number of Islamic studies graduates come from Universiti Utara Malaysia (Northern Malaysia University), Universiti Pertanian Malaysia (Malaysia University of Agriculture), and Universiti Sains Malaysia (Malaysia University of Science in Penang). Prominent Malaysia-trained Islamic scholars from southern Thailand include:

1. Kariya Langputeh, Lecturer in Arabic, Yala Islamic University (M.A. in Arabic from International Islamic University of Malaysia).
2. Dr. Ibrahim Narongraksakhet, Lecturer, College of Islamic Studies, Prince of Songkhla University (M.A. in Education, International Islamic University of Malaysia, and Ph.D. in Education from Universiti Malaya).
3. Dr. Abdullah Kharina, Lecturer, College of Islamic Studies, Prince of Songkhla University (Ph.D. in Islamic Studies from Universiti Sains Malaysia).
4. Dr. Mah-lazim Yalo, Ustaz, Lecturer in Arabic, Yala Islamic University (Ph.D. in Islamic Studies from Universiti Pertanian Malaysia).

Aside from these Islamic scholars, numerous prominent Malay-Muslims from southern Thailand have also graduated with degrees in social sciences, communications, and Malay language. While most of students in graduate programs obtained their first degrees from either Malaysian or Thai institutions, a number also graduated from degree programmes in universities in Egypt, Saudi Arabia, and Jordan.[80]

The nature of the Malaysia-southern Thailand tertiary Islamic education network is exceptional on three counts. First, while some enjoy scholarships and bursaries from their respective host institutions, in most instances students in Malaysia are self-funded.[81] This differs from the situation of Thai Malay-Muslim students studying elsewhere in the Islamic world, where they are usually funded either by host institutions, governments, or charities. Second, while there is a measure of Salafi-reformist influence among the Malay-Muslim cohorts studying in Malaysia, the scale of this influence is considerably less compared to that in Saudi Arabia or Jordan. Again, those sympathetic to Salafism tend to have come from Salafi-reformist private schools prior to pursuing tertiary education in Malaysia. Third, the connection between Malaysia and southern Thailand evidently derives from the shared language and culture of the two regions, not to mention geographical proximity.[82] Another possible reason for the popularity of Malaysia is the high regard which Nik Aziz Nik Mat, the charismatic Kelantan-based *ulama* and spiritual leader of the Malaysian opposition party PAS (Parti Islam Se-Malaysia), enjoys throughout the three southern Malay-Muslim provinces.[83]

At present, there are a number of Malaysian (and a handful of Indonesian) teachers teaching in Islamic private schools throughout southern Thailand. Most, however, are Malay language instructors and few are actually involved in teaching religion.[84] On the other hand, religious teachers from the southern provinces continue to teach in religious schools in Malaysia and Indonesia, though their numbers have dwindled significantly since the height of these exchanges in the early twentieth century.[85] In response to recent controversies regarding the alleged role of religious teachers in fomenting violence in the south, the Malaysian government has offered to provide Muslim teachers to instruct Thai Muslims in the "right" Islam.[86] This gesture, however, has not gone down well with the local community in the border provinces; it has also elicited telling responses from local Islamic leaders. These sentiments are captured in the remarks of a Yala-based *ustaz* who reacted in the following manner to the influx of Malaysian educators into southern Thailand: "For decades we have been teaching Islam to the people of Malaysia. We do not need to learn anything from them. Patani has a long and glorious legacy in Islamic studies".[87]

Indonesia

It is estimated that there are around 1,000 Thai students in Indonesian schools and that about forty to fifty students from the southern provinces register with tertiary institutions in Indonesia annually.[88] Of this figure, approximately 85 per cent pursue Islamic studies, while the rest enrol in academic degree programmes. Students from southern Thailand mostly study at the State Islamic University in Bandung, Muhammadiyah University in Medan, University of Surabaya in Surabaya, University of Indonesia and University of Jogjakarta in Jakarta, and Bandung Institute of Technology in Bandung.[89] It is further estimated that 75 per cent of graduates from Indonesia return to southern Thailand to take up positions as religious teachers and *imam* of mosques. While most graduates from Indonesia are mainstream Sunni in orientation (a smaller number of whom are Salafi), there has been a noticeable trend of students returning as Shi'a Muslims.[90] This is probably a function of the increasing popularity of Shi'a Islam in Indonesia.

Approximately 40 per cent of the Malay-Muslim students in Indonesia receive financial support from the Indonesian Ministry of Religion, while the rest are either self-funded or have access to financial aid from Islamic charities. As in the case of Malaysia and Egypt, the ideological underpinnings of those educated in Indonesia are predominantly Sunni in orientation, with most following the Shafi'i school of jurisprudence.

Beyond the practical issues of funding and proximity, enrolment trends away from the Middle East and towards regional Muslim countries have been influenced by the post-September 11 climate. As noted earlier, since the advent of the "Global War on Terror", the funding generated and disbursed by Middle Eastern governments (even some Gulf states) and Islamic charities in particular have come under intense scrutiny and pressure.[91] This has resulted in a discernible scaling-back of aid and financial assistance, including scholarships and student stipends, to various Muslim communities. Muslims in Thailand have not been spared from this, and insofar as students have had to rely on their own funds or on local *zakat* and *waqf* support, they are increasingly looking to institutions in Malaysia and Indonesia for more affordable tertiary Islamic education.

While much of the interest revolving around matters of external funding and influences in Islamic education in Thailand has centred on the role of Islamic governments and organizations, it should be noted that the U.S.-based Asia Foundation has for a long time played an important role in assisting Islamic schools in Thailand with modernizing their infrastructure and curriculum development, as well as staff/student training.

Since 1961, when *pondok* were encouraged to register with the government and to transform their curricula, the Asia Foundation has supported the creation of Islamic private schools by providing students in southern Thailand with general educational training and opportunities within the context of Islamic education. In its most recent initiative (2004), the Foundation launched a pilot programme for ten Islamic private schools (six from the southern provinces) that aimed to transform pedagogy in Islamic schools by introducing participatory learning methods and reducing the traditional emphasis on rote learning. The programme also aims to improve the level of English, mathematics, science, computer science, and civic education by redesigning existing curricula and introducing new teaching aids and study materials. As a benchmark, this programme employed successful Catholic schools as reference points as it attempted to draw up a model of how religious schools could excel academically while maintaining their religious/cultural heritage.

Through local Islamic councils the Asia Foundation has also provided scholarships for Muslim students from the southern provinces to attend universities in Bangkok, and has supported the training of staff from the College of Islamic Studies, Prince of Songkhla University. It is also interesting to note that Yala Islamic University has submitted a request for Asia Foundation funding in support of its English Language Institute, for language training for all its staff, as well as for field trips to Malaysia. Needless to say, while some quarters of the Muslim community in Thailand are prepared to work with the Foundation, others harbour suspicions about its intentions given that it is an American organization.[92]

ISLAMIC EDUCATION IN BANGKOK AND CHIANG MAI
Bangkok

Next to the southern provinces, Bangkok has the largest Muslim community in Thailand. Malays (mostly in Nong Chok district) are believed to form the largest Muslim ethnic community in Bangkok. The sizeable Malay-Muslim population traces its roots back to the historical wars between Patani and the Siamese state, where many Malays were either forcefully relocated or taken hostage (men, women, and children) back to Bangkok after the defeat of the Patani kingdom by Siam in the wars of the late eighteenth century.[93] The Malay-Muslims in Bangkok have played an instrumental and constructive role in Thai society as they provided much of the labour for major development projects. They were also responsible for building the vast majority of mosques in Bangkok and its outskirts. Compared to the Malay-Muslims, who were largely seen as aliens (if not enemies), the Cham, another major Muslim community from Cambodia, were viewed more benignly. This was because, historically, they had contributed to the military power of the Ayutthayan kingdom by forming a major line of defence in the face of the Burmese invasion of 1767. Nevertheless, according to Scupin, some of the later Cham arrivals to Bangkok were the war captives of subsequent Thai-Cambodian conflicts.[94]

Aside from the Malays and Cham, other significant Muslim ethnic minorities include Persians and Indonesians who arrived via historical trading routes. South Asians (Punjabi, Gudjarati, Sindhi, Bengali, Pathan, and Pashtun) also added to Bangkok's Muslim population when they came as traders as a result of the opening up of trade between Britain and Thailand under the auspices of the Bowring Treaty of 1855.[95] As noted earlier, South Asian Muslims played an especially important role in the development of Islam in Thailand by acting as conduits for the influx of Islamic reformist and modernist ideas. It was also South Asian Muslims who created the *Jamiyatul Islam*, which was modelled along the lines of the modernist *Jamaat-I Islami* formed by Abdul ala Maududi in Pakistan. The *Jemaat Tabligh*, discussed earlier, also has its roots in South Asian Islam. More recently, Muslims from the Middle East have been settling in Thailand, taking advantage of the opening of trade links between the region and the kingdom. Given the ethnic diversity of Bangkok's Muslim community, it should not be surprising to find that Muslim minorities are organized along ethnic enclaves. For instance, the Cham congregate in the Ban Krua area, Javanese and other Indonesian ethnic groups can be found in the Makassan area, and Persians are concentrated in Dhonburi. As is the case in ethnically diverse Muslim communities elsewhere in the world, Muslims in Bangkok often worship in mosques that are organized along ethnic lines.

There are approximately half a million Muslims and 118 mosques in Bangkok. There are also seventy-seven Islamic schools that teach religion on a part-time basis (in the evenings and weekends for Muslim students attending public/national schools). In addition to this, there are also an estimated twelve schools modelled the traditional *pondok* in southern Thailand that provide full-time instruction solely in Islam. These schools are mostly scattered in the outskirts of Bangkok and generally have small enrolments, mostly of ethnic Malays. In addition to these institutions, Bangkok has two Islamic private schools that provide a full curriculum comprising religious and academic/secular subjects — Santichon Islamic School and Bangkok Suksa School. Santichon is 60 per cent funded by the government, while Bangkok Suksa is privately funded (it had applied for government funding in 2007). The curriculum at Santichon consists of 35 per cent religious subjects and 65 per cent secular subjects. In terms of pedagogy, it follows the reformist model of integrating a religious dimension into all its academic subjects. Instruction in Islam is conducted in Arabic and Thai. This differs from southern Thailand, where Islamic studies subjects are taught in Arabic and Malay. Thai is not used in the southern provinces for instruction in Islamic topics.

Differences in the focus of Islamic education between the Muslim-dominated southern provinces and Bangkok are largely a result not only of demographic patterns (where one region has a larger Muslim population than the other), but also of how Islam itself has been received and integrated into cultural and societal norms. The importance of Islam in the history and traditions of the southern provinces should by now be abundantly clear. In contrast, Islam in Bangkok has evolved along an entirely different plane. As Scupin trenchantly notes, "the sociological fact that these Muslims (Bangkok Muslims) reside in an area which is predominantly Buddhist has definite consequence for the form of Islam in Bangkok.... [t]here are definite similarities between certain conceptual notions and practices of popular Islam in Bangkok and the general religious traditions maintained by the urban Buddhist".[96]

Chiang Mai

Numbering around 30,000, the Thai Muslims in Chiang Mai are predominantly ethnic Chinese, with Yunnanese (Haw) making up around half of the overall Muslim population. Other major ethnic groups among Chiang Mai's Muslim community include Bengali, Burmese, Pashtun, and a small but growing Malay community consisting of middle-class southern Malay-Muslims who have relocated as a consequence of the security crisis in the south. There are fourteen mosques in Chiang Mai. In contrast to the southern provinces, the dominant school of *fiqh* is Hanafi, reflecting South Asian and Chinese influences rather than the Malay influence one finds in the southern provinces.

Unlike in the southern provinces or even Bangkok, Islamic schools are not a prominent feature of the Muslim socio-cultural landscape in Chiang Mai. According to local opinions obtained in the course of research interviews and conversations, it seems that this is so because Chinese and South Asian Muslims are more "pragmatic" and do not privilege religious education in the same manner as their co-religionists in the south.[97] Muslim students attend public schools full-time during the week. On weekends, some attend general religious classes at mosques, committing three to four hours on Saturday and Sunday mornings. Some middle-class families engage private religious tutors for their children during the evenings.[98]

There are only three schools in Chiang Mai that integrate some religious education into their curricula, though the extent to which they can really be deemed "religious" schools varies. These three schools are Jitpakdee Attaqwa School, Santi Suksa School, and Fatih (Witt Thai Witthaya) School. Of these three schools, Jitpakdee Attaqwa School is the only one that has an exclusively Islamic curriculum.

Jitpakdee was formed in January 1971 by a Yunnanese Muslim businessman who had obtained support from several of his Middle Eastern business contacts to build an Islamic school for the Muslim community in Chiang Mai. Through these contacts, donations totalling ten million baht were procured from interests in Saudi Arabia, Kuwait, Tunisia, Egypt, Libya, and the United Arab Emirates. Since its formation, Jitpakdee has received intermittent support from the Saudi government. It should be noted, though, that this support has recently been curtailed as a consequence of the Thai government's scrutiny of funds originating from Saudi Arabia, much in the same way that Ismail Lutfi's charities in southern Thailand have suffered cuts in Saudi funding. Aside from Saudi assistance, the school has also been a beneficiary of *zakat* money from the Attaqwa Mosque and rental income from town houses in the vicinity owned by the mosque and built with *waqf* money. The school primarily teaches Arabic language as well as the Qur'an and *hadith*. While it could boast of an enrolment numbering several hundreds in the past, as a result of the moratorium on foreign aid Jitpakdee's intake has been reduced to 150 students (more than half being female). These students are supervised by twelve teachers. As a further consequence of funding cuts, the number of scholarships available to its students for religious studies overseas has been reduced markedly. Over the past few years the school has managed to send an annual average of only eight students abroad for tertiary education in Islamic studies, mostly to Saudi Arabia and Egypt.

Unlike Jitpakdee, Santi Suksa School has a curriculum that includes religious as well as general academic subjects, though it is weighted heavily towards the latter. While classified as a "religious" school, Santi Suksa is not an Islamic institution *per se*. It has both Muslim and non-Muslim students (who study their respective religions in fulfilment of the "religious studies" component of their curriculum). Much in the same vein, while Fatih School is recognized in Chiang Mai's Muslim community as an Islamic school because it is run by a Turkish foundation, it does not in fact provide any religious instruction at all — merely transportation for its Muslim students to attend the Friday *khutbah* at nearby mosques.

Notwithstanding the size of the Muslim community and the marginal nature of Islamic education, contestations between traditionalists and reformists have also found their way into Chiang Mai's Muslim social landscape, though at a predictably lower intensity than in the southern provinces. Three reasons, all specific to the Chiang Mai context, can be offered for this. First, unlike in southern Thailand or Bangkok, there are hardly any recognizably "Islamic" schools in Chiang Mai. Given the premise in this book that such contestations are often represented and expressed in the realm of education, the lack of bona fide religious schools has effectively blunted the ideological edges of the various camps. Second, differences have over the past two decades been contained and managed effectively by religious leaders in the community. Here, the role of Imam Mustapha demands special mention. Imam Mustapha is the long-serving chair of Chiang Mai's Islamic Provincial Committee and a widely respected leader in the local Muslim community by virtue of his qualifications as a graduate of Medina University, where he studied *dakwah*. Moreover, he previously served as a leader of the Chiang Mai branch of the *Jemaat Tabligh*. In other words, it is this diverse background that has allowed him to bridge the traditionalist, reformist, and *Tabligh* camps and manage the potential tensions arising out of them. Finally, there is a sense, possessing some normative force, that the Muslim community in Chiang Mai is in general more open to and tolerant of competing schools of Islamic thought compared to other regions.

Be that as it may, the tensions and contestations among these various "Islams" are, as earlier suggested, not altogether non-existent. For instance, the Arabic scriptures that hang on the *mizarab* wall of the Attaqwa Mosque and that were written in the style of Chinese calligraphy (reflecting cultural influences on the Muslim community in Chiang Mai) have been criticized as *bid'a* (innovation) by members of the small Salafi-reformist community in Chiang Mai, giving rise to heated debates about tradition and reform that have only recently abated (at least on this particular issue).

Although there are some broad similarities between the structure of Islamic private schools in the Muslim-majority south and some of those found in other Muslim-minority regions, there are a number of notable differences. For instance, there is a far larger number of Muslims studying in Buddhist and Christian schools outside the south.[99] This phenomenon is virtually non-existent in the Malay-Muslim south. At one level, this perhaps speaks to insufficient numbers of Islamic schools to cater for the needs of all communities. At another level, however, it indicates that the outlook of non-Malay Muslims in Thailand differs from that of their Malay counterparts, insofar as perceptions of and opinions on the primacy of formal religious education are concerned.

Notes

[1] Quoted in Chairul Fahmy Hussaini, "Islamic Resurgence in Iran: Impact on Singaporean Muslims" (M.Sc. dissertation, Nanyang Technological University, 2006/2007), p. 17.

[2] See Ernesto Braam, "Travelling with the *Tablighi Jamaat* in South Thailand", *ISIM Review* 17 (Spring 2006): 42. Braam suggests that up to 20,000 people conduct their *dakwah* every year in southern Thailand.

[3] Interview at Madrasah Tahfiz Alkuran, Yala, 11 December 2006.

[4] Married women are permitted to partake in *Tabligh* activities, but have to live with either relatives or female friends.

[5] According to Imtiaz Yusuf, there had been other attempts by the *Jemaat Tabligh* to build schools in Bangkok, but these were rebuffed by the Muslim community. Conversation with Imtiaz Yusuf, Bangkok, 14 January 2006. The figure of sixty was suggested by *Tabligh* members during an interview at Madrasah Tahfiz Alkuran, Yala, 11 December 2006.

[6] Interview with Pakorn Priyakorn, Secretary General, Islamic Centre of Thailand, Bangkok,; email interview with a local Malay-Muslim scholar, 2 February 2006.

[7] Given the nature of the *Jemaat Tabligh*, which effectively has a "revolving door" approach to membership, it is impossible to obtain definite figures regarding the

organization. Any Muslim can volunteer to do *dakwah* with the *Jemaat Tabligh* without necessarily committing to the organization itself in any formal capacity.

[8]   Interview at Markaz Tahfiz Alkuran, Yala, 11 December 2006.

[9]   Interview with a Tabligh member, Markaz Dakwah Yala, 11 December 2006.

[10] Horstmann, *The Tablighi Jama'at in Southern Thailand*, p. 15.

[11] Interview at Sasanu Patam School, Pattani, 14 February 2005.

[12] This view was expressed by several Malay-Muslim community leaders during field interviews conducted in Pattani in July 2005.

[13] Interview at Yala Islamic College, Yala, 18 January 2005.

[14] The *dakwah* movement in Malaysia, for instance, is focused on student organizations and university campuses. See A.B. Shamsul, "Inventing Certainties: The Dakwah Persona in Malaysia", in *The Pursuit of Certainty: Religious and Cultural Formulations*, edited by Wendy James (London: Routledge, 1995). Having said that, there are tertiary education students who are members of the *Tablighi Jemaat* in southern Thailand.

[15] The author was informed by Alexander Horstmann that the Thai chapter of the *Tablighi Jemaat* might have as many as 200,000 members.

[16] Dietrich Reetz, "Sufi Spirituality Fires Reformist Zeal: The Tablighi Jamaat in Today's India and Pakistan" (paper presented to the workshop titled "Modern Adaptations of Sufi-Islam", Berlin, April 4–5, 2003).

[17] Interview at Azizstan School, Yala, 11 January 2005.

[18] Ibid.

[19] Interview at Tabia Witthaya, Yala, 2 August 2006.

[20] We should bear in mind here that this criticism of the "lesser Hadith" is a common, often polemical, device through which Muslims contest and counter alternative traditions within Islam.

[21] Horstmann, *The Tablighi Jama'at in Southern Thailand*, pp. 24–25.

[22] Alexander Horstmann, "The Tablighi Jemaat in Thailand" (paper presented at the Ninth International Conference on Thai Studies, Dekalb, Illinois, 3–6 April 2005).

[23] Email interview with a local Malay-Muslim scholar, 2 February 2006. This scholar emphasized, however, that it is also possible that not all *Jemaat Tabligh* members are active in *dakwah* in their respective *kampung* (village). In fact, he suggested that most of the time *dakwah* activities are carried out outside of their local *kampung*.

[24] Interview with a Muslim scholar, Bangkok, 18 January 2006.

[25] Interview at Santichon School, Bangkok, 18 January 2006.

[26] See, for example, Numan Hayimasae, "*Hj Sulong Abdul Kadir (1895–1954): Perjuangan dan Sumbangan Beliau Kepada Masyarakat Melayu Patani* [Hj Sulong Abdul Kadir: Struggle and Contributions to the Patani Malays]" (M.Sc. dissertation, University Sains Malaysia, 2002), pp. 84–87.

[27] R.L. Winzeler, "Traditional Islamic Schools in Kelantan", *Journal of the Malaysian Branch of the Royal Asiatic Society* 48, no. 1 (1964): 92.

[28] Hasan Madmarn, "The Pondok and Change in South Thailand", in *Aspects of Development*, edited by in Scupin, pp. 49–50. See also Hasan Madmarn, *The Pondok and Madrasah in Pattani* (Bangi: Penerbit Universiti Kebangsaan Malaysia, 1999), pp. 22–23.

[29] Most are Chinese students from Xinjiang who are fluent in Arabic, though there are also a number of Malaysians, Cambodians, and Kazakhs. The school has also had an American and a Swedish student, both female, enrolled in recent times. Interview with Kariya Langputeh, Yala Islamic University, Pattani, 18 January 2005.

[30] Interview with Ahmad Somboon Bualuang, Pattani, 31 October 2006.

[31] Interview with Pakorn Priyakorn, Islamic Central Committee of Thailand, Bangkok, 25 January 2005.

[32] Ibid.

[33] Mamoun Fandy, "Enriched Islam: The Muslim Crisis of Education", *Survival* 49, no. 2 (June 2007): 78.

[34] Azyumardi Azra, *The Origins of Islamic Reformism in Southeast Asia: Networks of Malay-Indonesian and Middle Eastern 'Ulama' in the Seventeenth and Eighteenth Centuries* (Crows Nest, New South Wales: Allen & Unwin, 2004), p. 2.

[35] Surin Pitsuwan, *Islam and Malay Nationalism: A Case Study of the Malay-Muslims of Southern Thailand* (Bangkok: Thai Khadi Research Institute, Thammasat University, 1985), p. 129.

[36] Interview with a National Security Council official, Bangkok, 14 July 2005.

[37] Interview at Prasarn Witthaya School, Pattani, 3 January 2006.

[38] Of course, several *ustaz* interviewed have challenged that view. They contend that there are still some institutions of repute, such as Pondok Dalor, Thamma Witthaya Islamic Private School, and Yala Islamic University.

[39] Interview at Prathib Witthaya Islamic School, Narathiwat, 13 January 2005.

[40] Interview at Darun Witthaya Islamic School, Pattani, 13 January 2006.

[41] This was revealed in a casual discussion with locals conducted in Pattani, 18 January 2006.

[42] Of those who were locally trained, approximately thirty were not religious teachers but instructors in secular subjects.

[43] The figures from the defence and education ministries were obtained by my field researcher and relayed to me via an email report dated 7 July 2006.

[44] Email interview with the secretary of the Islamic Private School Association, 9 July 2006. It should be noted that this figure refers chiefly to Muslim students from the three southern provinces and does not include those from other regions in the country.

[45] Wan Kadir Che Man, *Muslim Separatism: The Moro of Southern Philippines and the Malays of Southern Thailand* (Singapore: Oxford University Press, 1990), p. 110.

[46] See Aurel Croissant, "Unrest in South Thailand: Contours, Causes, and Consequences Since 2001", *Strategic Insights* 4, no. 2 (February 2005): 9.

47 Figures obtained via email interview on 18 September 2007.

48 One should note, though, that these are annual, post-September 11 figures. There is a large number of Malay-Muslims who had gone to Saudi Arabia before the moratorium and who continue to study and reside there.

49 This was told to my field researcher on 19 September 2007 by an *ustaz* who was a Saudi graduate. The *ustaz* was, however, unable to furnish a reasonable estimate on the number of such cases. The membership figures of the Alumni Association of Saudi Arabia were furnished by a Saudi alumnus via email on 24 September 2007.

50 Email interview with a Saudi alumnus, 24 September 2007.

51 Interview at the *Persatuan Sekolah Agama Rakyat*, Pattani, 19 April 2007.

52 I would like to thank one of the anonymous reviewers for making this point. The extent of this oversight, though, remains unclear and difficult to ascertain.

53 "Students Come Home to Suspicion", *The Nation*, 31 October 2006.

54 Interview at the *Persatuan Sekolah Agama Rakyat*, Pattani, 19 April 2007.

55 Interview at the Islamic Centre of Thailand, Bangkok, 19 January 2006.

56 Interview with Hasan Madmarn, Pattani, 16 January 2006.

57 Interview at the *Persatuan Sekolah Agama Rakyat*, Pattani, 19 April 2007.

58 I mean by this that the majority of religious teachers on staff are known to be of Salafi orientation. There are, of course, Salafist and Wahhabi teachers scattered across the provinces in many other schools, and this may well contribute to the perception that some of these other institutions are also Wahhabi in orientation. Be that as it may, the schools listed here are characterized by the overwhelming number of Saudi-trained educators they have on staff as described by local education officials. It is important to stress again that not all Saudi educators are Wahhabi in doctrinal orientation and hence having a large base of Saudi-trained educators on staff does *not* mean that a particular school promulgates Wahhabi thought.

59 Students choosing to pursue secular degrees or courses, though, have to cover their own expenses.

60 Hasan Madmarn, *The Pondok and Madrasah in Pattani* (Bangi: Penerbit University Kebangsaan Malaysia, 1999), pp. 144–45.

61 Email correspondence with Hasan Madmarn, 2 April 2005.

62 Interview with Surin Pitsuwan, Bangkok, 13 July 2006.

63 Researcher interview at the *Persatuan Sekolah Agama Rakyat*, Pattani, 19 April 2007.

64 Email interview with an alumnus of University of Khartoum, 28 April 2007.

65 Interview with Ahmad-umar Japakiya, Yala, 20 March 2007.

66 Ibid.

67 This was the opinion of a senior Sudan-educated ustaz who was interviewed on 10 April 2007. This *ustaz* further suggested that seventy percent of Sudan-trained Islamic scholars in Thailand were traditionalists in terms of their theological persuasion, and the remaining 30 per cent were Salafi and Wahhabi. This is, of course, conjecture and difficult to confirm.

68   Ibid.
69   Ibid.
70   Interview at the *Persatuan Sekolah Agama Rakyat*, Pattani, 19 April 2007. According to the interviewees, these traditionalist schools are also coincidentally known to be linked to the separatist organization *Barisan Revolusi Nasional* (BRN).
71   Ibid.
72   Researcher interview at Samarnmit Witthaya School, Yingo, Narathiwat, 19 June 2007.
73   Ibid.
74   Ustaz Abdul Rahman Abdul Samad, a graduate in *shari'a* from University of Jordan, was a former chairman of the Islamic Council of Narathiwat.
75   Researcher interview at Samarnmit Witthaya School, Yingo, Narathiwat, 19 June 2007.
76   Interview with members of the *Organisasi Pelajar Lama Pattani Darussalam Pakistan*, Pattani, 17 November 2006.
77   Of these universities, the most popular are Aligarh and Nadwah Islamiah in India and University of Islamic Studies in Pakistan.
78   Interview with Nidae Waba, President, Islamic Private School Association, Pattani, 14 January 2006. Nidae could not provide a figure for Indonesia.
79   Researcher interview at the *Persatuan Sekolah Agama Rakyat*, Pattani, 28 May 2007.
80   Ibid.
81   Ibid. I was informed by an *ustaz* that funding from Islamic charities for studies in Malaysia has been scaled back over the past few years. Interview at Pattani Jihad Witthaya, Pattani, 14 January 2006.
82   This information was distilled from interviews with several *ustaz* and PSU lecturers who graduated from institutions in Malaysia.
83   Imtiyaz Yusuf, head of religious studies at Assumption University, Bangkok, and formerly associated with IIU in Malaysia, also informed me that Thai Muslims constituted the largest overseas student community at IIU. This comment was made at a meeting in Bangkok on 13 July 2006.
84   The author was informed that *Dewan Bahasa dan Pusaka* in Malaysia has regularly been dispatching language teachers to southern Thailand on short-term assignments. Interview with a Malaysian *ustaz*, Narathiwat, 26 April 2005.
85   Ibid. According to the interviewee, some of these *tok guru* have apparently also opened *pondok* schools in Malaysia and Indonesia, though it is unclear if the respective governments are aware of this development. This interviewee was also of the opinion that many of these Thai teachers do not return to Thailand for fear of being labelled separatists and militants.
86   This offer has apparently been taken up and teachers are being sent to Malaysia for training in religious instruction. See "Three *Pondok* picked to become models", *The Nation*, 31 March 2005.
87   Interview with an *ustaz*, Yala, 22 April 2005.

88   Interview at Sasanupatham School, Muang, Pattani, 25 May 2007.
89   There are currently no Islamic studies scholars among Malay-Muslim religious educators who have obtained a doctorate from Indonesia. The highest qualification obtained was by Ustaz Ahamakamae Wae-muso, who graduated from the University of Surabaya with an M.A. in Islamic studies and who now serves as headmaster of Sasanupatham School. Additionally, he is also *imam* of Banbana mosque in Muang and sits on the Provincial Islamic Committee of Pattani.
90   Prominent leaders of the Shi'a community in southern Thailand such as Anwar Budi and Ishak Budi were in fact graduates of Indonesian institutions.
91   Comments made by Surin Pitsuwan at a meeting in Bangkok, 13 July 2006.
92   This is the case not only within the Muslim communities in the south but also those in Bangkok.
93   See Raymond Scupin, "Muslim Accommodation in Thai Society", *Journal of Islamic Studies* 9, no. 2 (1998): 238–39.
94   Ibid., p. 240.
95   Ibid., pp. 244–45.
96   Raymond Scupin, "Popular Islam in Thailand", in *The Muslims of Thailand: Volume 1, Historical and Cultural Studies*, edited by Andrew D.W. Forbes (Bihar: Centre for South East Asian Studies, 1988), pp. 41–42.
97   This view was reinforced during my conversation with Suchart Setthamalinee, Chiang Mai, 9 January 2006.
98   Interview with Pam Kannaporn, Chiang Mai, 9 January 2006.
99   Interview with a senior administrator, Central Islamic Committee of Thailand, Bangkok, 25 January 2005.

CONCLUSION
Islamic Education in Southern Thailand: At a Crossroads

The quest for knowledge has always been viewed as an important responsibility and obligation for Muslims. This follows from injunctions in the Qur'an and *hadith* that among other things impress upon Muslims the need to "seek knowledge even as far as China" and "to seek knowledge from cradle to grave", and which further instruct that "the first thing created by God was the intellect" and "one learned man is harder on the devil than a thousand ignorant worshippers".[1] The pursuit of knowledge in Islam is understood by Muslims above all to be an expression of faith. Therein lies a fundamental difference between Islamic perspectives on education and modern, secular understandings of the function of knowledge, which tend to ascribe to knowledge an instrumentalist value towards the advancement of material interests. Islamic schools do not have as their primary task the supply of labour to the state or equipping citizens for the modern economy, particularly when such aims may entail compromises of faith and creed. This is not to say, however, that the considerations of physical welfare and the fulfilment of basic material needs are not a matter of concern for Muslim parents, teachers, and students alike. Indeed they are. The point to stress is that these concerns are seldom articulated as the foremost priority. Islamic schools are seen to provide Muslim students with specifically religious education and their concern is, above all, the matter of spiritual well-being. It is to this end that they follow distinct and long-cherished traditions of knowledge accumulation and dissemination. Any assessment of the Islamic education system, whether for the purpose of policy formulation or the study of a time-honoured tradition and institution, must necessarily bear this in mind.

Because of the place of knowledge in Islam, the Islamic school has through the centuries been considered a major social and religious institution of the Muslim world. This should not detract from the fact that Islamic education is in and of itself hardly a monolithic entity devoid of its own dichotomies and dissonances. Nothing could be further from the truth. On the contrary, what "knowledge" entails, who enjoys the authority to define it, and what the appropriate forms and structures are of the institutions and pedagogies through which it is transmitted — these questions are subjected to intense debate and contestation, not least from within Muslim communities themselves. Needless to say, such tensions are further amplified by the specific social and cultural conditions within which the quest for knowledge is pursued in any particular Muslim community. This book has attempted to plot out the struggles of Thailand's Malay-Muslim population in achieving and sustaining an education system that is infused with Islamic values and principles but which remains relevant for the community in the face of contemporary challenges, against its own peculiar social, political, cultural, and historical context. To this end, the book has focused on both the continuities and discontinuities in Islamic education primarily (though not exclusively) in the three Muslim-majority provinces of southern Thailand.

The reform of the traditional *pondok*, and more broadly of the Islamic education system in southern Thailand, has been a subject of considerable debate in both scholarly and policy realms. Much of this debate, however, has been informed by the imperatives of "counter-terrorism" and "counter-insurgency" and correspondingly stem from suspicions and allegations that Islamic schools are churning out militants. The prevalence of this mindset is unfortunate, for it not only obfuscates some very significant challenges confronting Islamic education that have little or nothing to do with terrorism or insurgency, but also limits and distorts analysis while marginalizing the very voices from within the Malay-Muslim communities and religious leadership that are in fact catalysts engaged in promoting reform. The fact that schools have historically been involved in the intermittent separatist movement is something that has been stressed on many occasions, not least in the literature on terrorism and insurgency. While such tracts are not entirely bereft of truth, their narrowness is unhelpful, particularly when they cause schools to become the focal point of counter-insurgency efforts in the minds of pundits and policy-makers without providing any nuanced understanding of Islamic education in southern Thailand. While we need to consider where to locate Islamic schools in the ongoing violence and to appreciate the role of education in perpetuating the notions of identity and difference or hegemony and resistance that threaten to polarize southern Thai society, we have to be equally conscious of the need to properly contextualize the link between schools and violence in all of its complexity. In this respect, rather than critique the security literature, this book has sought to supplement its observations by examining the form and content of Islamic education so as to provide crucial resource information and insights into very important yet incredibly opaque socio-religious institutions.

PERCEPTUAL GAPS

The preceding chapters have examined the policy, procedural, pedagogical, and philosophical underpinnings of Islamic education. It is well known that, historically, Islamic schools in southern Thailand have struggled to procure state recognition and accreditation. The creation of a modern bureaucracy and economy in Thailand in the early twentieth century entailed major changes in the traditional forms and structures of education. Aside from creating a modern bureaucracy that could sustain the rapid modernization taking place under King Chulalongkorn, there was another motive behind the project to transform education. It was during this period that the notion of a Thai "national" identity took shape around the mantra "Nation, Religion, Monarchy", which would eventually form the basis of a nationalist agenda that sought to assimilate minority ethnic groups.[2] By way of policies such as the enforced use of the Thai language and the introduction of the Buddhist belief system into the school curriculum, education became a means through which nationalism, assimilation, and integration were promoted. Concomitantly, the many attempts by the Malay-Muslim community to craft or recalibrate education policy have met with regular resistance, and on occasion overt violence. Such is the cyclical nature of this mutually reinforcing dynamic — while the current violence may in part be traced to Islamic schools, yet in the minds of many Malay-Muslims, the Islamic schools were themselves targets of assimilationist strategies. In other words, the recent targeting of Islamic schools and the attempts to reform these institutions on the part of the central state are just part of a long history of the politics of assimilation.

The friction between a consolidated national education system on the one hand and the autonomous, traditional Malay-Muslim *pondok* schools in the south on the other has on occasion been alleviated somewhat by more positive and conciliatory government policies such as the Pondok Educational Improvement Program, which facilitated efforts to transform Islamic education through government funding, to the extent that many Islamic private schools are today fully funded by the state. These policies have, however, proven double-edged, as the mechanism for funding has also in theory allowed for the closer regulation of Islamic schools by the state, a highly controversial provocative issue. More recently (since May 2004), the Thai government has required religious schools to register in exchange for further financial aid. In fact, apart from dangling the carrot of funding, government authorities have few efforts to examine the operations and curricula in Islamic schools. A commonly cited reason for this is the lack of experienced officials and personnel who are equipped with the requisite linguistic and cultural skills to scrutinize the curricula of these schools or to ensure that the funding allocated to them is funnelled to the right areas of development.[3] There have recently been, however, some more activist and culturally sensitive attempts, at least on the part of the Education Ministry, to make positive contributions to the transformation of curriculum. For instance, the Education Ministry has moved to propose the formalization of Malay as a first language.[4] The Thai government's realization of the need to recalibrate education policy in accordance with the specific conditions and contexts of the southern provinces, particularly in relation to questions of culture, identity, and ethno-historical memory, is further reflected in the latest articulation of government policy towards the southern provinces. Entitled *Education Development Plan of the Provinces along the Southern Border* (and referred to earlier in this book), this blueprint serves as a comprehensive articulation of the government's plans for transforming social, cultural, and economic space in southern Thailand through education.

Given the tendency among many to view Islamic education as static and medieval while the state is seen as a driver of change, it is worth noting that in southern Thailand many Muslims, including religious teachers, have stood at the forefront of demands for change, particularly in the context of growing internal and external pressures to modernize religious education. Organizations such as the Pondok Association and the Islamic Private School Association have been established to implement norms, procedures, and a set of universal standards for religious education and to oversee the general administration of *pondok*, Islamic private schools, and *tadika*. Likewise, tertiary education institutions such as the Yala Islamic University and the Princess of Narathiwatrajnakarin University have been created to provide much-needed educational opportunities that until now had only been available at the state-run Prince of Songkhla University. Of course, there are still substantial impediments to reform arising from within the community. Indeed, while it can be said that the Muslim elite, administrators, and school teachers are as much drivers of change as the government officials who oversee educational matters, some Muslim educators have posed obstacles to education reform. Oftentimes, these educators are themselves products of traditional religious education, hail from poor and lower-class families, and are predisposed to believe that any quest for reform threatens to open the doors of the *pondok* to a modernity that many see as an invitation to stray away from Islam. Indeed, for these traditionalist *tok guru* and *ustaz*, their essential task is viewed as the preservation, not innovation, of received tradition. It is at least in part because of this that institutional developments remain slow and standards are generally low when measured against secular yardsticks, notwithstanding efforts to bridge the gap between traditional and modern Islamic education as well as between religious knowledge and general academic subjects.

While some Muslim educators have highlighted their desire to maintain religious knowledge and practice as the cornerstones of Islamic education in Thailand, others acknowledge the need to find space in mainstream Thai education and to equip students with the necessary skills and qualifications so that they may advance to higher education or seek out employment in a way that does not compromise their religion. There is also another factor here that speaks to the socio-cultural currents that underlie the traditional structures and frameworks of Islamic education. Bearing in mind what Islamic schools represent for the Malay-Muslim community of southern Thailand, it is evident that the education system may be conceived of as a tool in the construction of the hegemonic nation state, in that it reproduces cultural capital and reconfigures power relations. Beyond the exigencies of development, the education system may be, or in this case has been, employed to impose a specific ideology, that of "Thai-ness" (expressed for instance in the preference for Thai as a medium of instruction as opposed to Malay). To be sure, this is not unique to Thailand. The sphere of education is, after all, often the prerogative of the state. Where it becomes a matter of concern is when the state seeks to homogenize a heterogeneous ethno-cultural landscape and in so doing overlooks, deliberately discounts, or even suppresses differences based on culture, religion, and language. The Thai state has a record of doing just this — instituting structures that effectively marginalize minorities, not least the Malay-Muslims of the southern provinces. The homogenizing efforts of the Thai state have, more often than not, elicited fierce reactions that in many ways further solidified and cemented identities along religious, ethnic, and cultural lines, and that focus on narratives of origin, ritual, heroism, symbols, and values.

It should be clear by now that Islamic education in southern Thailand cannot be divorced from the larger concepts of Malay-Muslim cultural identity and interpretations of history. Indeed, this book has attempted to demonstrate that in the Malay-Muslim community, the latter two precepts by and large inform approaches to the former, an important consideration in any attempt to understand the role of Islamic education in southern

Thailand today. The salience of issues of identity and history is further accentuated by simple demographics. What this means is that any prevailing "framework" for studying Islamic education in Muslim minority contexts cannot be applied to the case of southern Thailand for the simple reason that, unlike most other Muslim minorities, Thailand's Muslims are geographically concentrated in the southern provinces to the extent that they form an overwhelming majority. This explains not only the assertiveness and sense of entitlement of Thailand's Malay-Muslim community *vis-à-vis* the promulgation of their culture and religion, but also the sense of vulnerability and insecurity in the relationship with the central Thai state that quickly surfaces whenever the spectre of regulation is raised in relation to Islamic education.

Again, this does not to imply that the religious identity of Malay-Muslims in southern Thailand is an inherently static phenomenon. As Robert Hefner observes in his authoritative study on Islamic education, "Islamic education is characterized not by lock-step uniformity but by a teeming plurality of actors, institutions and ideas."[5] In recognition of this, the book maps out the reflexive questioning, active debate, and contestations within the community over what constitutes Islamic knowledge and education, how it has changed, and who has the legitimate right to appropriate and claim authority over this knowledge and its transmission.

COMPETING ISLAMIC DISCOURSES

Since Islam began to expand in the seventh century, divisions and discontinuities have emerged. For instance, religious law has come to be interpreted and elaborated by hundreds of schools, not to mention local traditions and customs. Such are the competing discourses in Islam that Muslims today are locked in intense debates over how holy scripture is to be interpreted and understood. The Malay-Muslim community in southern Thailand has hardly been immune to these tensions and contradictions, which clearly remain unresolved.

In order to understand the profound transformations that Islamic education in southern Thailand has undergone (and is undergoing), we must move beyond the optic of the relationship between the state and the Malay-Muslim community in the south. While this is undoubtedly an important dimension of the problem, such an approach tends to be overwhelmingly structural in its emphasis on the state. The crucial shifts taking place within local referents will tend to be neglected, and consequently, changing configurations of hegemony may be missed. The dilemmas that accompany pressures for change, this book has argued, are considerably more complex than implied by a state versus minority dichotomy. This comes across in the transformation taking place within the Malay-Muslim community itself, the discontinuities that accompany this process, and the competing Islamic discourses that have emerged. These transformations are expressed most profoundly in the rise of reformist approaches and their subsequent impact on the socio-religious landscape of southern Thailand, with their new interpretations of the faith and creed, as well as their new expressions of religiosity.

A major feature of this terrain in recent times has been the resurgence of the Salafi reform movement and its consequent competition with the mainstream, traditionalist Shafi'i-Sufi Islam that has long defined Muslim creed and practice in the Malay world (of which Yala, Pattani, and Narathiwat are a constituent cultural part). This contestation clearly has historical precedents and it echoes similar dynamics of many decades earlier, when a reform movement led by the indefatigable Haji Sulong sought to revive Muslim consciousness in southern Thailand by transforming the methodology, epistemology, and pedagogy of Islamic education. The new cohort of reformist scholars, most self-declared Salafis, are looking to reform Islamic knowledge and practice in the south in much the same way as Haji Sulong attempted. Based on an analysis of key works by Ismail Lutfi, arguably the most well-known and popular of the Salafi-reformists, as well as interviews with him and other Islamic teachers of similar theological and epistemological persuasion, the book unpacks the philosophical and ideological underpinnings of what is arguably the most influential version of reformist Islam in southern Thailand since Haji Sulong.

So far as may be ascertained, the brand of Islam advocated by Ismail Lutfi is an interesting marriage of fundamentalist Salafi ideology on the one hand and a reformist understanding of Islamic education on the other. While Lutfi betrays his Salafi roots by continually stressing a need to return to the Qur'an and *sunnah* in the pursuit of knowledge, he also demonstrates an acute awareness of the need to make this knowledge speak to the challenges of the modern world. In many respects, this duality is captured in the syllabus of reformist Islamic private schools and more noticeably in the curriculum and degree programmes at the Yala Islamic University. At another level, the vision of reform that Lutfi and his reformist colleagues promulgate contests many of the tenets of traditional Islam as practised in southern Thailand. Indeed, Lutfi has articulated his view that this brand of reformist Islam which marries Salafism and reformist ideas is in effect a rebuttal to traditionalist discourse and its conceptions of the sources of truth, knowledge, and authority, which in his view have been built on "*ilmu kurang*" or an apparent lack of true knowledge.

The seeming dualism embedded in Ismail Lutfi's comprehension of and approach to Islamic knowledge is not likely to sit very well with Western conceptions of social-scientific typologies and taxonomies, particularly if one is unable or unwilling to countenance nuances. For instance, the Muslim groups and movements that are conservative in their approach or perhaps even hostile towards Western values and interests may not be all that radical in their proposals for what they wish to achieve in society. Likewise, those who aspire to a "radical" transformation of the social order, such as the reformist Islamic scholars in southern Thailand with their desire for change in the traditional education system, may well eschew armed violence or extremist measures in the pursuit of their aims. As this book has shown, Lutfi's agenda is at once reformist, modernist, and fundamentalist. It is reformist in that it acknowledges the limitations of traditional Islamic education and the need for relevance in the face of modernity. Beyond this, the movement is also modernist in that it aims to integrate academic subjects such as science, technology, business, and finance into the curriculum of Islamic schools. Yet the agenda is at the same time fundamentalist in that it locates Islam, and in particular the Qur'an and *sunnah*, at the heart of its understanding of modern knowledge.

Given the tendency among some commentators to demonize Ismail Lutfi for purported links to terrorism and Wahhabism, the exposition of Lutfi's ideas in this book is intended in part to speak to these prevailing interpretations regarding the content and import of his religio-ideological proclivities. Here the book has argued specifically for the need to consider the nuances embedded in Lutfi's discourse. The close scrutiny of his work suggests that the Salafi-reformist Islam that Lutfi articulates responds to modernity not by rejecting or criticizing it — he is clearly comfortable with modern science and technology. Rather, borrowing an apt description from Roxanne Euben's pathbreaking analysis of Sayyid Qutb, Lutfi's notions of knowledge is more a "dynamic critique" rather than a "scripturalist reflex".[6]

As a reformist scholar, Lutfi deals with the controversial issues surrounding the difficult history of southern Thailand. His work on Islam and peace is an unequivocal statement against the illegitimate nature of the ongoing violence in southern Thailand currently being waged in the name of Islam. This position is reinforced in his warnings against the "false teachings" associated with the Khawarij, which were the progenitors of the practice of *takfir* (Muslims condemning fellow Muslims as infidels). Indeed, some have mistakenly accused Lutfi (by virtue of his alleged sympathies towards Wahhabism) of being a proponent of *takfir*.

Moreover, Lutfi's work on the classification of Muslim lands is important as it provides insight into how one of Thailand's leading Islamic scholars understands and conceptualizes the place of the Muslim-dominated southern provinces in the Thai geopolitical body. Unlike the discourse of southern Thai militants found in *Berjihad di Pattani* or the simplistic exegesis in *Jihad Fi Sabilillah Pengertian dan Bidang*, Lutfi's writing challenges the assumption underlying extremist Islamic thought, which is that the Dar Al-Harb automatically equates to hostility towards Islam and is therefore a legitimate target of *jihad*. When this text is read together with *Islam Penjana Kedamaian Sejagat*, where he persuasively reinforces the position on *jihad* that classical Islamic scholars have held through the centuries, Lutfi's writing makes it clear that not all Islamic scholars who invoke these traditionalist Islamic frameworks of international relations (i.e. Dar Al-Islam and Dar Al-Harb) are committed to the path of violence. On the contrary, Lutfi effectively uses precisely these frameworks to deny the ongoing violence in southern Thailand any religious legitimacy.

There is, however, one point that needs to be stressed about the Islamic reform movement in southern Thailand as it relates to historical trends of reform and the role of the religious establishment. Whereas the recognized standard-bearers of Islamic reform in the late nineteenth and early twentieth centuries, such as Jamaluddin Afghani and Muhammad Abduh, were middle-class professionals, those who spearheaded the Islamic reform movement in southern Thailand — Ismail Lutfi Japakiya, and before him Haji Sulong Abdul Kadir — were themselves part of the establishment of Islamic scholars. If anything, this indicates that there is still a strong tendency towards traditionalism even among the Salafi reformists.

KNOWLEDGE, EDUCATION, AND TRANSLOCALITY

Perhaps more so than any other religion, Islam conjures up images of adherents with malleable identities, allegiances, and political territoriality. This, one is often reminded, is epitomized by the abstract concept of the *ummah*, the universal body of believers, and the *hajj* pilgrimage, the convocation of Muslims regardless of race or nationality. Both these institutions draw attention to the salience of pan-Islam and the transnational essence of the religion. Notwithstanding the abstract nature of the *ummah* and of the relationships that define it, it is a concept that holds at least some measure of currency across the global Muslim community. This is arguably most clearly expressed in the local–transnational nexus of Islamic education.

For a long time, Southeast Asia's geographical distance from the Muslim core meant that "local cultures had developed idioms of Islamic practice largely in isolation from mainstream, scripturalist Islam", thereby giving rise to the syncretic form of faith for which the region has become famous.[7] Needless to say, things changed significantly with the advent of print capitalism and improvements in global communication and travel. The net result of this has been the emergence of a politics of authenticity "between itinerant students critical of oral traditions in their villages and those local religious leaders who insist on the correctness of their 'Islam' ".[8] Nowhere is this more evident than in the spread of Salafi and Wahhabi ideology, facilitating the enormous and penetrating expansion of Saudi influence into the remote villages of Pattani, Cotabato (Philippines), and Kampung Cham (Cambodia).

As with Islamic schools elsewhere, the *pondok* and Islamic private schools of southern Thailand are not insulated from broader trends across the Muslim world. This book has traced some of these transnational networks and discussed their impact on Islamic education as well as broader issues of culture and religion. From this exercise several trends emerge that are worth noting. First, given the tendency in mainstream Islamic praxis to see the Middle East and North Africa as the heartland of Islam and centre of religious knowledge, it is not surprising to see that an overseas education in the "heartland" remains highly prized in southern Thailand. In the eyes of local Muslims, teachers educated abroad command more respect than locally-trained scholars. This is particularly so in the case of Islamic scholars trained in the Arabic language and who by virtue of that have, in the minds of lay Muslims, been invested with the authority to access the original texts. To be fair, the transnational avenues of knowledge dissemination have not been exclusively one-way streets. Patani, as noted, developed a reputation as a centre of excellence in Islamic education. Not only that, prominent *ulama* from southern Thailand have spent, and continue to spend, much time in the *halaqah* in Saudi Arabia, thereby contributing to the kingdom's own reputation as the hub of Islamic knowledge and learning. The fact that southern Thailand's reputation as a hub of Islamic learning has been waning over the years cannot however be denied.

This transnational dimension of Islamic education has given rise to formal and informal alumni networks that, as with all conventional alumni organizations, serve as conduits for ideas. From the present study, it is clear that while a number of formal foundation-based local networks can be identified, most schools are by and large linked informally either through shared ideological proclivities (e.g., the Salafi reformists) or through alumni networks. In any case, transnationalism has its repercussions in terms of the accentuation of contestations and fragmentations within localities. As Peter Mandaville describes in his assessment of the transnational nature of Islam, "the resulting syncretisms and interminglings have bequeathed to Islam a rich body of cultural material replete with difference, hybridity and, at times, contradiction".[9] That säid, it is also the case, Mandaville continues, that "the relativisation of Islam which naturally occurs through travel allows Muslims to see internal hegemony, and translocality provides them with the intellectual environment in which to develop counter-hegemonic discourse".[10] This is the case not only with the Salafi-oriented reformist movement, which provides a cogent illustration of this phenomenon at work, but also the *Jemaat Tabligh* and, to a lesser extent, Shi'a Islam, all of which have emerged to contest the prevailing "internal hegemony" of the traditional religious leadership and mainstream Islamic knowledge and practice.

AT A CROSSROADS

Scholars who study Muslims in Thailand have accurately maintained that Thai Islam has enjoyed a long and vibrant tradition and that the country itself has been home to a wide variety of representations of Muslim identity. As this book has endeavoured to demonstrate, however, Muslim heterogeneity has also generated multifarious and variegated patterns of dissonance and contestations which have profoundly affected the realm of Islamic education. While differences between the state and Muslim society, as well as between Malay and Thai identities, have sparked considerable press and academic interest and coverage, the contestations and discontinuities that have emerged within the Muslim community as it seeks to negotiate identity and authenticity, modernity and tradition, must be more carefully studied and analysed.

In conclusion, while Islamic education in southern Thailand struggles to maintain its centuries-old reputation and status as a centre of Islamic learning, the discontinuities and fault-lines within the community itself have become increasingly noticeable as the Muslim ground has been disturbed by the emergence of Salafi reformists and other scripturalist constructions of Islam. This interplay of forces has been further complicated, if not exactly amplified, by the increasing assertiveness of the minority *Tabligh* and Shi'a Muslim communities. There is a distinct geo-cultural dimension to these issues of Islamic education and identity. It is clear from this study, for example, that the ethno-cultural imperative has been far more central to trends in Islamic education in southern Thailand than in other Muslim communities elsewhere in the country. Additionally, the number and demographics of Islamic schools in the south, as compared to elsewhere in Thailand, indicate differences in the level of Islamic knowledge and consciousness across the country. In other words, Islamic education is a dynamic realm where Muslim identities are contested and negotiated, and this book has used it as a point of entry to capture broader trends and tensions. Granted, it remains unclear how the Salafi-reformist challenge will pan out or if it can be sustained. After all, even as his popularity increases, Lutfi's ideas and theology are still met with much scepticism and caution by some, particularly those who cling to tradition. Nevertheless, the current fixation among scholarly and policy communities with Malay-Muslim violence has by and large ignored these deeper currents in Islamic education that will likely have significance consequences for notions of Muslim identity, community, and authenticity in Thailand in the future. The gradual disruption of traditional Muslim society with the influx of reformist ideas and the impact this may have on Muslim identity and community in the long run will be a phenomenon worth scrutinizing. While there should be little doubt that Islamic education institutions can function as catalysts of change, the dissonance within the Malay-Muslim community on issues of meaning, authenticity, and identity have found expression in educational structures and institutions and may well alter the nature and character of Islam in Thailand in the not-too-distant future — possibly in profound ways.

Notes

[1]   *Hadith* citations taken from www.twf.org/News/Y1999/0101-SSVision.html (accessed 21 September 2006).

[2]   See Craig J. Reynolds, ed., *National Identity and Its Defenders, Thailand, 1939–1989* (Melbourne: Monash Papers on Southeast Asia No. 25, Centre of Southeast Asian Studies, Monash University, 1991); Patrick Jory, "Multiculturalism in Thailand: Cultural and Regional Resurgence in a Diverse Kingdom", *Harvard Asia-Pacific Review* (Winter 2000).

[3]   "Tadika school transfer worries", *Bangkok Post*, 13 August 2005.

[4]   "Solutions for strife: Schools in South to teach Yawi", *The Nation*, 6 August 2005.

[5]   See Robert W. Hefner and Muhammad Qasim Zaman, eds., *Schooling Islam: Modern Muslim Education* (Princeton: Princeton University Press, 2006).

[6]   See Roxanne L. Euben, *Enemy in the Mirror: Islamic Fundamentalism and The Limits of Modern Rationalism* (Princeton: Princeton University Press, 1999).

[7]   Peter Mandaville, *Transnational Muslim Politics: Reimagining the Umma* (London: Routledge, 2001), p. 157.

[8]   Patricia Horvatich, "Ways of Knowing Islam", *American Ethnologist* 21, no. 4 (1994): 817.

[9]   Mandaville, *Transnational Muslim Politics*, p. 152.

[10]   Ibid., p. 179.

APPENDICES

APPENDIX I
Schools and Affiliated Foundations

Name of Schools in Yala (and foundation):
1. Darul Ulum Nibong Baru (Yayasan Darul Ulum Nibong Baru), Muang, Yala.
2. Tarbiartul Watan Mulniti (Yayasan Al-amin), Muang, Yala.
3. Thama Wittaya Mulniti (Islam Wittaya Foundation), Muang, Yala.
4. Prathib Wittaya (Yayasan Misbahhulmunir), Muang, Yala.
5. Pattana Wittaya (Yayasan Majlis Agama Islam Wilayah Yala), Muang, Yala.
6. Pattana Islam Wittaya (Yayasan Lutfi), Muang, Yala.
7. Sateri Islam Wittaya Mulniti (Yayasan Islam Wittaya), Muang, Yala.
8. Asasuddin Wittaya (Yayasan Muhamadi), Muang, Yala.
9. Darulhuda Wittaya (Yayasan Darulhuda), Raman, Yala.
10 Ma'had Islamiah (Yayasan Islam Suksa Bala), Raman, Yala.
11. Ma'had Dakwah Islamiah (Yayasan Islam Taklokhala), Raman, Yala.
12. Srifarida Baru Wittaya (Yayasan al-Ansar), Raman, Yala.
13. Suksawat Wittaya (Yayasan Suksawat Islam Wittaya), Yaha, Yala.
14. Islam Bachok Wittaya (Yayasan Islam Bachok Wittaya), Bannansetar, Yala.
15. Alawiyah Wittaya (Yayasan Abukar), Bannansetar, Yala.
16. Khairiah Wittaya Mulniti (Yayasan Muslim Thai-Muslim Betong), Betong, Yala.

Name of Schools in Narathiwat (and foundation):
1. Sukkan Sart Wittaya (Yayasan Sekolah Sukkan Sart Wittaya), Muang, Narathiwat.
2. Attarkiah Islamiah (Yayasan Islam Untuk Pendidikan), Muang, Narathiwat.
3. Islam Burana Toknor (Yayasan Islam Burana Toknor), Muang, Narathiwat.

4. Pattana Sart Wittaya (Yayasasan Kebajikan Dan pendididkan), Muang, Narathiwat.
5. Prathip Wittaya (Yayasan Aukaf al-Misbah), Ranget, Narathiwat.
6. Darussalam (Yayasan Darussalam), Ranget, Narathiwat.
7. Nahdhatulsubban (Yayasan Islam Untuk Pendidikan dan Kebajikan), Rusok, Narathiwat.
8. Siritham Wittaya (Yayasan Siritham Wittaya), Bachok, Narathiwat.
9. Darul Qurannulkarim (Yayasan Al-iman), Yingo, Narathiwat.
10. Jariatam Wittaya (Yayasan Jariatam Wittaya), Weang, Narathiwat.
11. Rahmaniah (Yayasan Sekolah Rahmaniah), Weang, Narathiwat.
12. Seangtham Wittaya Mulniti (Yayasan Seangtham Wittaya), Sungai Golok, Narathiwat.
13. Nuruddin (Yayasan Nuruddin), Takbai, Narathiwat.

Name of Schools in Pattani (and foundation):
1. Bamrung Islam (Yayasan Sokongan Pendidikan Seklah Bamrung Islam), Muang, Pattani. (This school is run by Dr.Ismail Lutfi).
2. Triam Suksa Wittya (Yayasan Untuk Pendidikan Sekolah Triam Suksa Wittya), Muang, Pattani.
3. Wattana Tham Islam (Yayasan Sekolah Wattana Tham Islam Pombing), Panaret, Pattani.
4. Anjamiah Al-Islamiah (Yayasan Sokongan Kebajikan Kampung Maruat), Panaret, Pattani.
5. Sart Sukksa (Yayasan Sekolah Sart Untuk Pendidikan), Saiburi, Pattani.
6. Samartdi Wittaya (Yayasan Sekolah Samartdi Wittaya Untuk Pendidikan), Saiburi, Pattani.
7. Saiburi Islam Wittaya (Yayasan Sekolah Saiburi Islam Wittya Untuk Pendidikan), Saiburi, Pattani.
8. Darunsat Wittaya (Masjid Darul Nasi-iin), Saiburi, Pattani.
9. Arunsart Wittaya (Yayasan Untuk Pendidikan Sekolah Arunsart Wittaya), Saiburi, Pattani.
10. Mulniti Aziztan (Yayasan Aziztanusorn), Khok Po, Pattani.
11. Songsermsart (Yayasan Abdulkadir Al-Qadi Littarbawi), Yaring, Pattani.
12. Al-Islamiah Wittaya (Yayasan Untuk Pendidikan Sekolah Insarilsunnah), Yarang, Pattani.

Name of Schools in Satun (and foundation):
1. Pattanakansuksa Mulniti (Yayasan Pattanakansuksa Wilayah Satun), Muang, Satun.
2. Seang Prathip Wittaya (Yayasan Untuk Pendidikan Sekolah Seang Prathip Wittaya), Muang, Satun.
3. Arunsart Wittaya Mulniti (Yayasan Untuk Pendidikan Sekolah Arunsart Wittaya Mulniti), Kuan Kalong, Satun.
4. Sasanatham Wittaya (Yayasan Kebajikan dan Pendidikan), Tungwa, Satun.

Name of Schools in Songkhla (and foundation):
1. Somboonsart (Yayasan Untuk Pendidikan Sekolah Somboonsart), Nathawi, Songkhla.
2. Pattana Sart Wittaya (Masjid Hikmah Ilummah), Tepha, Songkhla.
3. Thamsuksa Mulniti (Yayasan Thamasuksa Islam Anusorn), Hadyai, Songkhla.
4. Thayai Wittya (Yayasan Untuk Pendidikan Sekolah Thayai Wittaya), Hadyai, Songkhla.
5. Songsermsart Wittaya Mulniti (Yayasan Sekolah Songsermsart Wittaya), Hadyai, Songkhla.
6. Pattana Wittaya Mulniti (Yayayasan Muslim Mulniti), Bangklam, Songkhla.
7. Bustanuddin (Yayasan Untuk Pendidikan Sekolah Bustanuddin), Chana, Songkhla.
8. Damrongsart Wittaya (Yayasan Untuk Pendidikan Darul Naim), Chana, Songkhla.
9. Jariatam Suksa Mulniti (Yayasan Untuk Muslimat dan Muslimin Wilayah Songkhla), Chana, Songkhla.
10. Kiamuddin (Masjid Ban Hua Din), Chana, Songkhla.
11. Sasana Bamrung (Yayasan Untuk Pendidikan Darul Naim), Chana, Songkhla.
12. Sangkom Islam Wittaya (Yayasan Untuk Pendidikan Darul Naim), Sadao, Songkhla.
13. Pattana Sart Mulniti (Yayasan Untuk Pendidikan Pattana Sart), Sadao, Songkhla.

APPENDIX II

Schools with a Substantial (Majority) Number of Saudi-trained Teachers

Yala Province:
1.   Asasuddin, Muang.
2.   Alawiyah, Bannangsta.
3.   Thamma Wittaya Mullanithi, Muang.
4.   Phatana Wittaya, Muang.
5.   Phatana Islam Wittaya, Muang.
6.   Suksawad Wittaya, Yaha.
7.   Islahiyah, Muang.

Pattani Province:
1.   Bamrung Islam, Muang.
2.   Triam Sueksa, Muang.
3.   Mahad Darul-Maarif, Muang.
4.   Azizsathan, Khokpho.
5.   Sasanupatham, Muang.
6.   Wattanatham Islam Phoming, Panareh.
7.   Al-Islamiyah Wittaya, Yarang.
8.   Sasana Samakki, Nongchik.
9.   Ratprachanukroh, Thung yang Daeng.

Narathiwat Province:
1.   Darussalam, Rangeh.
2.   Attarkiyah Islamiyah, Muang.
3.   Buranah Islam Tokno, Muang.
4.   Sengtham Wittaya, Sungaipadi.
5.   Suksan Sasana, Muang.
6.   Samanmit Wittaya, Yingo.

APPENDIX III

Schools with a Substantial (Majority) Number of Egypt-trained Teachers

Yala Province:
1.	Satree Islam Wittaya School , Muang.
2.	Asasuddien School, Muang.
3.	Sri-Farida Baru School, Raman.
4.	Darawite School, Yaha.
5.	Pratheep Wittaya School, Muang.
6.	Sasana Islam Wittaya School, Yaha.
7.	Islam Bajoh Wittaya School, Bannangsatar.
8.	Somboon Sasana School, Yaha.

Pattani Province:
1.	Addirasah Islamiyah School, Panareh.
2.	Azizsatan School, Khokphoe.
3.	Jongraksat Wittaya School, Muang.
4.	Attarbiyah Islamiyah School, Maikaen.
5.	Somboon Sasana Islam Wittaya School, Panareh.

Narathiwat Province:
1.	Nirandorn Wittaya School, Muang.
2.	Jariyatham Wittaya School, Waeng.

GLOSSARY

adil	just
ahl harb	people at war
ahl 'ahd	people of the covenant of peace
akhlak	ethics
alim	scholar
aqidah	belief in the articles of faith
ayat	phrases from *hadiths*
balai	huts
balaisoh (Thai)	prayer halls, usually smaller in size than mosques
balai surau (Malay)	prayer halls, usually smaller in size than mosques
bantu-membantu	mutual help and support
belas kasihan	empathy
berkat	blessed
berkenal-kenalan	getting to know one another through interaction
bid'a	innovation
bumi Patani	Patani land
dakwah	propagation of Islam through word and action, calling the people to follow the commandments of Allah and his messenger Prophet Muhammad
damai	harmonious
Dar Al-Islam	house of Islam; land ruled by a Muslim ruler and where the *shari'a* is held as the rule of the land
Dar Al-Harb	house of War; land ruled by non-Muslims or where the *shari'a* is not recognized as the law of the land
Dar Al-Muwada'ah	land ruled by non-Muslims and in no hostility agreement with land ruled by a Muslim ruler

Dar Al-'Ahd	Dar Al-Islam with autonomous rule under a non-Muslim ruler
Dar Al-Kufr	land of disbelief
Dar As-Sulh	land of peace treaty
dharurat	emergencies
dikir barat	a type of Malay cultural performance
dirampas	seized
falak	astronomy/astrology
fara'id	Islamic law on succession/inheritance
fard'ain	describes knowledge that is a religious obligation
fard kifayah	describes knowledge that is obligatory not for all, but for a sufficient number of such Muslims in the community
fatwa	decree issued by Islamic leader or *imam*
fikiran Melayuisme	Malay nationalist thought
fiqh	Islamic jurisprudence
fitnah	disbelief
gerai-gerai makanan	food stalls
gotong-royong	working and aiding one another in achieving mutual goals
hadith	a series of authenticated sayings and declarations recorded by Muslim scholars who tracked the chain of sources concerning what the Prophet said, did, or tacitly approved
hafiz	Muslims who have committed the Qur'an to memory
hajis	a term used to bestow honour and respect on men who have completed their pilgrimage in Mecca, also known as 'hajj'
halal	permissible in Islam
halaqah	study circle; scholastic circles
hanafi	one of the four dominant Islamic legal traditions in Sunni Islam; dominant in most of South and Central Asia
haram	unclean
haramain	two holy lands — Mecca and Medina
hijab	headscarf worn by Muslim women
hijaz	the Arabian Peninsula where non-Muslims who possess the proper permits are allowed to enter and stay for a period not longer than three days
hijrah	the migration of the Prophet and his followers from Mecca to Medina in AD 622.
ijtihad	independent judgement; the ability to exercise reason and formulate a specific opinion in the absence of a precedent
ilmu	knowledge
imam	leader or a person who leads the prayer
iman	faith

isha	evening daily prayer
istiwa' 'ala al-arsy	God's position on the throne
Jahili	people of the ignorance
jahiliyya	literally means ignorance; also describes the pagan practice of the days before God's revelations to the Prophet Muhammad
Jawi	Malay version of Arab script
Jemaat Tabligh	an Islamic grassroots *dakwah* (missionary) movement that is primarily focused on the purification of the Islamic community
jihad	the Qur'anic injunction for believers to strive and struggle with their entire being to carry out the commandments of God as part of their submission to God's will
jihad qital	armed *jihad*
jihad fi sabililllah	struggle in the way of Allah
jizya	tributary tax
kafir	infidels
kalam	theology
kampung	village
Kaum Muda	the "New Generation" as they are known in the Malay world. At times associated with, though not confined to, Salafis who attempt to reform Islam by taking it away from its traditional association with syncretism and re-orienting it towards scripturalism
Kaum Tua	the "Old Generation" who espoused traditional models of religious education and practice, at times including subscription to some elements of pre-Islamic beliefs and practices
keadilan	justice
kedamaian	harmony
kehidupan	everyday living
kemanusiaan	humanity
ketua kampung	village head
kesejahteraan	peace
khaek	a pejorative term which literally means "dark-skinned visitors"; historically used by Thais to describe the Malay-Muslims in southern Thailand
khutbah	sermon delivered on Fridays and special occasions
kitab	texts
Kitab Kuning/Jawi	classical Malay religious literature written in Jawi script and produced by Patani scholars
madrasah	a type of Islamic school

masjid	mosque
magrib	sunset daily prayer
mazhab	the traditional schools of Islamic jurisprudence or *fiqh* that anchor much of traditional Islam
Muhayid state	a state that has entered into a peace treaty with an Islamic state
mujtahid	jurist
mujahideen	struggler (a Muslim engaged in a *jihad* or holy struggle)
mukmin	people blessed by God
mulniti	Islamic foundations
munafikin	hypocrites
musafir	a traveller
nahwi	Arabic grammar
pasar-pasar	marketplaces
peperangan	war
pondok	traditional Islamic schools
qadi	Islamic judge
qira'at	recitation of the Qur'an
qiyas	analogy
qunut	act of standing or special supplications in a standing posture during dawn prayer
Ramadhan	the ninth month of the Islamic year when Muslims fast during the day
Salaf	three generations of the community of elders and companions of the Prophet. These include the companions of the Prophet (the *Sahabah*), their students the "successors" (the *Taabi'een*), and their students (the *Atbaa Taabi'een*)
Salafi	those who attempt to reform Islam by taking it away from its traditional association with syncretism and re-orienting it towards scripturalism
Salafus-Saaleh	pious predecessors
sarf	grammar and conjugation
sejahtera	peaceful
Shafi'i	one of the four legal traditions in Sunni Islam; dominant in Southeast Asia
shari'a	Islamic way of life, including Islamic law
shirk	innovation
shura	councils consisting of groups of elders who in the context of the *Jemaat Tabligh* meet to vet the readiness of followers to conduct their *dakwah*, which is usually either three days a month or forty days a year.
sifat 20	twenty attributes of God

sunnah	the actions and teachings of the Prophet
suri rumah tangga	housewife
surah	verses from the Qur'an
tabligh	Islamic missionary effort
tadika	Islamic kindergartens
tafsir	Qur'anic exegesis
thawb	white robes
takfir	the highly politicized exercise of labelling fellow Muslims as infidels that is often associated with radical Salafis and Wahhabis
taqiya	turbans
taqlid	uncritical acceptance of textual sources
tarikh	history
tariqahs	Islamic mystical brotherhood
tassawuf	spirituality
tauhid	oneness of God; unity of God
tiga wilaya	three provinces — the local nomenclature for the Malay-Muslim provinces of Narathiwat, Pattani, and Yala
tok guru	*pondok* religious teachers
tolong-menolong	helping one another
ulama	religious scholars
ulama Jawi	distinguished scholars of Islam from the Malay world
ummah	the community of Muslim believers
ustaz or babo	religious teachers in Islamic private school
usul-addin	principles of Islam
usul al-fiqh	principles of jurisprudence
uswah hasanah	role model
Wahhabism	refers to a particular brand of Salafism rooted in the historical evolution of Islamic thought and praxis in the Arabian Peninsula. Wahhabism advocates for a return to the tradition of the Prophet and his companions and is grounded principally in the religious thought of one particular Salafi thinker, Muhammad ibn Abd Al-Wahhab
waqf	Islamic endowments
wayang kulit	Malay cultural performances
wira shuhada	martyrs
yayasan	Islamic foundation
zakat	Islamic tax system; almsgiving which constitutes one of the five pillars of Islam
zikr	supplication
zimmis	protected minorities

BIBLIOGRAPHY

Books

Abdul Malik, Mohd. Zamberi. *Umat Islam Patani: Sejarah dan Politik* [Patani's Muslims: History and Politics]. Shah Alam: HIZBI, 1993.

Abdullah, Wan Mohd Shaghir. *Syaikh Ahmad al-Fatani*. Kuala Lumpur: Khazanah Fathaniah, n.d.

Al-Fatani, Muhammad Nur bin Muhammad bin Ismail Ismail. *Kifayah Al-Muhtadi* [Provision for a Person Who Receives Guidance]. Pattani: Muhammad An-Nahdi and Sons Publication House, 1932.

Al-Talimbani, Syeikh, Samad. *Hidayatul Salatin*. [Guidance for Sultans]. Pattani, n.d.

Alatas, Syed Farid, Lim Teck Ghee, and Kazuhide Kurada, eds. *Asian Interfaith Dialogue: Perspectives on Religion, Education, and Social Cohesion*. Singapore and Washington D.C.: RIMA and The World Bank, 2003.

Allen, Charles. *God's Terrorists: The Wahhabi Cult and the Hidden Roots of Modern Jihad*. London: Abacus, 2007.

Aphornsuvan, Thanet. *Origins of Malay Muslim "Separatism" in Southern Thailand*. Asia Research Institute Working Paper Series No. 32. Singapore: Asia Research Institute, 2004.

Askew, Marc. *Conspiracy, Politics, and a Disorderly Border: The Struggle to Comprehend Insurgency in Thailand's Deep South*. Washington, D.C.: East-West Center Washington, 2007.

Azra, Azyumardi. *The Origins of Islamic reformism in Southeast Asia*. New South Wales: Allen & Unwin, 2004.

Bangnara, A. *Fatani Dahulu dan Sekarang* [Fatani Now and Then]. Selangor: Penal Penyelidikan, 1977.

Bashah, Abdul Haleem. *Raja dan Dinasti Jembal dalam Patani Besar* [King and Jembal Dynasty in Patani]. Kelantan: Pustaka Reka, 1994.

Berjihad Di Pattani [The Conduct of a Holy Struggle in Pattani]. Author's personal copy, 10 August 2004.

Chapakia, Ahmad Omar. *Politik dan Perjuangan Masyarakat Islam di Selatan Thailand, 1902–2002* [Politics and Struggle of the Islamic Community in Southern Thailand, 1902–2002]. Bangi: Universiti Kebangsaan Malaysia, 2002.

Che Man, Wan Kadir. *Muslim Elites and Politics in Southern Thailand.* Penang: Universiti Sains Malaysia, 1983.

Che Man, Wan, Kadir. *Muslim Separatism: The Moro of Southern Philippines and the Malays of Southern Thailand.* Singapore: Oxford University Press, 1990.

Cornish, Andrew. *Whose Place is This? Malay Rubber Producers and Thai Government Officials in Yala.* Bangkok: White Lotus Press, 1997.

Delong-Bas, Natana, J. *Wahhabi Islam: From Revival and Reform to Global Jihad.* London and New York: I.B. Tauris, 2004.

Dulyakasem, Uthai and Lertchai Sirichai, eds. *Knowledge and Conflict Resolution: The Crisis of the Border Region of Southern Thailand.* Nakhon Si Thammarat: School of Liberal Arts, Walailak University, 2005.

Euben, Roxanne L. *Enemy in the Mirror: Islamic Fundamentalism and The Limits of Modern Rationalism.* Princeton, NJ: Princeton University Press, 1999.

Fatani, Ismail Lutfi. *Ikhtilaf Ad-Darain wa Atsaruhu fi Ahkam Al-Munakahat wa Al-Muamalat* [The Effect of Two Dars (Dar Al-Islam and Dar Al-Harb) on Islamic Personal and Transaction Laws]. Cairo: Dar As-Salam, 1990.

———. *Ikhtilaf Ad-Darain wa Atsaruhu fi Ahkam Al-Munakahat wa Al-Muamalat* [The Effect of Two Dars (Dar Al-Islam and Dar Al-Harb) on Islamic Personal and Transaction Laws]. Second Edition. Cairo: Dar As-Salam, 1998.

Fathi, Ahmad. *Ulama Besar dari Fatani* [Patani's Revered Ulama]. Kelantan: Pustaka Aman, 2001.

Forbes, Andrew D.W., ed. *The Muslims of Thailand: Volume 1, Historical and Cultural Studies.* Bihar: Centre for South East Asian Studies, 1988.

———. *The Muslims of Thailand, Vol. 2: Politics of the Malay Speaking South.* Bihar: Centre for South East Asian Studies, 1989.

Gilquin, Michel. *The Muslims of Thailand.* Translated by Smithies, Michael. Chiang Mai: Silkworm Books, 2005.

Gunaratna, Rohan, Arabinda Acharya, and Sabrina Chua. *Conflict and Terrorism in Southern Thailand.* Singapore: Marshall Cavendish, 2005.

Hikmatullah, Hassan. *Jihad Fi Sabilillah Pengertian dan Bidang* [The Understanding and Call for Struggle in the Way of Allah]. Undated.

Horstmann, Alexander. *Class, Culture and Space: The Construction and Shaping of Communal Space in South Thailand.* Tokyo: Research Institute for the Languages and Cultures of Asia and Africa, 2002.

Japakiya, Ismail Lutfi. *Hayat Tayyibah: Dari Kalimat Tayyibah Hingga Masakin Tayyibah* (The Good Life: From A Good Word to A Good Abode). Pattani: Majlis Al-Ilm Fattani, 2001.

————. *Islam Agama Penjana Kedamaian Sejagat* [Islam as the Pathway to Harmony]. Alor Star: Pustaka Darussalam, 2005.

James, Wendy, ed. *The Pursuit of Certainty: Religious and Cultural Formulations*. London: Routledge, 1995.

Janchitfah, Supara. *Violence in the Mist: Reporting on the Presence of Pain in Southern Thailand*. Bangkok: Kobfai Publishing Project, 2005.

Keyes, Charles F. *Reshaping Local Worlds: Formal Education and Cultural Change in Rural Southeast Asia*. New Haven, CT: Yale University, 1991.

————. *Thailand: Buddhist Kingdom as Modern Nation-State*. Boulder and London: Westview Press, 1987.

Loos, Tamara. *Subject Siam: Family, Law, and Colonial Modernity in Thailand*. Ithaca, NY: Cornell University Press, 2006.

Madmarn, Hasan. *The Pondok and Madrasah in Pattani*. Bangi: Penerbit University Kebangsaan Malaysia, 1999.

Maulid Klang Organising Committee of Thailand. *Holding Fast to the Ideology of Harmony Among Thais*. Bangkok: Islamic Committee of Thailand, 2006.

McCargo, Duncan, ed. *Rethinking Thailand's Southern Violence*. Singapore: Singapore University Press, 2006.

Ngah, Mohd. Noor. *Kitab Jawi: Islamic Thought of the Malay-Muslim Scholars*. Singapore: ISEAS, 1983.

Nik Mahmud, Nik Anuar. *Sejarah Perjuangan Melayu Patani, 1785–1954* [History of the Struggle of the Patani Malays, 1785–1954]. Bangi: Penerbit Universiti Kebangsaan Malaysia, 1999.

Pitsuwan, Surin. *Islam and Malay Nationalism: A Case Study of the Malay-Muslims of Southern Thailand*. Bangkok: Thai Khadi Research Institute, Thammasat University, 1985.

Reynolds, Craig J., ed. *National Identity and Its Defenders, Thailand, 1939–1989*. Melbourne: Monash Papers on Southeast Asia No. 25, Centre of Southeast Asian Studies, Monash University, 1991.

———— *National Identity and its Defenders: Thailand*. Chiang Mai: Silkworm Books, 2003.

Riddell, Peter. *Islam in the Malay-Indonesian World: Transmission and Responses*. Hawaii: University of Hawaii Press, 2001.

Roff, William R. *The Origins of Malay Nationalism*. Oxford: Oxford University Press, 1967.

————. *The Origins of Malay Nationalism*. Second Edition. Kuala Lumpur: Oxford University Press, 1994.

Ruohomaki, Olli-Pekka. *Fishermen No More: Livelihood and Environment in Southern Thai Maritime Village*. Bangkok: White Lotus, 1999.

Scupin, Raymond, ed. *Aspects of Development: Islamic Education in Thailand and Malaysia*. Bangi: Institut Bahasa Kesusasteraan dan Kebudayaan Melayu, University Kebangsaan Malaysia, 1989.

Shiraishi, Takashi. *An Age in Motion: Popular Radicalism in Java, 1912–1916.* Ithaca, NY: Cornell University Press, 1990.

Sugunnasil, Wattana, ed. *Dynamic Diversity in Southern Thailand.* Chiang Mai: Silkworm Books, 2005.

Syukri, Ibrahim. *Sejarah Kerajaan Melayu Patani* [History of the Malay Kingdom of Patani]. Pasir Puteh, 1958.

———— *Sejarah Kerajaan Melayu Patani* [History of the Malay Kingdom of Patani]. Translated by Connor Bailey and John Miksic. Athens, OH: Ohio State University Press, 1985.

Taryoto, Andin H. *Studi Persiapan Program Kemandirian Ekonomi Pondok Pesantren: Laporan Penelitian* [Establishment of Autonomous Economic Programs in Pondoks and Pesantren: A Research Report]. Bogor: Pusat Penelitian Sosial Ekonomi Pertanian, Badan Litbang Pertanian, 1997.

Thomas, M. Ladd. *Social-Economic Approach to the Integration of Thai Islam: An Appraisal.* Urbana-Champaign, IL: Center for Southeast Asian Studies, Northern Illinois University, 1967.

Wyatt, David K. and Andries Teeuw. *Hikayat Pattani* [The History of Pattani]. The Hague: Martinus Nijhoff, 1970.

Wyatt, David K. *Thailand: A Short History.* New Haven, CT: Yale University Press, 1984.

Yusuf, Imtiyaz and Lars P. Schmidt, eds. *Understanding Conflict and Approaching Peace in Southern Thailand.* Bangkok: Konrad-Adenauer-Stiftung, 2006.

Zaman, Muhammad Kamal K. *Fatani 13 Ogos* [Fatani 13 August]. Kota Bahru, 1996.

Articles

Albritton, Roger. "Political Diversity Among Muslims in Thailand". *Asian Studies Review* 23, no. 2 (1994): 233–46.

Al-Helmi, Zahidi and Muhammad Jihad. "*Rahsia dan Iktibar disebalik Kejatuhan Pondok*" [Lessons from the Demise of Pondoks]. *Imam* 2 (December 1989): 34–37.

Braam, Ernesto. "Travelling with the *Tablighi Jemaat* in South Thailand". *ISIM Review* 17 (Spring 2006): 42–43.

Bradley, John. "Waking Up to the Terror Threat in Southern Thailand". *Straits Times*, 27 May 2004.

Bruinessen, Martin van. "Kitab Kuning: Books in Arabic Script Used in the Pesantren Milieu". *Bijdragen tot de Taal-, Land- en Volkenkunde* 146 (1990): 226–69.

Burr, Angela. "Religious Institutional Diversity — Social Structural and Conceptual Unity: Islam and Buddhism in a Southern Thai Coastal Fishing Village". *Journal of the Siam Society* 60, no. 2 (1972): 183–216.

Che Man, Wan Kadir. "The Thai Government and Islamic Institutions in the Four Southern Muslim Provinces of Thailand". *Sojourn* 5, no. 2 (1990): 255–82.

Davis, Anthony. "Thailand faces up to southern extremist threat", *Jane's Intelligence Review*, 1 October 2003.

Forbes, Andrew D.W. "Thailand's Muslim Minorities: Assimilation, Secession, or Coexistence?" *Asian Survey* 22, no. 11 (1982): 1056–73.

Gowing, Peter. "Moro and Khaek: the Position of Muslim Minorities in the Philippines and Thailand". *Southeast Asian Affairs*, Institute of Southeast Asian Studies, 1975.

Human Rights Watch. "No One is Safe: Insurgent Attacks on Civilians in Thailand's Southern Border Provinces". *Human Rights Watch* 19, no. 13(C) (August 2007)

International Crisis Group. *Southern Thailand: Insurgency, Not Jihad*. ICG Asia Report 98, 2005.

Japakiya, Ismail Lutfi. "Status and Roles of Ulama in the Holy Qur'an and Sunna". In *Holding Fast to the Ideology of Harmony Among Thais*, edited by Maulid Klang Organising Committee of Thailand. Bangkok: Islamic Committee of Thailand, 2006.

Kersten, Carool. "The Predicament of Thailand's Southern Muslims". *American Journal of Islamic Social Sciences* 21, no. 4 (Fall 2004): 1–29.

Khoury, Nabeel A. and Abdo I. Baaklini. "Muhammad Abduh: An Ideology of Development". *The Muslim World* 69, no. 1 (1979): 42–52.

Liow, Joseph Chinyong. "The *Pondok* School of Southern Thailand: Bastion of Islamic Education or Hotbed of Militancy?" *IDSS Commentaries*, August 2004.

————. "International Jihad and Muslim Radicalism in Thailand? Toward an Alternative Interpretation". *Asia Policy* 2 (July 2006): 89–108.

Matheson, Virginia and Hooker, M.B. "Jawi Literature in Patani: The Maintenance of an Islamic Tradition". *Journal of the Malayan Branch of the Royal Asiatic Society* 61, no. 1 (1988): 1–86.

Scupin, Raymond. "Muslim Accommodation in Thai Society". *Journal of Islamic Studies* 9, no. 2 (1998): 229–58.

Suhrke, Astri. "Loyalists and Separatists: The Muslims in Southern Thailand". *Asian Survey* 17, no. 3 (1977): 237–50.

Vatikiotis, Michael. "Resolving Internal Conflicts in Southeast Asia: Domestic Challenges and Regional Perspectives". *Contemporary Southeast Asia* 28, no. 1 (April 2006): 27–47.

Winzeler, R L. "Traditional Islamic Schools in Kelantan". *Journal of the Malaysian Branch of the Royal Asiatic Society* 48, no. 1 (1964): 91–103.

Yusuf, Imtiyaz. "Islam and Democracy in Thailand: reforming the Office of Chularajmontri/Shaikh Al-Islam". *Journal of Islamic Studies* 9, no. 2 (1998): 277–99.

Dissertations and Unpublished Papers

Dorairajoo, Saroja. "From Mecca to Yala: Negotiating Islam in Present-Day Southern Thailand". Paper presented at the symposium Islam in Southeast Asia and

China: Regional Faithlines and Faultlines in the Global Ummah, City University of Hong Kong, 28 Nov–1 Dec 2002.

Dulyakasem, Uthai. "Education and Ethnic Nationalism: A Study of the Muslim-Malays in Southern Siam". Ph.D. dissertation, Stanford University, 1981.

Hayimasae, Numan. "*Hj Sulong Abdul Kadir (1895–1954): Perjuangan dan Sumbangan Beliau Kepada Masyarakat Melayu Patani* [Hj Sulong Abdul Kadir (1895–1954): Struggle and Contributions to the Patani Malays]". M.Sc. dissertation, Universiti Sains Kebangsaan Malaysia, 2002.

Horstmann, Alexander. "The Tablighi Jama'at in Southern Thailand". Paper presented at the Ninth International Conference on Thai Studies, Dekalb, Illinois, 3–6 April, 2005.

Hussaini, Chairul Fahmy. "Islamic Resurgence in Iran: Impact on Singaporean Muslims". M.Sc. dissertation, Nanyang Technological University, 2006/2007.

Langputeh, Sukree. "The Islamization of the Discipline of Public Administration in a Thai Higher Education Institution: The Experience of Yala Islamic College". Paper presented at the International Workshop on Voices of Islam in Europe and Southeast Asia, Nakhon Si Thammarat, 20–22 January 2006.

Madmarn, Hasan. "Traditional Muslim Institutions in Southern Thailand: A Critical Study of Islamic Education and Arabic Influence in the Pondok and Madrasah Systems of Patani". Ph.D. dissertation, University of Utah, 1990.

Mansurnoor, Iik A. "Intellectual Networking among Muslim Scholars in Southeast Asia with a Special Reference to Patani Works on Society, Coexistence and External Relations." Paper presented at the First Inter-Dialogue Conference on Southern Thailand, Pattani, 13–15 June 2002.

Moawad, Darwish. "Southernmost Thailand Violence: Illiteracy, Poverty, Politics, Illicit Drugs Trafficking, Smuggling, and Nationalist Separatists — not Religion and Culture — the Issue". Paper presented at UNESCO Conference on "Religion in Peace and Conflict", Melbourne, Australia, 12 April 2005.

Narongraksakhet, Ibrahim. "Developing Local-based Curriculum Guidelines for Islamic Private Schools in Southern Thailand". Ph.D. dissertation, Universiti Malaya, July 2003.

Osman, Mohd Taib. "*Hikayat Seri Kelantan*" [The History of Seri Kelantan]. M.A. dissertation, Universiti Malaya, 1961.

Reetz, Dietrich. "Sufi Spirituality Fires Reformist Zeal: The Tablighi Jamaat in Today's India and Pakistan." Paper presented to the workshop entitled "Modern Adaptations of Sufi-Islam", Berlin, April 4–5, 2003.

Sachakul, Kanniga. "Education as a Means for National Integration: Historical and Comparative Study of Chinese and Muslim Assimilation in Thailand". Ph.D. dissertation, University of Michigan-Ann Arbor, 1984.

Tamimi, Azzam. "*Muhammad Ibn Abd Al-Wahhab dari Pembangunan Semula Abad Ke 18 Aktivisme Abad Ke 21*" [Muhammad Ibn Abd Al-Wahab from 18th Century Revivalism to 21st Century Activism]. Paper presented at *Seminar Antarabangsa Mengenai Syeikh Muhammad Abdul Wahab* [International Seminar on Syeikh Muhammad Abdul Wahab] Kangar, Perlis, Malaysia, 16–17 March 2006.

Zakaria, Abdul Rahim. "The Legacy of Haji Sulong in the Contemporary Separatist Struggle in Thailand's Restive South". M.Sc. dissertation, Nanyang Technological University, Singapore, 2005.

Web Sources

Abuza, Zachary. "A Conspiracy of Silence: Who is behind the escalating insurgency in southern Thailand?" *Terrorism Monitor* 3, no. 9, May 6, 2005. <http://jamestown.org/terrorism/news/article.php?articleid=2369684>.

"Al-Qunut in salatul fajr". <http://www.usc.edu/dept/MSA/law/fiqhussunnah/fus2_13.html>.

Croissant, Aurel. "Unrest in South Thailand: Contours, Causes, and Consequences Since 2001". *Strategic Insights* 4, no. 2, February 2005. <http://www.ccc.nps.navy.mil/si/2005/Feb/croissantfeb05.asp.>.

Hassan, Abdullah Zaidi. "Syaikh Ahmad Bin Muhammad Zain Al-Fatani — Pemikir Bangsa" [Syaikh Ahmad Bin Muhammad Zain Al-Fatani- The Nation's Thinker]. n.d.<http://www.geocities.com/traditionalislam/syaikh_ahmad_alFatani.htm.>

Holt, Andrew. "Thailand's Troubled Border: Islamic Insurgency or Criminal Playground?" *Terrorism Monitor* (Jamestown Foundation)2, no. 10, 20 May 2004. <http://www.asiamedia.ucla.edu/article.asp?parentid=11383>.

Jory, Patrick. "Multiculturalism in Thailand: Cultural and Regional Resurgence in a Diverse Kingdom". *Harvard Asia-Pacific Review*, Winter 2000. <http://www.hcs.harvard.edu/~hapr/winter00_millenium/Thailand.html>.

Kaplan, Fred. "Rumsfeld's Pentagon Papers". *Slate*, 23 October 2003 <http://slate.msn.com/id/2090250>.

"Killings at Pattani's Krue Se Mosque and a Cover Up Enquiry". *CounterCurrents.Org*, 6 May 2004. <http://www.countercurrents.org/hrachr060504.htm>.

Prasetyo, Teddy. "Thailand: Buddhism-Islam dialogue aimed at ending violence and promoting greater religious understanding". *Current Dialogue (World Council of Churches)* 46, December 2005. <www.wcc-coe.org/wcc/what/interreligious/cd46-12.html.>.

Government Sources

Ministry of Education — Thailand. *Education Development Plan of the Provinces along the Southern Border*. Bangkok: Ministry of Education, 2006.

Ministry of Education — Thailand. *A Brief Report on Development of the Islamic Private Schools in Regions 2, 3, and 4 in the Fiscal Year 2000*. Bangkok: Office of Private Education Committee, Ministry of Education, 2001.

Report of the Independent Fact-Finding Commission on the Krue Se Incident. 24 April 2005 <http://yuwathut.mfa.go.th/web/463.php?id=9873>.

Newspaper Articles

"*Al-Ghazaly Modern Syekh Nawawi Al-Bantani*". www.sufinews.com, 8 April 2004.

"Crown Prince to open Islamic college headquarters in Pattani". *The Nation*, 6 March 2004.

"Imam admits contact with separatists". *The Nation*, 1 September 2004.

"Planning for a peaceful future in the South". *The Nation*, 28 August 2005.

"Shadowy group behind violence". *Straits Times*, 1 May 2004.

"Solutions for strife: Schools in South to teach Yawi". *The Nation*, 6 August 2005.

"Southern Front". *Time*, 11 October 2004.

"Students Come Home to Suspicion". *The Nation*, 31 October 2006.

"Tadika school transfer worries". *Bangkok Post*, 13 August 2005.

"Teaching Thai: Innovative approach blends in Malay". *The Nation*, 14 August 2005.

"Thai districts impose martial law". *BBC News*, 3 November 2005.

"The (un)making of a militant". *New Straits Times*, 12 September 2005.

"Three *Pondok* picked to become models". *The Nation*, 31 March 2005.

"TRT MPs fund body linked to militants". *The Nation*, 2 April 2004.

"TRT MPs propose shutting down *Pondok* schools". *The Nation*, 14 September 2005.

INDEX

ABOUT THE AUTHOR

Joseph Chinyong Liow is currently Associate Dean and Associate Professor at the S. Rajaratnam School of International Studies, Nanyang Technological University, Singapore. His research interests are Muslim politics and Malay-Muslim communities in Southeast Asia.